ISBN: 9781290356565

Published by:
HardPress Publishing
8345 NW 66TH ST #2561
MIAMI FL 33166-2626

Email: info@hardpress.net
Web: http://www.hardpress.net

THE

ROMANCE OF THE STREETS.

THE

ROMANCE OF THE STREETS.

BY A

LONDON RAMBLER.

London, the needy villain's general home,
The common-sewer of Paris and of Rome,
With eager thirst, by folly or by fate,
Sucks in the dregs of each corrupted state.
Forgive my transports on a theme like this

DR. JOHNSON.

London:
HODDER AND STOUGHTON,
27, PATERNOSTER ROW.
MDCCCLXXII.

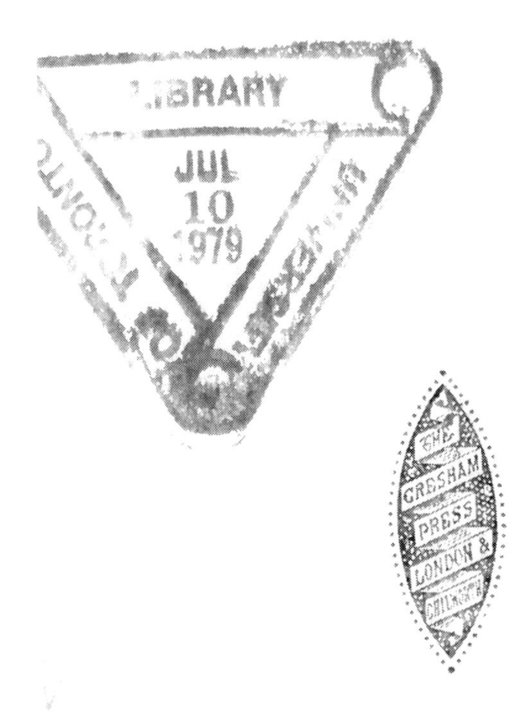

UNWIN BROTHERS PRINTERS BY WATER POWER.

CONTENTS.

I.

LONDON ARABS.

THE

ROMANCE OF THE STREETS.

LONDON ARABS.

We live in an age when it is not fashionable to undervalue the benefits of knowledge; and most Christians admit that education should be permeated by religion. Education which does not borrow something from the Word of Inspiration, will, in the end, turn out unsatisfactory; for though a purely secular training may become a mental discipline, and in a slight degree conduce to moral progress, it will be discipline and progress of a very heathen sample. A mind stored with knowledge, while wanting a sanctified conscience, resembles a richly-laden but rudderless barque, unable successfully to make way against the current. She is water-tight and comfortable only so long as no breakers discover her weakness.

Parliament has lately decided on promoting the weal of the poor by authorising School Boards to provide for the education of those who, without some rescuing agency, would continue in ignorance. This is well, so far as it goes, if care be taken that such education is based on Bible morality in the true spirit of Christianity. It seems perfectly reasonable to unbiassed minds that the State—which can never become an acceptable religious teacher as such—should yet provide for the training of children whom misfortune precludes from a better discipline. We read the Bible in our day-school classes, so that its precepts may at least leaven our teaching, without supposing that the secular tutor is to usurp the functions of an exponent of Gospel truth. Should he set himself up as a religious teacher, he almost necessarily becomes sectarian, and an engenderer of sectarian animosities. Happily, it is not my province here to inquire whether a Christian State is strengthened in religion and morality by the bulwarks of an Established Church. I only desire that the Government shall extend the province of the day-school teacher, meanwhile leaving religion as much as possible to its recognised teachers.

In all ages ignorance has been the bane of the poor population, for from ignorance spring vice and improvidence. What the consequences would have been had our dangerous classes still remained untouched by Christianity, while multiplying and sinking lower and yet lower in depravity, can be best pictured by calling to mind how hordes of barbarians swept the fruits of civilisation from the world in the olden time, to reduce to chaos the labours of ages. There is a germ of evil in every ragged untutored child, which may expand into proportions such as we little suspect. A spark from a cowherd's lantern sufficed to destroy Chicago.

Yet who has not sometimes encountered one of an almost extinct school of political economists, whose sympathies are not with the schoolmaster? In face of the contrary testimony of history, we are assured that ignorance is the best security for the obedience of the poor and the prosperity of the opulent. Not very long ago a justice of the peace was heard declaiming on the bench against 'the evils of education.' If such persons are honest in expressing what they believe, we may recognise their honesty but doubt their judgment. Probably such would rejoice in reintroducing a condition of affairs such as existed in the early part of last century, when only 27,000 children were found in all the charity schools of England! Though open to conviction, we have not yet discovered that England's prospective dangers are based on copy-books and grammars, nor that a spread of knowledge among the poor will injuriously affect our national industries. Nevertheless, though seldom pushing them into print, many deal privately in hushed-up objections to a spread of education, and parade as impending dangers what we regard as vanquished enemies. Objections, long ago exploded, but supposed by some to be inimical to national progress, are marshalled in argumentative array, and pointed out as assuming a threatening front. But Christian philanthropists have no time for dealing with objections; while God and conscience bid them go forward, they pursue their calling in faith and hope.

That is surely an odious doctrine which teaches that the moral world is daily sinking lower in iniquity. Not only are such views disagreeable, they cannot be logically maintained without inverting the testimony of history, or by calling good evil, and evil good—a procedure they cannot afford to adopt who regard the voice of our national annals. But, able to rejoice in believing that the world progresses towards the goal of good, we must sorrowfully admit that its present condition is bewilderingly bad. In our every-day conversation, we talk of the prosperity of this or another nation, while knowing that the condition of the most advanced in civilisation is entirely unsatisfactory. What is the present condition of England? The impoverishment of the industrial classes, consequent on the stagnation of trade, has been a dismal topic of discussion during several years. A mere novice in political science knows that stagnation of trade means increase of pauperism; and pauperism is synonymous with blighted hopes, broken hearts, desolate hearths, and with more misery than can be known, and with more than most would care to listen to could it be described. Whence spring these national disasters? Are we to chronicle them as mere gigantic misfortunes? Have vice and ignorance nothing to do with their occurrence? Have Christian teachers no antidote for this long train of evils?

Now, though in the province of philanthropy we do not yield a first place to ragged-school teachers, they certainly rank among our most honourable workers. The gifts of well-disciplined agents in this department are enviable endowments, commanding a large share of that double blessing which refreshes the spirit of both giver and of receiver. Teaching the poor is confessedly a work of self-denial; but on 'good ground' self-denial yields a return of a hundred-fold.

It was indeed giving expression to a noble idea, when our philanthropists, with Lord Shaftesbury for a leader, resolved on proving what could be done in cleansing the stream of London life at the fountain-head, and so deliver the men and women of another generation from crime and degradation, by rescuing the children. A recent Report of the Ragged-School Union thus explains the origin of the movement:—

'A few humble individuals (mostly Sabbath-school teachers), seeing the forlorn and destitute condition of thousands of poor neglected children in our London streets, and knowing that some few schools were carried on under considerable difficulties for the benefit of such, met in a ragged-school-room or loft near Streatham-street, Bloomsbury, to form a union of such schools, to assist in extending their operations and in increasing their number. Mr. John Branch, of the City Mission, presided on that memorable occasion, and after some deliberation as to the best course to be pursued, it was moved (by one who, by God's good providence, has been spared to act as honorary secretary from that time to the present), "That an association be formed to encourage and assist those who teach in ragged-schools, to be called THE RAGGED-SCHOOL UNION." This proposal was seconded by Mr. S. R. Starey (at that time a worker in Field Lane School), and passed unanimously.'

Since that day the working of the Ragged-Schoo Union has been a prolonged illustration of the proverb,

'Prevention is better than cure.' The magistrates of future generations will, it is hoped, be saved considerable business by its purifying action. Schools are not only cheaper, but more effective for good than prisons and convict-yards.

Then it must be remembered that other schoolmasters than those of the 'Union' are abroad; and if children are not trained in courses of rectitude they will come under the discipline of tutors in crime; and by their depredations—to say nothing of the cost of punishment—will entail on the nation a hundred-fold more expense than is incurred by their timely education. Thieving has become a science, with its recognised professors, who lecture their classes in the dark recesses of our London rookeries. Fagin, in 'Oliver Twist,' is no mere literary creation. Fagin resided in Spitalfields, and conducted an institution where young persons could be initiated into all the arts of dishonesty.

This chapter will illustrate the counteractive influence of ragged-schools.

However rough may be the subjects on first taking them in hand, the truth instilled in the ragged-class soon yields due return. One evening, while out walking, a teacher observed a company of his pupils debating something with earnestness, as though it were a matter of moment. What could it be? It might be a dispute relating to marbles, or about the 'squaring' of a few halfpence. But it was nothing of the kind, however. One of the party being in a state of destitution more than ordinarily pressing, his companions had subscribed eighteenpence for the unfortunate fellow's benefit, and were arranging the best method of laying out the money. After standing aside and listening to their dialogue, the teacher discovered himself; and one of the lads, on being interrogated, answered, 'We've been trying to raise a trifle for that poor fellow, for he's got nothing to eat,—he's got no home.' Then they discussed how they could procure him clothes and employment, and one actually walked four miles to beg him an old coat. This from boys who were obliged to seek a precarious living in the streets, and who, in some cases, had not themselves a bed to lie upon!

In many instances the children of our ragged-schools are orphans, the proportion of these being much greater in the lower ranks than among ordinary Sunday scholars. The rent-collectors of poor districts are in bad repute, and though often unjustly vilified, their treatment of destitute children is sometimes heartless and inexcusable; for when a family is broken up by death, the hapless offspring of departed parents are turned adrift to shift for themselves. The following, it may be feared, is a sample of what too often occurs in London:—

One Sabbath afternoon, as a ragged-school teacher was returning home, he suddenly came up to a disconsolate-looking lad, whose deplorable condition so excited his compassion that he supplied him with temporary lodging and passed him into a Refuge. The grateful subject of this solicitude told an affecting story. His mother died during his infancy, and his father had lately sunk into a drunkard's grave. After seeing his father's remains committed to the earth, the now friendless boy returned to London with a sufficiently heavy heart, doubtless cogitating by the way how he should contrive to keep together the humble home. Home? He had no home! On reaching the room whence he came a few hours before, to follow the corpse to its last resting-place, he found some men removing the furniture as payment for debts overdue; and thus he himself was turned into the street. The first night he slept in a cart, and afterwards selecting a dry arch, he relinquished its accommodation by direction of the police. Then fortune favoured him. By special permission, he nightly huddled into the boot of an omnibus in a neighbouring yard; but while thus irregularly lodged he set an example to those who would fain excuse dirt by the plea of poverty. How he should keep himself and his shirt cleanly was a problem not to be solved without some trouble; and only after due consideration and search was a hot-water pipe found by the river-side, where he could easily wash his linen. Admitted to the Refuge, this boy turned out an honest and worthy character.

He who picks up moral beings like the above, to restore them to respectability and usefulness, does what is worthy of being acknowledged by the Victoria Cross of philanthropy. Sometimes, in the lowest state of poverty, a lad will be found who, for some cause or another, has left home to become involved in ruin. In a wretched and foul lodging-house, a teacher, while canvassing for scholars, once met with a case of this description, and thus reports his experience in the monthly organ of the Ragged-School Union:—

'"They are mostly boys, you see," said the landlord,

referring to his customers, "and you will find them a complete lot of riff-raff. . . . There is no doing much with them. But I have one boy I should like you to see; he has been well brought up, but now he is lost." "Lost!" said I, the word ringing dolefully in my ears; "lost!" "Yes, lost, sir; but I'll bring him to you." He soon appeared in the street, and by the light opposite I could perceive that his sallow-looking countenance betokened both mental and physical suffering. He had evidently once moved in a very superior station to the one he now occupies. The very touching and affecting replies to the questions that I put to him made it both difficult and painful to elicit from him his previous history. "The reason I appear so different to the others is owing to my former position; I have moved in a very different sphere to the one you now see me in." I remarked to him, "You appear ill," and proffered my assistance to procure for him medical advice, for which he thanked me, observing that he felt the doctors could do but little for him now. "I shall not trouble any one long." I invited him to see me on the following morning, when his attenuated form, as seen by the light of day, prompted the most compassionate feeling. He then related to me the story of his life. "I was brought up very respectably, and received an expensive education. My uncle and my father were at the expense of my education jointly. My father was then captain of a ship. In consequence of his inability to pay his share for my education, I was obliged to leave school. He is now reduced through his extravagance; in fact, he is so poor that he is unable to keep the five children dependent upon him; it is not likely he can afford to keep me. After the death of my mother, I was apprenticed on board a merchant-vessel trading to North America. When I returned last voyage, the captain discharged me out of pity. He could see I was not strong enough, and my cough was so troublesome as to make it difficult to perform my duties; in fact, everything was irksome to me. I had never been taught to look for a livelihood by my own exertions, but should not have minded that, had I been strong enough. Had my mother been living, I should not have gone to sea. My uncle was for two years mayor of Waterford, and is very rich. He will have nothing to do with me now. I met one of his sons in the street the other day, when he said to me, 'You must know my father well enough to know that it would be of no use whatever again to apply to him.' Indeed, I have made up my mind never to trouble him again. I have a knowledge of Latin, and can read French pretty well, but cannot now speak it. I do not think of my former history much during the day, as I employ my time in reading, but cannot help thinking of it during the night; but I do not wish to think of it much."'

But we have not yet done with romance, though, alas, the life-story of divers of these children of the streets is romance in crime. The tragical scenes of sensational fiction do not always surpass the following account of the early associations of a boy received into the Westminster Refuge.

His father being by profession a coiner of base money,

attained to a high standard of excellence in his art, if 'excellence' may be applied to such employment. The home, workshop, and warehouse of this desperado were situated in a court—long since demolished—which in its day 'seemed as if purposely adapted as a fortified retreat for robbers and outlaws. Hidden in front by the houses in Old Pye-street, and the only entrance to it being by a dark narrow passage from the most notorious part of Duck-lane, it was never frequented by visitors except on business.'

In this retreat, where the police entered only in companies, lived the coiner's family—himself, wife, and two children, and the last were in course of training for the same nefarious business. The attic, or laboratory, where the man worked, was actually a mint in miniature, and, approached by a dark staircase, was purposely rendered difficult of access; only one person in a stooping posture being able to enter at once. The boy of our story, at the date of the collapse of the establishment, being about twelve years of age, already showed a precocity in wrong-doing beyond his years. One part of the daily business consisted in collecting pewter from the marine stores of London; and this, night by night, they converted into flash coin, and so skilfully was the transformation effected, that the chief artificer won a rare reputation among distinguished 'smashers,' and drinking propensities only hindered his becoming a capitalist. These people being cowards at heart, shrink from the risk of passing their own manufactures; and in an instance like the present there was no need to incur the danger, the man's profits sometimes reaching as much as three or four pounds in a day. The coin, if well done, fetches about a third of the value of good money.

It happened that a former accomplice or 'friend' of this coiner turned traitor, and supplied the police with information, besides giving them a plan of the premises, so as to enable them to effect an easy capture. The attack being planned, the assaulting column, consisting of twenty constables, headed by an inspector, approached; and when they surprised the ruffian in his den, their force proved to be not one too many. Indeed, so desperate a resistance was offered, that only by being literally overpowered could the coiner be brought to bay.

The representatives of law and justice now supposed their victory complete; but in the meantime agencies were working against them, the existence even of which they little suspected. Mrs. 'Smasher,' instead of being judiciously detained, was incautiously allowed to remain unnoticed, and she soon proved the potency of a woman's interposition by hastening into another house to acquaint the leader of a gang of thieves with the state of affairs at 'the mint.' On receipt of this stirring news the 'ganger' rushed into a public-house near at hand, and marshalled his men by calling them to arms in a few terse sentences. 'The mint' was surprised and stormed; and those enemies of their craft, the police, were even then in possession. Worst of all, their smasher-in-chief was in the clutches of the law. 'Chaps!'—this by way of peroration—'surely you won't see the poor fellow served like that!' The party started up at hearing this summons, and hastened to the court, where now a peculiar whistle was heard proceeding from the coiner's den—a well-known signal for his 'pals' to rise. In a few minutes the stairs were filled by a dauntless company, who were resolved on compelling the police to raise the siege. This being actually accomplished, the coiner escaped, to return soon after to his occupation and to defy the law. For a time he remained unmolested; but at length was again suddenly surprised by fifty policemen, when, escaping through a trap-door, he got clear away, and still remained untaken. Not to be for ever outwitted and defied, the police finally succeeded in effecting a capture; though such was the violence of their prisoner that he tore the officers' clothes, bruised their limbs, and behaved as though he would shake the cab into ruins which conveyed him to the station. Being brought to trial, this determined criminal received a sentence of thirty years' transportation; but after serving a tenth of that term, he, by good conduct and many signs of true penitence, earned a ticket-of-leave. The son, who was rescued from an apprenticeship of lawlessness and a life of crime by ragged-school agency, grew up grateful for having been assisted in escaping the degradation of his father's business, and turned out an intelligent, promising scholar. 'It was a miserable life,' he said; 'we were always in terror. Although living at the top of the house, if we heard any one at the bottom of the stairs, father would spring to his feet and stand listening at the door until he knew who it was.' One part of this boy's singular discipline consisted in practising the swallowing of coins, so that they should readily be put out of sight in case of urgent need. Five or six shillings seem to have represented the extent of his juvenile capacity; but the more accomplished sire 'bolted' crown-pieces with ease! Ultimately this interesting scholar was sent out as an emigrant to Australia.

The above relation sufficiently proves the correctness of what was before remarked—that schools are not only cheaper, but far more effective than prisons in preventing crime as well as in reforming the criminal. The best of prison discipline frequently serves only to harden. Thus a certain boy having been sentenced to seven days' imprisonment for stealing half-a-crown, would on regaining liberty probably have lapsed into a confirmed thief, had he not been helped to a better course by the ragged-school. How fatal in its evil corrupt fruit is a first sin. That half-crown was expended in treating divers dissolute companions of worse character than the actual transgressor; for when at their instigation the thief refused to repeat the offence, he was informed against and convicted. On leaving prison, perhaps he was fortunate in being compelled to regard his old comrades as enemies; for, separated from bad companions, he became more susceptible of the good influence of the teachers, by whom he was instructed, apprenticed, and put in a way of doing well.

Opportunities of acting the good Samaritan in the streets of London are seldom wanting to those who desire them, for objects on whom to bestow compassion are plentifully scattered abroad. The ragged juvenile outcasts who throng the river-side and romp beneath dry arches, are not always inveterate thieves. Some are striving hard, and amid very terrible surroundings, at least to put on a show of honesty. Boys of this order loiter about railway stations and markets, watching with hunger-sharpened eyes the extent of each pedestrian's luggage, and noting the weight of articles marketers purchase, hoping that a chance may somewhere turn up of earning a trifle by carrying the load.

One winter night, such a one was discovered at Billingsgate. Homeless, ragged, and starving, he wished to do what was right, but in the unequal struggle he succumbed to want and cold. Having no alternative but that of stealing, or applying to the relieving officer, he chose the last; and, while walking to the workhouse, he met the lady who resolved on becoming his friend. When admitted to the school, this lad's physical condition was dreadfully reduced, as was shown by his skin being covered with sores. In very pity several class-mates purchased him a shirt, so that the rough clothing should cease to be a torment. Helped to this degree, the ragged scholar soon delighted in helping himself. The friend who first noticed him now procured employment for him, and, with his foot on the bottom round of the social ladder, he ascended to a respectable station. Still progressing in well-doing, in faith, and in temporal prosperity, he finally desired to be enrolled among the teachers of the school, in order to enjoy an opportunity of leading others in the way in which he had himself been led.

These are large results, won by humble agents in a field sufficiently repelling to many respectable Christians; but since the Bible assures us that 'lack of knowledge' is equivalent to destruction of soul, even ragged-school teachers may beware of underrating the importance of their labours. Ignorance is the blighting curse resting on the poor children of the streets. The instinct of animals supersedes in a large measure *their* need of education. The higher the creature in the scale of being the weaker are its instinctive powers, so that with man, ignorance is the parent of a myriad of evils. The experience of our teachers and missionaries shows that we strike at the root of social and even political wrong by diffusing Christian knowledge; for Christianity no less truly carries temporal good in one hand than she does salvation in the other. What is ignorance—ignorance of God—but the gaunt tyranny of the powers of darkness, whose empire of misery and of degradation our persevering workers are invading, and whose ascendency their endeavours tend to curtail.

Hence it follows that the work of reclamation, as prosecuted by the city missionary and the ragged-school teacher, is a national benefaction. The good result of their labour so infuses itself into the every-day life of the nation, that our present contracted vision is unable to trace its extent. If the heart of England is beating more healthily than of yore, these philanthropic agencies have tended to the purifying of the national life. After adducing examples like those already given, is it too much to say that Christian work among the poor even tends to the repression of worldly poverty? The evangelist in London is constantly proving that the natural effect of the Gospel is to socially raise those whom it reaches, however low their condition.

Undoubtedly, one chief hindrance to the spread of

religion is the difficulty of making people realise their lost state—to see themselves as God sees them; for once engender dissatisfaction with present circumstances, and you create a desire for something better. This is just what our Christian workers in the low parts of London are doing. Both by precept and example, it is theirs to show that fear of God begets respect of self, while both are compatible with a due enjoyment of temporal blessings. What are the effects of their teaching on the lowest classes, on those who are already criminal, and who as children threaten to become so? Young persons instructed in the fear of God and in habits of industry will not *willingly* live to prey on others. A very little Bible truth suffices to beget in the degraded a sense of degradation, and every outcast man, woman, or child is a hopeful subject when brought to know the sense of shame. 'This school,' said a youthful thief, 'has done me a great deal of harm since I've been here. I'll tell you why. Me and some of my pals here get our living how we can; 'cause why, we've got no characters, and nobody won't employ us; we can't starve, don't you know, and what's a cove to do? Well, they're always preaching about God seeing you and the like of it, that it makes a cove afeared; it takes all the pluck out of *me*, I know. I never thieve now unless I am forced to do it from hunger. If I go after a hankercher, when the pinch comes I begin to think about God Almighty, for, as they say, you know, fear makes cowards of us. I've been for a good many things, and had many hair-breadth escapes in my time, but have never been lagged yet; no, never had the key turned on me once yet. It's my luck, I suppose, or, as they say, the Almighty's goodness.' This testimony is satisfactory, even though somewhat ludicrous. Physical pain is no more certainly a sign of life than shame in a sinner is the best omen of repentance; and because the teaching of the ragged-school begets this sense of shame, and a yearning in the heart of the child after something better than has satisfied the parents, the seed sown by its agency is yielding as fruit some of the fairest things of human nature. The good received by the children redounds to the parents. A profane drunkard once burst into tears when his little girl crept from her bed to rebuke him:—'Father, my teacher says, if you get drunk and swear so, you will never go where God is.' That man forsook his evil habits, began spending his evenings at home, and was soon a regular attendant at public worship.

What strange innovations in the moral world would be effected by a wider diffusion of the sacred oracles. The world is wide enough for all; but those taught in moral rectitude and in Bible precepts will more readily help themselves than those of a lower caste. Are not our busy teachers rescuing their constituents from the sad fate of having to grope through life in mental and spiritual blindness, while the more fortunate find opportunities of making their way? While knowledge is power, while the education of the well-to-do strengthens its subjects in the power of self-help and promotes self-respect, the knowledge carried into the dark retreats of great cities is also of surpassing potency. Numbers raised in respectability by relationship to Christ, are, as we hope, but the sample-drops of a hovering shower. Even as regards the present life, Christianity includes far more than the world supposes. All who are reached by its benign influence appear to become further removed from the dangers attending false steps in life and from the miseries engendered by improvidence.

What are the qualifications of an efficient ragged-school teacher? He must be animated by a kind heart, possess a strong nerve, and, being himself quick to learn his scholars' wants and idiosyncrasies, he must be apt to teach, and of winning manners; he must also master the knack of commanding obedience and attention. If a paid agent, he is poor in worldly gear; but yet though constantly associating with poverty in its worst form, he is ever tempted to devote an undue proportion of his slender means to affording relief to those who are poorer than himself. To-day, perhaps, one of his class is dinnerless, and a piece of bread must needs be doled out to prevent the child from fainting; to-morrow, a scholar may be missing, and on calling at the lodging, fever and destitution may call for still more urgent action and more Christ-like self-denial.

What of the ragged boy? Did you, my reader, ever properly realise that the urchin who keeps pace with omnibuses, turning summersaults more to the risk of neck and limb than the passengers' profit, and who eagerly opens your cab-door, or begs the privilege of carrying your parcel, is *your* brother? The bare idea of so undesirable a relationship is no doubt entirely disgusting. Yet you need not superciliously turn aside; for when rescued, and allowed to partake of a little of that knowledge which has made *your* way to differ from *his* hard lot, he too is found to carry the divine image. Only give him a few opportunities, or as he would express it, let him have 'a chance,' and the subject taken from the slum, or the thieves' rookery, will not so disgrace his friends as would at first appear. He offers good material for philanthropists to mould, and genius sometimes lights up his hunger-pinched features. That matchless definition of a parable, 'An earthly story with a heavenly meaning,' was given by a ragged scholar. He is grateful for a little help, but if left to himself he is not given to harbouring vindictive feelings against persons better off, and who suffer him to drag on his existence in wretchedness and ignorance. In the hardest seasons, unless more than usually depressed by cold and want, he is not very subject to lowness of spirits. 'Hi, clean yer boots, sir!' 'Cigar-lights, three boxes a penny!' 'Hecho and Hevenin' Standard, third edition!' are familiar sounds, seldom pitched in a key betokening dulness within. True, the boy is ignorant, excepting in things he should not know; for he has been schooled in no better discipline than want, hard usage, and ill-words. His home—should he have one—is an attic in some foul court or obscure alley, where few would find it convenient to be clean and honest. His genius, like that of his brothers and sisters the world over, is quicker at progressing in vicious courses than in learning what is good; and by associating with 'pals' older than himself, he is, while yet a child, initiated into the ways and mysteries of crime, and learns that to be 'plucky' he must steal, and swear, and fight. Nevertheless, he never loses his reverence for those whom he knows to be sincere in their professions, and honest in their prayers and endeavours for his reclamation. 'At times they exhibit a shrewdness, and I may say a generosity, which are remarkable,' said Charles Stovel, in a speech at Exeter Hall. 'Passing down Rosemary-lane one night, a handkerchief was extracted from my pocket by a lad, who ran away with it. Soon afterwards, however, he returned and said, "Please sir, is this yours?" "Yes, it is," I replied. "Take it," said he; and then he added, "Please, sir, give me something for bringing it back." "No, my boy," I said, "I must not do that, but I will leave for you with my friend here a little book." The boy came next day to the house of my friend, and said, "Please, sir, was not that a minister?" "Yes," was the answer. "Ah well," said the boy, "I will never rob a parson, for God's sake.'" If rescued in time, the ragged boy will reward his deliverers; but if left to himself he will not disappoint his 'schools and schoolmasters' by growing up true and honest. On the contrary, while himself swiftly traversing the broad road to destruction, he will unwittingly inflict heavy revenge on those whose apathy, not to say cruelty, has provided for him no better fate.

We may delineate the ragged boy, and explain his wants and aspirations, while suggesting plans for his amelioration; but sometimes he can write about himself far more effectively than can any mere beholder. The following account is from a lad admitted into the St. Giles's Refuge some years ago, and who, emigrating to Australia, rose to competence and respectability:—

'I have reason to bless the day I first entered the ragged-school. If I had not been admitted, I do not know what would have become of me, for I had lost my character with keeping bad company in a common lodging-house in Queen-street, Seven Dials, where vice, and drunkenness, and misery, in all its shapes, are open to the mind of the young beginner. There is the hoary-headed old man on the same footing with the boy. The old man swears and blasphemes, and the boy thinks he has a right to do so too; at least, such were my ideas. We used to sleep seven or eight in the same room, without any regard to age; and I daresay, sir, you can form an idea of the state of a common lodging-house better than I can describe it. Suffice it to say, there wickedness and crime are carried on to a great extent. I was in a good situation at the West End; *but unfortunately I lodged out.* I had a friend or relation who lodged in this common lodging-house, and he induced me to lodge there, too; *and that, sir, was the beginning of my fall.* I soon learned the art of gambling, and would play cards with the oldest man in the house, and he was seventy-six years of age. At last, not being able to meet the demands for the money I lost, I robbed my employers of half-a-sovereign, to squander it away in the kitchen, where from twenty to thirty men and boys spend their evenings, drinking and gambling. I was not suspected by my employers, as I had been with them some time, and they had a good opinion of me. I soon became careless, and dissatisfied with my situation, because my wages were not sufficient for me to gamble with and support myself.

I left, and from bad I came to worse. During the six months previous to my being admitted to the Institution I had no less than five different places. At last I lost my character altogether, and no one would employ me. What was I to do then? My only alternative was either to plunge deeper into crime, and become a thief or else a vagrant. From the first I shuddered, and the latter I was too proud to do. I could not starve, so I made application to the parish I was born in, to see if they would do anything for me. One of the officers told me, if I would go to his house at Fulham, he would employ me. I went, and only staid a fortnight. I left in a clandestine way, and stole a new coat belonging to him, for which I was apprehended, and sent to the house of correction for ten days. I then began to see how dreadful was my situation, and resolved, if I could only get another opportunity of earning an honest living, I would take care of it. For some misdemeanour I committed, I was confined in solitary confinement, and on bread and water for two days. I then, for the first time for a very long while, prayed to God sincerely to assist me. I came out of prison on a Saturday night, at eight o'clock. It rained very hard, and I had not a penny in my pocket, and no one to give me a night's lodging, for I was ashamed to go near any of my relations; for although they were poor they were honest, and to the present day they do not know that I have ever been in prison. Such were my prospects. I had to wander the streets that night, and the following week I was much the same way situated; but I had determined to be honest. At last,

Providence directed me to this Institution. How different are my prospects now to what they were then! For I feel convinced, if I had not been admitted, I must have become a thief or an outcast of society; and perhaps, instead of going out to Australia as an emigrant, I might have gone as a convict. I have reason to look on myself as a brand saved from the burning; and when I am far away on the mighty deep, I will offer up a prayer to Almighty God to bless the labours of the committee and subscribers of this Institution.'

The reformation of characters once all but hopelessly involved in the meshes of crime and ignorance, is the choicest reward we can offer the ragged-school teacher. The Bible is indeed a power among the ragged children, and not unfrequently it is almost startling to witness how a mere child will tremble when accused by conscience, after being instructed in the nature of right and wrong. A girl of a West-end ragged-school, on account of her condition of general destitution, was received into Lisson-street Refuge; and there she endeavoured to excite compassion by a false story of poverty and orphanage. Calling to mind, however, what she had heard in the class about the terrors which will one day overtake evil-doers, she was dismayed, and one night was observed lying in sleepless terror. In reply to the matron's inquiries she cried, 'I cannot sleep; I am so unhappy. Let me speak to you alone. I have something to tell you which I have not courage to say to governess. I have tried for many days to make up my mind to tell her, but cannot do so.' This girl was not an orphan, as she had represented; on the contrary, she ran away from home to fall grievously into sin. This young creature, restored to her mother and to a respectable station, was saved by the Ragged-school Refuge.

The above illustrates the working of the Refuges; for an agency seeking to benefit neglected children, temporally as well as spiritually, would be incomplete without the REFUGE. Would the reader like to take a peep into one of these institutions? Here is a description, from the organ of the Union, of one situated in Marylebone:—

'The "Grotto" is one of several houses now open to the thousands of friendless wanderers in this large city, where they can obtain shelter and food and are partially clothed. Its two *distinctive* features are: First —that it admits boys at a more advanced age than any Refuge in London. This, though of course adding difficulty to the work, has proved an untold blessing, as it gives to many a second chance, and meets the case of numbers who, having made a false start, are brought to the verge of ruin, and who would be without hope of escape if it were not for a home such as this. Even limiting ourselves to the winter that is just past, three different lads have voluntarily said, "If it had not been for the Grotto, I should have been on the gallows." One of them—a very clever fellow—had joined a gang of forgers, the second had been taught the first lessons in the college of thieves by a "professor," and the third was being gradually trained to be an actor in the "Jack Sheppard" school, "where the pieces mostly end in murder." All these are now rescued, and one has himself become an active worker for God. The second feature in which the Grotto differs from most other Refuges is—that no subscription or influence of any sort is needed to procure the admission of a lad. So long as there is room the doors are at once open to all who apply, at all times; the only title they need is being homeless and friendless.

'The great object of the promoters of the Refuge is, that these poor and homeless outcasts of society should be brought to the knowledge and love of the Friend of sinners, who Himself, when on earth, had not where to lay His head; and to seek to manifest, by words and deeds of love, that God is love, to those who have grown up with the fixed idea that both God and man are against them. We are deeply thankful that in many cases this message has proved the means of real conversion, shown forth in a new life, and in numbers more we have every evidence that the seed has taken root, and prayerfully and hopefully we look for its one day bearing fruit—resting on the promise, "In due season ye shall reap." Every effort is made to obtain satisfactory situations for the boys on leaving, and to keep up a kindly feeling after they have left. The constant affection with which the Grotto is spoken of by the "old hands," and the eager way in which they return to it after some years of absence, to see the Home and visit their comrades, is most gratifying, and tells in unmistakable terms of lasting good sought and found there. It has been ascertained, that of those who have been admitted since the Grotto first opened its doors for the reception of these vagrants, upwards of one hundred are now doing well, and have become respectable members of society. We have had most encouraging visits from many of them this winter. One, whom we had almost despaired of ever hearing of again, returned with eleven years' good character from sea. Another, whose case for a long time seemed quite hopeless, now writes from Canada, that his master will not part with him, as he is the only one he can trust for being always sober. The other day we had a visit from one, originally found in the streets on a stormy night, who has now been eight years in one situation, and whose mistress has just died, leaving him a legacy. Another has just called, leaving half-a-sovereign to "save," as he said, some other fellows. Cases might be multiplied. . . The work which occupies several hours a day consists principally in chopping wood and making it into bundles for firewood, and in picking hair for upholsterers; and it is supposed that each boy shall average one hundred bundles of firewood a day and forty-five pounds of hair.'

The working of these institutions only needs to be known to be appreciated. Take the following samples of the inmates which were found in one establishment by a visitor on a certain occasion. A little girl, the child of a dock-labourer, having lost her mother, had been subjected to gross ill-usage after her father's second marriage, frequently having been shut out from home all night. Another girl of fifteen, turned adrift with her sisters into the streets by those who should have protected her, had been saved from impending ruin. One child had brought on illness by walking from Liverpool, and she would have been lost but for this timely asylum. A similar youthful adventurer tramped to London in hope of finding employment, but, disappointed, sat for a fortnight on London-bridge, sleeping by night in an empty garret, to which a kind woman allowed her access. Such are specimens of the juvenile characters which the Refuge snatches from ruin and prepares for places of useful industry.

Illustrations of good effected are the best arguments for the need of these institutions. What heart will not be touched on reading a story like the following? One winter evening, when the air without was damp and chilly, a scholar of Gray's-yard school cried playfully to his fellows, 'Now let us run home.' Another little fellow standing there, precocious beyond his years, answered, '*I wish I could say that.*' He had not even a wretched home wherein to rest his wearied body. Yet, forlorn as he was, he would yet obtain a little schooling. On losing his mother, he soon found himself abandoned by a drunken father and left to his fate. By day he ate such food as charitable persons bestowed, and by night slept on staircases where he could. Unless assisted by some rescuing agency, such unfortunates as the above could scarce do otherwise than lapse into vicious courses.

Another instance will show the beneficial working of the St. Giles's Refuge. One day a missionary was told of a girl thirteen years of age, whom the abandoned women of a house in Westminster were retaining in servitude. Having lost her father, her mother also was virtually lost, for she lay on a drunkard's death-bed in a neighbouring workhouse. The missionary boldly entered the brothel and found the child securely tied to a bedstead, there being some danger of her running away. The little prisoner was released and taken to the Refuge, and properly succoured by her new friends. News of this deliverance reached the mother's ears, and, repenting of her evil ways, she gave her daughter a blessing, and expressed her gratitude to those who had rescued her from sin worse than slavery. Here innocence was snatched from the yawning gulf of crime and immorality, and trained for respectable service and happiness.

A lad of fifteen applied for admission, saying he only just remembered his mother, while his father had been stricken down by accident. After wandering about, picking up a few casual pence by opening cab-doors and carrying parcels, he felt that want and exposure were undermining his constitution, and, half despairingly, he applied at the St. Giles's Refuge. On being admitted, his condition was indescribably shocking, his flesh having been eaten into by vermin. The morning after his admission he awoke with cries of pleasurable surprise. 'I have not felt so well nor lain so nicely for many months.'

Take another example. One spring afternoon, a gentleman interested in the work of rescuing neglected children was walking along Holborn, when a sad-looking object attracted notice in the form of a girl, evidently in an abject state of destitution. She dragged her way slowly along, half despondingly, now stopping at one window, and then at another, apparently surveying most wistfully all the stock of a richly-stored jewellery establishment. The gentleman presently accosted the outcast: 'Have you no home?' 'No, sir.' 'Have you no parents or friends?' 'No, sir.' These replies being true and straightforward, the girl was directed to proceed to a Refuge near the spot, and wait until the gentleman should return. The shivering creature obeyed the directions given, and at the Home manifested great impatience at the delay of the gentleman, declaring that should he not come, she would watch for his reappearance in Holborn, for he surely intended to befriend her. When really taken in she became excited with joy; and when washed, clothed, and refreshed by a night's sleep, she scarce resembled the ragged outcast of Holborn-hill of the previous afternoon. Losing her father when six years of age, and latterly her mother, she had not slept in a bed for months; and her only home being the streets, she lodged wherever an opportunity offered, fortunate if able to lie down in a cab or creep into a cart. But even in this forlorn condition the wanderer did not want friends. There were kind hearts about to give her a little food, one benevolent policeman especially distinguishing himself by frequently treating her to a hot breakfast. What a fact for moralists to think about? A girl of tender years alone in the inhospitable streets! 'I wish I was in heaven with my poor mother!' she once exclaimed. 'Nobody cares for me here. I have been two or three times to the Serpentine to drown myself, but so many people were there that I could not.' To such the Refuge is a last resource, a very door of hope.

Other waifs and strays have been met with in the

streets by persons when about their daily business. Thus, while walking near Charing-cross, a gentleman observed four girls, two more ragged and forlorn than their companions, sitting on the steps of St. Martin's Church. He watched them a minute, and then, approaching, inquired if they would like to enter St. Giles's Refuge. They joyfully embraced the offer. Though two were strangers to the other two, they had casually met, and, as common subjects of misery, became friends.

By the agency of the ragged-school great numbers of these children have been moved from a miserable lot, in squalid courts and alleys, to a life of healthful industry in the colonies. There they readily obtain desirable situations, and the letters continually coming home, filled with expressions of gratitude and hope, are very encouraging to their instructors. A gentleman of an Australian port was surprised at the appearance of a number of good-looking, well-conducted emigrants, who wished to be recognised as 'Lord Shaftesbury's boys;' and through this adventure became a life-long benefactor of London ragged-schools. When will the urgent need of the children of our streets inspire others who are blessed with abundance also to befriend the outcast? The nation does not sufficiently appreciate the evils which are alarmingly rampant in the recesses of great cities. Is it not cheaper and safer to nip sin in the bud than to battle against it in its maturity—to reform the child than to punish the adult? The sapling may be bent and cultured; the strong tree is obstinate and unyielding.

Is it not highly becoming to exercise sympathy for children who show so touching a sympathy one for the other? A lad on earning a penny has been known to bestow a loaf on a breakfastless companion; and a scholar, on losing a widowed mother, has had his class-mates cluster around to pray for his comfort and even to make a collection on his behalf. These are indeed the true subjects of misfortune, and their necessity calls for compassion and help. Who else but Christians shall help them, when their ignorance in many cases extends to knowing nought of parents and relatives? *Who* are these City Arabs? A theory has been ventured, that not a few of our street adventurers are the offspring of aristocratic sires—infants abandoned by baby-farmers, and who, sheltered by the very poor until able to care for themselves, find their way into the criminal ranks by their surpassing genius in wrong-doing!

When will the world arrive at a right estimation of the evils of ignorance, by which poverty, crime, and drunkenness are supported—the evil triad which blight the lives of our outcast children? Looking at the subject as political economists, we ask, Has not popular ignorance favoured oppression? In states where social progress has been hindered by tryanny has not a 'lack of knowledge' alarmingly prevailed? To be effectively matured dark designs require darkness. Popery rose to ascendancy by proscribing the Bible and discouraging schools. Despotism prospers without senators and constitutional advisers. But the dread of one monarch is the glory of another, and here we are fond of claiming that things are ordered for the people's good. In England circumstances favour the philanthropist. The English are lovers of liberty and progress. The pure religion of Christ is their heritage. The mephitic atmosphere in which cruelty and tyranny thrive could not be breathed on our free shores. Why do we differ from less fortunate neighbours? Has not a spread of divine knowledge, partial as it is, repressed abuses in the State, and literally been to our senators wisdom? Even a spread of mere secular knowledge raises the poor by teaching them self-help and self-reliance; but the higher learning of the Bible blesses the soul. Ragged-schools have proved that Christian knowledge discourages crime, by engendering in the minds of the young abhorrence of mean and dishonest courses. By teaching the outcast to realise his value by the estimate of the cross, we lay the basis of moral restoration; and every sinner restored to honour and usefulness is gain to the nation at large.

In our crusade against ignorance and its attendant miseries, we are not moved by enthusiasm for what at the least is but a day-dream of ignorance itself—equality. Levelling may produce ruin; it can never benefit the masses. As things are at present constituted in modern society, distinct classes are as necessary to complete the national fabric as are the lesser and more imposing parts of architectural designs to the symmetrical proportions of noble buildings. He who raises the poor from degradation, not only leaves untouched every social distinction, but becomes in fact a promoter of harmony among classes. Each ragged-school teacher, in an eminent degree, is a peacemaker in a troubled world. The word spoken in his class is seed yielding fruit in the children, and also at the home fireside. By each well-prepared lesson he distributes good first learned of Christ. By sowing the germs of religion and moral rectitude among the neglected populace, we raise them in the respect of their fellows, and beget in them also a becoming bearing to their superiors. Christianity teaches just notions of the relative positions of rich and poor, and sympathises with the trials and privileges common to both.

This is not all. Unless to prevent revolutionary crises proper means are used,—such as instructing betimes the rising generation of the poor,—are not the opulent classes liable to become, what history shows us they have frequently been, the victims of the subjects of ignorance? Are they not liable, in some such sudden and overwhelming conjuncture, as in the collapse of France, to fall a prey to those who, possessing none of the learning which conduces to a life of rectitude, are yet sufficiently cunning to seize opportunities of avenging themselves on those whose strange indifference, or unchristian apathy, has allowed ignorance to blight their lives? Is it not a worthy work to promote harmony among our too widely separated classes? Are those forbidding moral gulfs, preventing the lowly from approaching us, and across which we refuse to go to them, necessary for preserving a sombre background to our gentility? It would not appear so. It seems rather that class dangers, springing from ignorance, jealousies, and bickerings, are healed for ever by a liberal diffusion of Christian and secular knowledge, through the agency of the teachers of the poor.

Thus, as we grieve over the vast amount of squalid wretchedness of London, and ask, Whence does it spring? the answer is, from IGNORANCE. Ignorance of God and of moral duties is the heaviest calamity which can befal a mortal. In proportion as moral beings depart from God they lose respect for themselves, and they who respect not themselves are lost to honour and honesty. Truly enough 'knowledge is power.' It is more. It is a revolutionary power in the best sense, as the history of ragged-schools abundantly proves. What does it effect? Out of rough and unpromising human materials, it moulds valuable and respectable members of society. The day has come for the exercise of true charity, which consists in discouraging mendicity, and in responding to the cry from the children who, running wild in the fœtid courts and alleys of this great city, involuntarily send forth their appeal from the streets.

The ragged-school teachers, in their daily toils, it is easy to believe, would feel the crosses of their life-work to be insupportable were they not lightened by extraordinary encouragement. Some of these half-clad, uncouth natures, who, till assisted by the mission agency, were subjected to evil influences on all sides, have received what, in time of trial, has conquered evil and asserted the supremacy of good. A newspaper-boy once picked up a parcel containing £350, and, dazzled by the vastness of the prize, and concealing his fortune from his associates, he made for Liverpool, intending to emigrate and be a great person in a foreign clime. But at Liverpool conscience awoke, and the teaching of the class rose in condemnation, till he could not proceed. When he would have stepped on board the ship, a voice within said, '*The money is not yours!*' and so, returning to London, he gave the parcel to his mother—an extremely poor but honest creature—who unhesitatingly returned the whole to its lawful owner. Now, how did that boy profit by ragged-school teaching, in a temporal sense merely? Instead of three hundred and fifty, he received only twenty pounds; yet, by being apprenticed with that amount, it went further than any ill-gotten gain, for it introduced him to a good position for life. The owner of the money also discovered that schools redound with blessing on the heads of their promoters.

It is not uncommon for truth to progress in the hearts of these children until they unwittingly set high Christian examples. One boy was heard rebuking some others for playing marbles on the Sabbath, and, unsuccessful in his appeals, he told his teacher that they refused to heed his words. 'What did you do?' was asked. 'I went home and prayed,' he answered. A training which can produce scholars of this sample should supply the labour-market with good material. This it evidently does; for the emigrants from the London schools find eager employers on landing in Australia and other places.

Then the kindly natures of many of the children reared under circumstances entirely unpropitious is sometimes very gratifying, and they frequently become a means of conversion to their profane relatives. One little Mary, at the date of her admission to a West-end school, presented a saddening spectacle. Spending their earnings in vicious indulgences, her parents had allowed her to roam in ragged freedom, supplying her with little beyond what she herself procured. But, quickly intelligent, Mary soon learned to read, and, influenced by Bible truth, began influencing others. Her home was a filthy den, and in which, half starved by day, she had only a little straw to lie upon at night. A change was at hand, however. One afternoon, when the school was being closed, Mary inquired if the books were to be given out.

'Why do you wish for one to-night?' inquired the teacher.

'Mother likes me to bring them home,' replied the child; 'for she reads them to father, and he has left off drinking since she read to him "Roger and his Home." When she began to read he did not like it, and said, "I have had enough of *that*;" but she said, "I must go on," and read it several times. He told her again and again he did not like it, when she replied, "You *must* like it." Now we are very happy, and have a few things about us to make us comfortable.'

Indeed, every endearing trait of human character can be found in the ragged class, if only diligently sought. The sensitive nature of the children, after conversion, recoils from their degrading surroundings. One daughter of a low drunkard desired, when dying, to be carried to the workhouse, to be out of hearing of her father's voice. Then, do we look for energy of character? A boy with a lame leg has been known to arrange with another to carry him to school, because he would not stay away on account of a mere inability to walk. Do we look for self-denial? A few shillings left by a visitor among the girls has been voluntarily surrendered to aid a case of distress. Do we look for the enviable capacity skilfully and delicately to rebuke remissness in duty? 'Will you not say your prayers, mother?' asked a little girl at bed-time. 'It's late and cold,' replied the woman. 'I will pray for you,' cried this better-instructed ragged-scholar;

and, falling on her knees, she offered her petition. Thus praise continues to issue from the mouths of babes and sucklings. Their behaviour often strangely contrasts with the profanity of unnatural parents, who seem to think their duty consists in training children to vicious habits. Teachers hear of infants of five or six years being dosed with intoxicants; and one child was known to be stupefied with spirits twenty or thirty times before the age of seven!

Doubtless, too, genius sometimes is found among the children of the street, and this, if judiciously trained, will make way in what is ennobling, instead of merely excelling in criminality. A story told by the Bishop of Cork, at a meeting in London, will show what valuable human gems are occasionally to be picked up in the street.

'There was once a little boy in Ireland, playing marbles and joking very much, and a clergyman who was passing by heard his jokes, and took a fancy to him. He sent him to Trinity College, Dublin, where he distinguished himself, and was at last called to the bar. At the bar he also distinguished himself, so he went on and on, and at last took a house and furnished it with all the accompaniments of respectability. Now in those days a journey from Cork to Dublin took a very long time, and this old clergyman, who had not for many years been able to see anything of the lad he had brought up, was very anxious to go and see him. He had heard of his progress, and intended many times to take the journey. At last he made up his mind, and set off, and after some time he reached Dublin, found his way to the square where this boy lived, and found the house. He was a plain country clergyman, and did not look very grand; and when the door was opened by a powdered servant, his questions were answered very haughtily. The clergyman asked, "Is your master at home? I want to see him." "He can't be seen," said the servant. "But I must see him," said the old gentleman. "You *can't* see him, then," said the servant. "Show me up to the drawing-room," said the clergyman; "your master will see *me*." There was something in his manner, something in his voice, that startled the servant, and so, after "humming and hawing," he showed him upstairs into a very nicely-furnished room. The old gentleman walked in, took a chair, and put his feet on the fender. Presently the door opened, and in walked a fine-looking gentleman, and, seeing a stranger with his feet on the fender, he said, "What do you want, sir?" The old gentleman looked around, and immediately their eyes met. The gentleman rushed forward, threw his arms round his neck, and exclaimed, "My dear old friend, you are welcome; the fender is yours, the furniture is yours, all that I have is yours, my more than father." And who is this I am speaking of? Why, the first lawyer of his time—JOHN PHILPOT CURRAN, Master of the Rolls.'

Though not exactly belonging to the history of ragged-schools, the above will show that the truest charity consists in seeking the deserving, and in making them the recipients of our bounty. This is so far superior to indiscriminate alms-giving, that ragged-school teachers class the latter among the evils of the age; and it is a serious hindrance to their success. One course is fraught with blessing; only evil can spring from the other, as could be shown by many instances.

On a Sunday morning in winter, a lady, while walking to church along a West-end thoroughfare, observed that a certain crossing was kept by a young girl of a good expression of countenance, but otherwise in a poor condition as regards clothes and cleanliness. Being of too considerate a nature to drop the customary penny and walk on, the lady questioned the child, and found that she resided in the notorious Church-lane, St. Giles's, but was one who had known better days. Shortly after, the lady inquired for the girl at the address given, where she lived with an old Irishwoman, their home being a loathsome cellar. Her history, though a sad one, was interesting, because she had not fallen into gross vice. Her father, a journeyman carpenter, emigrated to Canada, where he lost his wife, after which he himself returned to England and died. The orphan entered into service, but, thrown out of employment by the removal of the family, she was soon distressed for means of living. She necessarily left her lodging, and accepted the offer of the Irishwoman, who showed kindness by recommending her to take to a broom. Of a sensitive nature, she did violence to her feelings by adopting this course, but in the main preserved her character. Being on the downward road, however, the agency of the ragged-school came only just in time to rescue her from lower degradation, and to place her in a respectable situation.

Sometimes the case is reversed; and the unfortunate juvenile, overtaken by want, instead of being sought in his haunt by a kind gentleman or a philanthropic lady, will crave shelter or advice at the hands of those he imagines will befriend him; *e.g.*, the city missionary, the teacher, or even the pew-opener of a church. A boy, brought by his father out of Essex, and forsaken at the railway terminus in London, was taken into a Refuge after telling his story to the keeper of a chapel after service one Sunday night, and he subsequently went out as an emigrant. Another instance, quite as remarkable, was that of an Irish lad, who, having accompanied his parents from Ireland to Wales, lost them both by death at Cardiff. Being quite alone in the world, and utterly destitute, he went to Bristol, where for a time he gained a precarious livelihood by selling newspapers in the street. When that employment failed, he resolved on walking to London to seek better fortune. Arriving in the capital, without any home to go to, or money to supply immediate necessaries, he wandered about in a desponding condition, finding neither the employment nor the succour he had expected. Then a happy thought occurred. In Bristol he had been instructed at a ragged-school, and there he never received aught but good treatment and wise counsel from the teachers. Possibly similar institutions existed in London. At any rate he would look, and make special inquiries. To his great joy a school was actually discovered in a yard of Drury-lane, the superintendent being a city missionary, to whom the starving and footsore lad told his story, and, according to his faith, found in him a friend and adviser. On being admitted into St. Giles's Refuge, his conduct was so exceptionally satisfactory that he became a communicant, and won the attachment of all the other inmates, who called him 'Happy Jack.' Ultimately he emigrated to South Africa, and from there he sent home letters filled with expressions of gratitude and details of abounding prosperity. On one occasion he remitted £12 for a consignment of goods, with a further request that an apprentice should be selected from the institution—a lad 'with a high forehead,' betokening undeveloped talents for stitching and closing. This little life-story affords another instructive insight into the beneficial operation of school refuges.

Cases of the above description might be multiplied. When the children are taught and fitted for respectable stations, the benefit they themselves derive being the only return for the cost and trouble incurred, the teachers have still their reward; but when the ragged scholar progresses in good till he becomes in turn an effective teacher, the moral triumph is doubly complete, as is shown in the following example :—

A certain intelligent lad was sufficiently unfortunate, not only to have dissipated connections, but parents who were professed abettors of infidel sentiments. Having arrived at the age of seventeen, entirely uncared for as regards education, he coveted a little learning, but nervously shrank from invading the precincts of the ragged-school. At home he had heard Christians spoken of contemptuously, 'parsons' being especially denounced as impostors and hypocrites. Going to school he called 'unbending himself,' and for long he refused to stoop to the humiliation. At length scruples were overcome, and after attending the classes for a time, he made surprising progress, reaching to the higher rules of arithmetic and even to the Latin grammar. Still improving rapidly, he applied for permission to teach in the Sunday-school, to the great surprise of his superiors, who explained the responsibility of such duties and the mischievous results springing from indiscretion or unfitness on the part of those who undertook them. But being thoroughly in earnest, and understanding the nature of the work, he went to his minister, and told him he desired to identify himself with the Church of Christ. Being a youth of rare promise, he afterwards entered a training college, whence he was taken by the Bishop of Sydney to preside over a school in Australia. These are moral victories, well repaying for a little garment-soiling, or the inconvenience of going out of our ordinary way. Being conquests which only Christian gentleness can win, they are beyond the reach of the corrective hand of the law. Christian kindness triumphs where harsh correction only hardens.

Then do we seek for romance? It is seldom that fiction excels the interest attached to many histories connected with ragged-schools. Take the following autobiography of a boy, who was introduced to a situation in a warehouse, where, with the companion referred to, he rose into a comfortable station. The story would be marred were it given in any words but those of its own subject:—

'I was born in Glasgow, some eighteen years ago. I am a soldier's son; disease abroad killed my father, and the cholera took away my mother. In one year my three sisters and I were made orphans, without a penny, and scarcely a friend. My sisters found employment in the neighbourhood where we lived. I went to live with an uncle,—a man without a heart. Oh, sir, he was ill, ill to me! After a few years I saddened and sickened under his care, and at last ran away. With a companion, Charlie Brunton, I resolved to visit England. We set out, meeting our expenses by walking from town to town. After six months, we found ourselves within fifty miles of London. Here I separated from Charlie, who found regular employment, and I did not. The day we parted we spent the afternoon and evening together, and separated at midnight, under a tree, in silence. "Ah, Charlie, before you and I meet again," I said, "we'll know both sides of the shilling." Our arms were round each other; we stood speechless, and tore ourselves asunder. So ragged and woe-begone was I now that I was refused work. As I passed people stared and whispered; I felt I was suspected. Worst of all, sir, I was reduced from working and travelling to begging and travelling. My spirits, like lead, sank to the bottom of my heart. Well do I remember sitting under a hedge to eat the crust I had not earned, calling upon death to finish the ball. I knew enough of my Bible to believe suicide was sin, and that the rope and the river were not always the shortest cuts to happiness. My conscience would not let me murder myself, and at that time to me the cross of Christ was unknown. I was pained at the heart, and I seemed to move in thick darkness. I was in despair, with only courage and reason enough left to finish the twelve miles between me and London. After a sleepless night, without one bit of cheer, one ray of hope, I took the road, believing that in the evening body and soul would finish their acquaintance on the pavement of the city. I arrived late in the evening at the west end of

Oxford-street, and spent the night out of doors. I was forced to beg, so as to get a crust and a few coppers, and was able to pay threepence for a night's lodging in one of our cheap lodging-houses. May God keep me, sir out of those dens all the rest of my life! They are worse than hells, these places—they would make devils worse than they are. Men and women lying all of a heap—drinking, swearing, and snoring in all directions; two or three tallow candles stuck in bottles, at intervals, round the room, and the walls glittering with sweat. My circumstances were now dreadful. I saw I MUST become a thief if I remained there, and have any peace. Sir, I have fallen into many sins in my time, but I am not a thief—never was. Such an assembly met there one night that I rose from the fire and walked out; the street, sir, was heaven to it. I staid out all night, and caught cold, and was seized with a kind of ague. I thought I must surely die. In this condition I crawled down to London Bridge; I sat and trembled in a corner; I asked nothing; the crowd passed on. Towards five in the afternoon a gentleman turned aside, asked me a few questions, and gave me a shilling. He took out his card, and wrote the address of the school you found me in on the back of it. There I was received, and sheltered for a day or two. I gradually got better, and took to street-work again, and was able to earn a little, enough to keep me in board and humble lodgings. That gentleman's card let daylight in upon me. I now became a regular attendant in Miss L——'s Sunday-class, and much good I have gotten there. The sour feelings towards men, and the harsh ones towards God's providence, which sprang up in me during my trials, wore away. I felt happier, somehow;—it's hard to hate, sir. It makes one miserable—just like having a live coal in the palm of your hand. Yet I was no holier in my heart; all that dear lady used to tell us of Jesus did not move me; and I am sure of a Sunday night she used to drag her whole class to the foot of the cross. I again turned ill, and was unable to work, and was once more out of a home. I was so ill that I was again compelled to ask for shelter beside the school-stove; that very night you came on a visit to it. That was a night of nights to me. At that school-stove I was joined by a companion—one of my Sabbath class-fellows. We sat together; he was sad, and I was sadder. That night, however, he seemed softer in his manner than he used to be, and spoke oftener of the Bible. We bewailed our fate; I said I was becoming hopeless and heartless; he made no reply, and I stared into the fire. At length, looking me full in the face, and laying his hand on my shoulder, he said "*Tom, do you know,* I INTEND TO PUT GOD TO HIS WORD TO-MORROW." I did not understand him. He said, "Do you remember that lesson of Miss L——'s, two Sundays ago, about prayer? I can't get it out of my mind. She said so often and so earnestly, and looked at us so, 'Lads, God hears and answers prayer.' Now we have been nearly this whole day without bread; and she said the very ravens, when hungry, prayed, and got answers too. Now, if I live, Tom, I'll pray to God to-morrow. Do you pray?" I was silent; but my conscience answered—No! Here he looked earnestly up in my face, and said, "Will you join me?" So sincere did he look, for my life I could not say, No. After a little more talk we stretched ourselves upon the bench, and fell asleep. The morning bell was rung; we started to our feet, washed, and were turned out for the day. When we reached the bottom of the stair, the morning was raw, cold, and very dark. "Now, Tom, do you remember your promise?" whispered a voice beside me; "you said you would." My companion was at my side. I demurred. *There was no place.* Pointing to one of the dry arches, "This will do, Tom; come on," he said. In he went, and I followed. Having reached the far end, he fell on his knees and burst into prayer. The exact words I can't remember, but it came from his heart. The burden of it was—Bread, work, and pardon. We both came out; we wiped our eyes; we had both been crying. I had not opened my mouth, but I remember saying, as I grasped his hand, "Now for it." We turned down the street in the dark, and at the bottom took our stand—hungry, quiet, and waiting. We felt as if watching an experiment. Time wore on: there was nothing on the move. "I fear," said I, "we are two bad ones; we are not to be heard." My companion replied, "Wait, Tom, wait; we cannot command God." This shut my mouth: we stood in silence. An hour had passed away. But, sir, I was wrong; God DOES hear and answer prayer. A little man, in great haste, came up to us: "Carry this bag for me to Euston Station," and laid it down. My companion shouldered it, and I supported it from behind; we arrived at the station; he threw down two shillings and disappeared. We grasped each other's hand, we looked each other in the face, and not a word we spoke. At last I said, "What fools we were to be running at men's heels and cringing for coppers, when God is so liberal. I'll doubt His word no more." We spent that day by ourselves: that day Jesus tied our hearts to Himself. And now, sir, this day I am here; and from that hour I have had bread, a coat, and a home. I believe it will be so to the end.'

Though it is the richest return the school can achieve, for the teachers to be able to point to those who are both socially and spiritually raised by their discipline, they have frequently to be content with the assurance that their scholars are happy in another state. Sometimes disease, aggravated by want and exposure, thins the class; but otherwise even worse calamity conduces to the same end.

One summer afternoon a number of scholars belonging to a Westminster school were bitten by a mad dog, and five died of hydrophobia. One of the victims was a little fellow of eight years, of a sweet disposition, and possessing good capacities. From his infant lips his mother heard the Gospel, it having been his custom to repeat at home the texts and hymns learned at school. Lying in pain and weakness, he was an example of Christian patience, and unconsciously became to beholders an affecting plea for ragged-schools. When not incapacitated by the nature of the complaint, he sang verses committed to memory in health, and presented a very cheerful aspect. One day, when the end approached, both teacher and doctor stood by the bed, the latter observing to the disconsolate mother, 'I fear your son cannot live much longer.' 'I am glad to hear it,' directly cried the sufferer. 'Why, my little man?' inquired the surgeon.

'Because, sir, I am going home;' and then, turning to his teacher, he continued, 'Do not leave me yet, for I shall soon go home.' Complying with the ragged scholar's request, the visitor sat until the neighbouring clocks chimed the midnight hour, when the spirit of the child was released, to be numbered with the lambs of the fold above. How true is it that much of the good resulting from mission-work in London will not be manifest until the day of universal reckoning.

But while these gratifying results of earnest labour abound on all hands, let it not be supposed that the way of ragged-school teachers is not uphill, nor that they are never depressed by dark discouragement, springing from unconquered evil in the pupils themselves, or from the depravity of abandoned parents. Our meaning may be illustrated by the history of an unfortunate member of the Shoe-black Brigade.

The Shoe-black Society is an offshoot of the 'Union,' and its history includes some strange insights into the byways of London life. Many children have found this employment a door to comfort and respectability. One poor boy, when he entered the school, seemed to give much promise, and, upon joining the Brigade, he prospered until he had money in the bank. But this story of prosperity reached the ears of a drunken father, who, caring nothing for his son's welfare beyond coveting his money, forcibly withdrew him from school, drove him into the streets, sold his clothes, and squandered the proceeds. In a destitute condition, the late scholar would not, for shame, seek renewed acquaintance and help at the hands of old friends, which might have been done without risk of denial. On the contrary, utterly desperate, and not caring what he did, he fired a stack, was imprisoned for three years, and was probably thereby converted into a life-long criminal!

A singular chapter might be written on the trials of these neglected children of the streets—trials which happily do not often end in disaster and ruin as in the above instance. One shoe-black, on losing a mother dearly beloved, shrank from the idea of having her buried by the parish. Insisting on paying for the funeral by instalments, he raised the final payment only a week before his own decease. Apparently dying of a broken heart, the expenses of his own funeral were subscribed by his fellow scholars. Another boy became overjoyed at finding a long-lost mother, but was plunged into desponding grief at that mother's unconcern at the meeting, and complete indifference to his welfare.

But while speaking of the trials of ragged-school scholars—trials peculiar to their position, or such as are common to human nature—we must not overlook the hardships of labour which mere infants are often compelled to undergo. To most persons such a scene as the following would constitute a new phase of human life:—

One day a visitor entered a certain room, where was found an old lady superintending the making up into shirts of a heap of material. The operatives were a number of little girls of five years and upwards, the eldest, who was invested with the authority of a monitor, appearing to be not more than ten. Though silence was a rule of the establishment, it could only be nominally maintained, from the impossibility of controlling infant tongues.

One would begin to cry because her next companion had made her lose her thimble. Another would show signs of distress on being taunted, in a low voice, by a neighbouring vixen, with the reminder that her father was transported. 'And he was not transported,' the daughter maintained, in her eagerness to defend the family honour, 'because he had gone in a bootiful sip.' Then the dispute waxed more serious, and being sufficiently loud to reach the ears of the crone in command, she, according to her humour, coaxed or beat her constituents into order. Blood from the tender fingers of the workers smeared the seams they were sewing. Not unfrequently one would fall asleep; but the dame was not over hard in respect of the sleeping, for at five years of age, sleep by day is almost as much a necessity as it is a luxury. The occupants of a room like this are borrowed children; and their mothers, who go out to work, are glad to be relieved for the consideration of their offspring being supplied with 'not half enough to eat.'

There is yet another class of children deserving compassion and assistance — the natives of a foreign land, and who, brought hither by base deceivers as marketable commodities, endure a miserable existence. These are the Italian organ-boys of London, who, being kidnapped — their experience warrants the use of the term — are subjected to misery and hardship from day to day. The story of one of these unfortunates is thus narrated in Ferretti's 'Brief Narrative of a Mission in London:'—

'I believe I am nine years old, and am a Piedmontese. My father is a poor peasant, who labours hard to support his family by his work. The produce had been scanty, and to remedy in some degree our misfortunes, we had need of a loan of at least fifty francs; but we knew no one who would do us this kindness. One fine day the curate, or Catholic priest of the parish, came to my father, accompanied by a gentleman, who offered to lend us the fifty francs without interest. My father thanked him, and promised to pay him by little and little, in the course of a year. With this money my father purchased a cow, for the maintenance of his family, and other provisions of which we stood in need. A week had not elapsed when the gentleman returned with the curate, and informed my father that, as in consequence of urgent affairs he must immediately return to England, he should want in two days' time the fifty francs that he had lent him. My father was thunderstruck. What could he do in such circumstances? The cow could not be sold again, except at a heavy loss. The curate then said to my father—"This gentleman has a very lucrative business in England; he is a good Christian, and has under him many boys, whom he instructs in the profession of music, which he follows. In England gold coins are picked up in the streets. It is a Protestant country, it is true, but there are Catholic churches for the Italians, where the holy mass is celebrated every day. Take my advice: you have two sons; give one of them to this gentleman for the fifty francs which you owe him. He will take him with him to England, take good care of him, teach him the business, and in a few years he will return to Piedmont, loaded with money." My father was obliged to consent, to the great sorrow of my dear mother. We left in the diligence, and, arrived at the confines, I found other boys, accompanied by their conductors, who were waiting for us. We were told that it was necessary to pass through France on foot, as far as the sea. It took us a month, and during the journey I never slept on a bed, but in huts, upon straw, and often in the fields in the open air. Happily it was summer. Our food was a piece of bread and cheese in the morning, and the same in the evening. My master, however, went to the inn to eat and sleep. We were all knocked up with fatigue, and I cannot tell you what I and my companions suffered during that journey of thirty days on foot. The smallest of us, who was in delicate health, was so reduced by hunger and fatigue, that he fainted on the road, and was carried to the hospital, where he died the next day, far from his native country, and the mother whom he loved. At length we arrived at Boulogne, and were rejoiced at the sight of the sea, considering that our master could not oblige us to go over on foot. Unfortunately, however, the sea was so rough that I disembarked at the port of London more dead than alive. The master, who by deceit had bought me in Italy for fifty francs, sold me again for a hundred to the master to whom I belong. Now hear how he treats me. In the morning, before we go out, we receive (we are fifty in all) a basin of hot water, which they call tea, and a piece of hard bread. Till late at night I wander through the streets of London, asking charity, to the sound of this violin which you see. If I had been a little bigger, my masters would have put a small organ on my shoulders. They wanted to give me a little shrine, with the image of the Madonna in it; but I resisted this, because I had heard that those persons who show the Madonna to Protestants have every now and then stones thrown at them by the boys, and I never like to have stones thrown at me. The priests advised the masters to make the boys go about with those shrines, saying that this is the surest means of converting the English, who, as you know, are heretics, and believe neither in the Madonna nor in the Pope. If I am not able to bring him the whole sum, he beats me and sends me to bed without my supper, which consists of some bad soup, sometimes so bad that not even a dog would eat it. My bed is made of a little straw, on which we stretch ourselves without undressing. In Piedmont I enjoyed good health, but here, what with the smoke of the chimneys, the fogs, the fatigue, hunger, and beatings, I am certain I shall soon die. Oh, my dear mother! my dear mother! perhaps I may never more see you on earth. . . . . Know, sir, that these masters of Italian boys have no bowels of compassion, and are worse than the wild beasts. I have perceived that they maltreat us for their own interests. . . . . This is what I mean: if we have a pale face, if we are thin, or lame, we excite the pity of ladies, and then the master becomes rich.'

Thus have I endeavoured by illustration and otherwise to give a many-sided view of the work of ragged-schools. Enough has been said to show the vastness and importance of the work in which the teachers of the poor in London are engaged, as well as to demonstrate that abundant encouragement exists for perseverance in well-doing. These times call for large-hearted charity, but it must be charity of a sterling kind would we forward the good work of street philanthropy. Helping the poor is something quite different from the foolish habit of indiscriminate almsgiving. A little judicious assistance may put the neglected child in the road to industry, comfort, and respectability; unthinkingly to toss him a sixpence may only foster the indolence which usually ends in crime and misery. A gentleman, while passing over London-bridge, observed a boy in one of the recesses, and awaking him, found that he was a native of Hampshire, who never knew his father, but he had been used to out-door labour. By sending him to a Refuge the basis of that prosperity which he was destined to enjoy in a foreign land was laid; but had the passenger given a donation, and passed on, who can tell where the boy's disasters would have ended? What shall be done to extirpate mendicity and to secure to the poor the coins now thrown to beggars? Nearly twenty years ago, the 'Times' declared that, 'In London . . . . we have reduced the poor to the lowest scale of morals. It has come to this, that you will encounter more beggars of one sort or another, in a walk from Westminster-abbey to Oxford-street, than you will in a tour from London to Switzerland.' Unfortunately, this condition of affairs shows few signs of improvement; but street almsgivers should remember that by their misdirected kindness they hinder the work of reformation, and frustrate the operations of the best friends of the destitute; and the manner in which the custom affects ragged-schools is shown by a correspondent of the organ of the 'Union,' *e.g.*:—

'Near Beauvoir Town, London, there is a row of houses inhabited by very poor people. In one of the rooms of one of these houses lived a pair, the father being a drunkard, the mother a hard-working woman, but fond of her 'drops.' Her children, while she was out at work, were left to be educated in the streets, but with food at home. The boy, however, before he was five years of age, had learned that jumbles, hard-bake, and tarts were pleasanter eating than bread and butter, and were to be obtained by asking — that is, begging. Not long after this he inducted his sister, about three years younger, into the mystery. Of course the humble fare at home was left untouched, and the mother was not long in discovering that keeping a family need not be so expensive as some people make it, and their story of not having had anything to eat often now became a true one. We have once or twice tried to induce the boy to attend a ragged-school, but labour or restraint in any form is very distasteful to him. For twelve years we have watched him, and now we find him, at the age of seventeen, sending forth his sister early to sweep a profitable double crossing, one half of which he takes possession of at about nine a.m. From the pastry-cook's near at hand they breakfast as the money falls in, until between eleven and twelve, when the boy hires a velocipede, and takes an airing for about three or four hours up and down Kingsland-road and the adjoining streets, sometimes singly and sometimes accompanied by another 'Arab.' He then descends to earth again, assumes the brush, but only to beg, and as soon as the penny-gaffs open, both he and his sister and friends are taking their pleasure again. The boy works only on Sunday. He then sweeps a profitable crossing near Beauvoir Church.'

Let the facts given speak for themselves; and if,

beside instructing and warning, they excite sympathy for the work of reclamation going on in the London streets, they will not have been written in vain.

Education has happily become a leading question among social reformers. Besides secular education comes the still greater duty of Christianizing the people; for after all, a proper bearing of the creature towards the Creator is so closely connected with true progress, and reformation of manners in general, that it should be promoted by all means in our power. Undoubtedly the Christian teacher ranks high among political and social reformers. We may disagree as to what should be the constitution of common schools; but with a mighty empire of sin to invade, the cross of Christ becomes the rallying-point of faithful labourers. None wish to see the secular schoolmaster become an agent of religious partisans, for merely making proselytes is not spreading religion. Religious teaching is lifeless unless it reaches the heart, as is well understood by those who aim at amending the outward life of the low and degraded by reaching their souls. The sowing which will yield its best return hereafter is found to bring forth its first fruits on earth. The knowledge of the day-school, it is true, more concerns the body and its welfare than the soul; but still the soul is benefited, for even spiritually it is an advantage to possess a healthy and well-regulated body. Thus the day and Sunday-school teachers of London districts are banded together in a blessed alliance in the work of reclaiming from the empire of vice and ignorance many of the Creator's fair provinces. Ever bending with good fruit are the branches of the True

Vine. Plucking and eating only stimulate their bearing. Our fathers did more than a Sabbath day's work in founding Sunday and Ragged-schools. They planted a system of national education, the fruits of which, as lasting as time, are gladdening every day in the year.

Though Christianity has had chiefly to do with bringing in an era characterised by a grateful spread of general knowledge, and a becoming solicitude for the welfare of the rising generation of the poor, it is in accordance with its spirit to harmonise, not to annihilate, class distinctions. We are as far removed, probably, as the most conservative desire from inconveniences likely to arise from artisans and housemaids beguiling their leisure with the Talmud and with the philosophy of the Schools. Our hopes in raising the lowly are not Utopian. We believe that none so aptly fall into their proper places in life as do those who are instructed in Bible principles. It is certainly a loss to the body politic when persons formed by nature for manual labour usurp the office of teachers, or when skilled workmen become bad commoners. Yet, in accordance with the liberal spirit of our faith, the highway to advancement should be open. The prizes of time, as the good things of Providence, should be had in fair competition. Gradually, but surely, education is opening the avenue of progress to all comers. Christian workers may draw courage from a survey of the situation, for in due time there will be victory. How many of the religious and political blessings which we now possess are directly or indirectly the results of the labours of our sleeping fathers! The promise of an auspicious future is written in the experience of the past.

The first step towards temporal prosperity, as well as the first lessons in the higher life, have often dated from the Ragged or Sunday-school.

Subtle arguments have been used before now against aiding or inciting the industrial orders to rise from their humble condition. By passing into superior stations do not we inherit perplexities peculiar to change of fortune? Notwithstanding all drawbacks, is it not better that the road to honour and competence should be select? Would Milton's old age have been blighted by penury and hard usage, had ignorance shielded him beneath her wing? and is not social comfort of more worth to a man than are his poems to posterity? Would not Cromwell have pursued a serener course had he only concerned himself with the field and the fold? While garnering wisdom and rising into usefulness, man encounters trial. What though some great souls may have been eclipsed by 'lack of knowledge;' did they not live without being vexed by extravagant desires? and did they not pass away, free from the mockery of being lionised in death? Truly, we may answer, If wanting knowledge ever redounded in blessing, many nameless graves and wasted lives can trumpet the benefits of popular ignorance. But if the world is to grow in goodness, and fallen man is to repair the now marred image of his Maker; if we are to render to a brother a brother's due; if the harmony of classes is to be encouraged; the peaceful welfare of the nation to be advanced; if social crimes are to be repressed, and political evils to be cured; then we must extend, with diligent hands and yearning hearts, the sum of all good—that Divine knowledge which, on account of the creature's inability to scale its height, sound its depth, measure its length, or comprehend its breadth, is called, in the words of inspiration, THE UNSEARCHABLE RICHES OF CHRIST.

The missionary and the teacher in London may at least rejoice that they live in an age when all efforts of a philanthropic kind command so universal a sympathy. Old prejudices against educating the poor commonly emanate from those who have not themselves very deeply drank at the Pierian spring. Christian workers must learn to be deaf to objectors and cavillers. They must not grow alarmed at imaginary difficulties. They must consider well the vastness of the blessing communicated. The City missionary and Ragged-school teacher may properly think meanly of themselves as a means of good; but let them beware of underrating that grace which they are the instruments of conveying to susceptible youth or needy age. 'How feeble I am,' each is tempted to cry. Yes, and how poor a thing in itself is the glass which collects the noontide rays; but how potent are the burning beams when concentrated therein! The faithful Christian teacher, however lowly, is a medium which the Sun of Righteousness condescends to use while diffusing those beams that transform our moral winter into a summer of fruitfulness. Yet, on the other hand, while persevering in his course, the evangelist may beware of accepting the world's estimate of his labour. He is warranted in rating his weekly toil as highly as does his Master. Only they who are themselves subjects of Christ know the blessedness of Christianity. Only they who enjoy rich privileges are competent to speak their worth.

Who were properly acquainted with the quality of the banquet — the guests who partook of it, or the cynic Diogenes, who scowlingly left the viands untasted, as things in the world he could do without? Was the Greek indeed wise in his generation? Would the relishing of a feast have vitiated his taste for homely fare? And will a due share of knowledge render the poor less happy by making humble duties distasteful? Will it not rather, when coupled with early discipline, tend to the lightening of life's burdens and cares, by rendering each humble subject of its influence more contented and happy in his little sphere?

Then it will be well for teachers in our several schools to take into account the progressive nature of their work. The natural and political world are analogous in this—nothing stands still. Science tells us that what are called the Everlasting Hills, in common with the surface of the earth, are continually changing. With reverence we say, it is the same with the religious world. Though the Gospel is for all time, and in its essence remains immutable, it yet assimilates itself to man and to his varying position and diversified wants. It keeps pace with human progress. A teacher whose limited knowledge would not have hindered him a generation ago, would not to-day shine among his fellows. The earnest teacher must strive to keep creditably ahead of the intellectual growth of his more intelligent scholars. Let all who have their hearts as well as their hands in the work, brace themselves up for assuming higher ground as necessity may require; so that while our countrymen are eagerly seizing on newly-won political privileges, the children—many of them rescued from crime and vice—taught in a higher science than such as pertains to temporal prosperity only, may grow up into yet worthier custodians of the liberties of England.

If the good accruing to the nation from Sunday and Ragged-schools be so great as would appear from the foregoing pages, do they not claim wider sympathy and larger support? Would that none were given to dealing in that small and hackneyed objection—How little am I able to effect! Is that a valid excuse for indolence or unconcern? Let each examine himself as to the origin of such a murmur. Is it the child of vanity or of indifference, rather than of humble self-abasement? Is it pride yielding the fruit of spurious humility? Suppose this objection to active work were universally adopted, no labourers would be left in the field, since the ablest are nothing apart from Christ. The broadest valley and the chastest mountain scene are composed of atoms. Each bud, tree, or plant, unitedly producing the grateful effect of the whole, is in itself something very insignificant. But let each cease to act the part appointed by the Creator, and what confusion would ensue! No, let each and all continue. Nature has not a blade more than is needful, nor a superfluous bird's note, for completing the harmony of her system. Then let none shrink from this great work of rescuing for God the Arabs of our streets. Let us proceed, and in that borrowed strength, without which the strongest arms are weak and the most successful lives vanity. 'Sunday-School Union' and 'Ragged-School Union' are pleasant names; and here, in the holiest sense, UNION IS STRENGTH.

II.

THE FALLEN.

THE FALLEN.

I PURPOSE devoting this chapter to a difficult and untempting subject. To write effectively on such a theme, judiciousness and delicacy are indispensable; but the mark aimed at will be missed if the task be approached with too fastidious a sensitiveness. An appalling evil has to be looked into, and the morality of individuals will gain nothing by our not facing the enemy boldly. Let our commiseration be awakened for a class who drew forth the sympathy of Christ. We do not palliate, but condemn sin, when our hearts are drawn out in tenderness towards transgressors.

The numbers of fallen women abounding in large towns have commanded a large share of the attention of philanthropists; and not bare of encouraging symptoms is the present aspect of labour among their ranks. Happily experience proves that kindness and earnestness in the work of benefiting these fallen daughters are a sure road to the fount of feminine feeling—the heart of woman, which no amount of guilt and misfortune renders altogether obdurate and proof against good impressions.

None who were witnesses will readily forget the scene of the first Midnight Meeting, nor will many who merely perused the printed report soon have the impressions effaced which their reading left on the mind. When curiosity at the strangeness of the gathering subsided, and the objects of the promoters were explained by the several speakers, sounds of sobbing arose in different parts of St. James's Hall, and some of the auditors were carried out in a fainting condition—overcome by the remembrance of happier days, which the appeals of their new-found friends awakened. Of its attendant wide-spread ruin, and of the proper means of curing this evil, many earnest and able writers have treated; and were a similar discussion the object of our present chapter, little need be done besides following the beaten track; only shunning that abhorrent principle which would license the sinner and legalise the vice. My task will rather consist in showing, by illustrations from life, how the fallen are continually being rescued by an agency worthy of being strengthened by the prayers and contributions of all charitable hearts. For this, as well as for all other evils, Christianity is the only panacea.

It is unjust to imagine that poor creatures would willingly choose a course of life they are too often driven into by despair; for well they know despair must cling to them to the very end of the dark short road they travel—the road literally leading unto death! There may be an outward show of mirth and carelessness, but this counterfeit is only a mockery of light-hearted girlish glee. They who would make the discovery need not go far to witness the misery endured by those whose life-prospects are hopelessly eclipsed, and who are in themselves striking and shocking examples of the darkness which envelops broken hearts. In the vicinity of a brilliant concert-room was once encountered a showily-attired girl, about twenty years of age, whose experience and state of mind illustrated the truth of the words, 'The way of transgressors is hard.' 'My friend, will you take a tract?' said the missionary. Startled, and gazing as if bereft of speech, the girl needed to have the question repeated, before giving the curt rejoinder, '*Can't* read.' 'I am sorry for that,' returned the other, little suspecting the hidden meaning of *can't*. 'Perhaps some one will read it to you.' But the woman trembled, and her eyes flashed wildly, as she added, 'CAN'T read; must not read. *If I read I think;* AND IF I WERE TO THINK I SHOULD GO MAD.' Having said this she hurried off, and was lost sight of in the darkness.

The Mission in London employs specially-appointed missionaries to these unfortunates, who could not be properly reached by ordinary visitation. There are several thousands of fallen women in the parish of Marylebone alone, and some years ago a gentleman subscribed the entire salary of a missionary, who, he desired, should devote himself exclusively to their benefit. The majority of the girls are very young—ranging from sixteen to twenty years of age. By their way of living they dig for themselves an early grave; for the strongest constitutions, after adopting a career of shame, do not survive more than ten years, and the average only last about half that period. It seems infinitely shocking to write about the marketable value of human flesh and blood; but such is the degrading nature of sin, it depresses to the level of supply and demand what is precious beyond the powers of arithmetic to calculate! A girl on entering this service of sin, if blooming with health and personal attractions, may sometimes command almost her own terms, and live in grander style than anything to which she has been accustomed. But when her roses fade, flatterers depart, and it is a fearful step downward when the victim, ceasing to live as the toy of a gay paramour, takes to the street. Her whole life is then a rapid descent in degradation; for a dreaded day soon arrives, when attractions intended by God to adorn the home of virtue, do not suffice to allure common profligates. The doomed one must descend low and still lower, and at length she is fortunate if in her misery she is permitted to share the home of a thief, a sharper, or a costermonger! But in the majority of instances, the fragile frame will not bear up till the end of this terrible ordeal. The girl will die on a bed of pain and remorse in a hospital-ward; or, hidden from the world, which thinks nothing of her longer than she can minister to its vicious selfishness, her shattered frame slowly succumbs to disease in some obscure garret or cellar—Death being literally the wages for which she has lived.

The missionary whose errand of mercy obliges him to mix with these characters is soon recognised as a friend, and then trusted as a confidant, until he can at any hour safely enter the worst haunts of iniquity to hold religious converse with the inmates. This arises from the girls knowing him to be at heart their friend, and one with whom they can advise when in anguish or perplexity.

Overflowing with sadness and romance are many of the stories to which the evangelist listens. Some of these fallen daughters were formerly respectable governesses, till conquered by misfortune or treachery. Others ranked still higher as children of professional men, such as surgeons, naval and military officers, or even preachers of the Gospel, the daughter of a dissenting minister and also the wife of a clergyman having been found among them; and, stranger still, as it will appear to many, even a lady who has been presented at Court was once discovered in the purlieus of degradation! Thus all classes contribute to the evil; but they are generally best acquainted with religion whose origin has been comparatively lowly — a fact supposed to testify to the efficiency of Sunday-school teaching.

The facts picked up by the visitor are fraught with instruction and warning. One girl, of liberal education, whose birth and fortune originally fitted her for a very different position, told a remarkable story. Her parents died before she came of age, but, inheriting £2000, she boarded with a relative. Gay in youthful spirits, and inexperienced in the ways of the world, she, in an evil day, became acquainted with a smart military officer, who in time, wielding a strong influence, persuaded her to settle in London and live with him, under promise of marriage. When, after spending half her money, this paramour absconded, the girl's first thoughts were of returning to her friends, with what means were preserved intact. Just at this conjuncture, however, a medical student of London University made advances, and won her affections. This young man persuaded his intended wife to emigrate with him to Australia, where they could unitedly push their fortune. In Australia they failed to prosper, after losing nearly the whole of the thousand pounds; and disliking the country, soon returned to England. They were now again in London, but unmarried, and because unable to earn a competency as yet, the young man assured the girl he would make her his wife when fortune smiled on his endeavours. Being once more alone in the world, and in abject poverty, the poor creature resorted to the usual shifts of persons in her unfortunate situation. One article of small value went after another, and clothes were sold, till nothing more remained to sacrifice. She still occasionally heard from the young surgeon, who still professed unwavering attachment, and buoyed up by promises, she strengthened herself in resisting dark temptations. Then, at length, she thought herself rewarded, and grew overjoyed by hearing that he, for whom she still harboured a strong affection, was appointed a medical officer in the navy, at the same time receiving the assurance, probably given in good faith, that he would raise her to honour and happiness as soon as circumstances allowed. She now bravely endured the hard striving which youthful imprudence had entailed; and though involved in debt, fondly hoped to see the day when all would come right. It was while in this condition of mind and estate that she was shocked by the horrifying news of the death of her intended husband, by the sinking of his ship in the Black Sea. Stunned by this blow Reason reeled; and, encompassed with poverty, and terrified at future prospects, she took a last relic of better days—a silver thimble—and pledging it, purchased with the proceeds a quantity of laudanum, which, on returning home, she swallowed, thinking thus to end her misery. Though prostrated by the poison, the prompt means used by the hospital surgeons, blessed by Providence, saved her life; and when carried before a magistrate to answer for her short-sighted folly, the intended suicide was handed over to a missionary for lodgment in an asylum. As will be shown in our progress through this work, each missionary is aided and advised by an able superintendent; and one of these gentlemen sent the young woman of the present narrative into the country for a month's change of air, so that her shaken system and broken spirits might recover from the shock sustained. Thus attended to and encouraged, after six months' stay in an asylum, she gave satisfactory evidence of having experienced a saving change of heart. Then affliction yielded its blessing, until the world, as a stepping-stone to another, became better than anything she had hitherto known. Friends obtained for her a situation as schoolmistress; and starting anew in life by emigrating to Australia, she lived a blessing to herself and others.

The experience of London city missionaries embraces some phenomena in social life of which, but for their labours, the world would remain in ignorance. Happily the instances are not rare wherein the visitors become a means of restoring the erring. We also obtain an insight into causes which lead to so deplorable a disaster as daughters departing from virtue. Sometimes the evil arises from associating with bad companions, but still oftener, base-hearted men occasion the calamity. In a few cases girls turn aside into immorality as mere wantons, or they are decoyed into the same wicked path by hired procurers.

While visiting the fever-ward in Whitechapel workhouse, some years ago, a missionary discovered a girl, seventeen years of age, in whom, on hearing her history, he evinced considerable interest. She listened with attention or even eagerness to religious instruction, and soon showed she had not been instructed in vain. She was the only child of a respectable tradesman, her family residing at Islington. Having lived for two years in her shameful profession, she needed not to be told that the way of transgressors is hard, for she earnestly longed to be aided in returning to friends and home. Yet while desiring reconciliation, she shrank from the idea of presenting herself before the parents so signally disgraced; but this sensitiveness was rather commendable than otherwise. The address was produced where the unfortunate creature formerly resided; but on inquiry, her friends were found to have removed, and not without perseverance against difficulty were they finally discovered. Endeavours to trace the parents by means of a directory entirely failed. Being a tailor, the father was inquired after at houses of call, and a former fellow workman of his was discovered, but nevertheless the family could not be traced. What more could be done, the missionary might well inquire while standing by the bed of the slim girl, a mere child, who replied to his best words by speaking of home, and of loving ones who would receive her could they be found. Not to be baffled, it was inquired if no other friends existed to whom he could make application; and it appeared that a relative lived in the country, who probably could tell something. This clue led to the desired information; and on being apprised of the situation, the girl's mother, who had worn out her strength during two years of anxiety, woe, and physical exertion in prosecuting the search after this only daughter, immediately put in an appearance. Having made all possible inquiry, she and her husband had also explored London in various directions, hoping they might possibly cross the path of their fugitive child. Suspecting the profession adopted by the wanderer, her mother, emboldened by despair, invaded the precincts of the most notorious haunts of iniquity—places where, under ordinary circumstances, no one valuing respectability could for a moment think of entering—and with heartrending curiosity scanned the features of the abandoned inmates, catching at mere straws, and hoping against hope in the agonising anxiety of discovering a daughter's fate. But, until blessed by this interposition of the missionary, the dreadful comfort —better than suspense—of knowing the worst had been denied. Now, however, the prodigal was discovered, and in the workhouse fever-ward lay like one restored from the grave. There remained one other trial—what would her father say to this sum of sin and shame? That consideration indeed weighed heavily on the poor invalid; for it was truly a sore ordeal, this first treading the threshold of home after a long and disgraceful absence. But in the mean time the parent heard something about the forgiving spirit and loving forbearance exemplified by Christ; and then, attended by the missionary, the girl was taken home. 'Such a scene

I never witnessed,' said the evangelist. 'It was indeed a scene to see father and mother and child meet together after so long an absence, after so many sleepless nights and anxious days on both sides; for the child was as anxious to see and be reconciled to her parents as they were to find her, and it was with great difficulty, during her illness, that I buoyed up her spirits. She often in tears despaired of ever seeing them again, and would beg of me not to let her go back to the miserable and degrading life she had led. To see her, as first on her knees before her mother, and then with her arms around her father's neck, she implored pardon; to see the father weep, the mother weep, the child weep, was a scene which I think would have melted a heart of stone.' The occurrence of such things in our midst should lead to something more practical than melting 'hearts of stone.' Sympathy and feeling are admirable, but substantial help is better. Who will aid the good cause?

Surely no class of sin-cursed unfortunates endure misery more urgently needing attention than the thousands of fallen females in London. As will be inferred from the examples given, numbers of these girls have life-histories belonging to them as sadly affecting as they are instructive and interesting. While shocked at the sin which has provoked them, their trials still excite our pity. It must at least encourage the evangelist when seemingly brazen-faced outcasts, by whose recognition in mock phrases of affection decent men consider themselves affronted, are readily moved by Christian kindness. During the calm of one Sabbath evening, a missionary entered a room where four of the 'gay' species were employed over making or mending dresses. An appropriate chapter being read, the divine word was illustrated by the relation of the story of one who, like the listeners, turned aside to evil, and who, while she might have remained cheerful and useful, sank into the grave a victim of sin, but who yet lived long enough to repent and lay hold of the righteousness of Christ. Presently the eyes of the girls filled with tears, and himself affected to a like degree, the visitor exhorted them to embrace virtue while there was hope and acceptance.

Leaving this group, the missionary proceeds on his way, sowing the seed of righteousness; but as it is Sabbath evening he must needs refresh his spirit in God's house. On the way thither, one is encountered corresponding in character to those just addressed, and being a stranger, the woman passes a familiar salutation. 'Nay, come with me,' is the reply given. When the girl finds herself approaching a church, she halts suspiciously with signs of confusion, thinking there must be some mistake. But, no; there is no mistake; and her companion, insisting on having the bargain fulfilled, she is soon joining in long-neglected public-worship, 'confounded and affected.' Yet she has made a discovery; the man in whose character she was so greatly mistaken has rightly judged her need, and proved himself worthy of confidence. Then comes the sad relation, the same in effect as what is too often poured into the ears of His servants, who is touched by sympathy for all oppressed by the woes inseparable from sin. By the hearth, in the virtuous home of her childhood, she drank in the teachings of God-fearing parents; but these died, and young, desolate, and inexperienced, she drifted into a condition of life, sufficiently abhorred, and from which she would fain escape; and when she declares her intention of forsaking sin, the missionary is rewarded for his assiduity. Will the Church refuse to stretch out her helping arms to such subjects as these? By strengthening the London City Mission we contribute to a great moral reformation.

Further to illustrate the successful working of the Mission, the following is given:—One summer evening, while passing through a bad district near Gray's-inn-lane, one of the visitors knocked for admission at a house of immoral character. A girl as yet not degraded to the level of the other lodgers, answered the summons; and on being asked, 'What do you here; have you a mother?' the young creature, who presented a very juvenile appearance, burst into tears. Being further asked if she would leave the house, she replied with an eager affirmative, and accordingly was taken away, committed to the care of the missionary's wife, and rescued from ruin. This girl, brought up in a humble but pious home, went into a respectable place of service, whence she was decoyed by a couple of worthless women, such as roam the streets, seeking any means of making infamous gains. These hags, after selling the girl's clothes, turned her adrift and left her to her fate. Unable or ashamed to return home, the victim was reached by the Mission when just on the brink of that abyss in which thousands of fair creatures are annually engulfed in physical and moral ruin.

But though the poor oftener fall into temptation than their well-to-do neighbours, the affluent are still subjects of the tempter. A gentleman of fortune in one of the provinces possessed an only daughter, on whom he and his wife lavished every luxury, and introduced to the complete round of worldly pleasure. When in her eighteenth year this young lady left home with a man of her own social station; but not fulfilling the usual promise of marriage, her lover soon absconded in search of new attractions. Weighed down by the misery of her forlorn condition, the girl made an unsuccessful attempt at suicide. This offence entailed a short imprisonment, which, however, failed in exercising a beneficial influence, for on coming anew into the world, she lapsed into a life of shame, and added drunkenness to her other sins. Afterwards she suffered several terms of imprisonment; but this and the discipline of the penitentiary seemed only to harden, until a slight impression was produced by the conversation of the missionary. As a partially reformed character, the girl entered service; but becoming shockingly addicted to drinking, she necessarily relinquished a desirable situation, and at last contracted so bad a name that none would allow her shelter but the missionary himself, with his wife's consent. Having respectable and Christian connexions in Australia, who formerly vainly sought their transgressing sister, she decided on trying her fortune in a new country. The evangelist, who had so assiduously promoted her good, accompanied her to Gravesend, as did also a lady who manifested peculiar interest in the case. Just prior to parting, the latter took a ring from her own hand, and 'put it on the finger of the poor friendless girl, as a token of remembrance, so that when she looked on it she might think of the giver and her advice.'

The thoughtful philanthropist will scarcely decide whether to exult or despond while walking abroad in our great London. The imposing edifices and pleasing signs of commercial prosperity may well elate the spirits by exciting native pride; but, on the other hand, the wickedness and squalid poverty everywhere peering through the gilded surface, must depress a charitable heart. Then we may look with complacency on the endeavours made—inadequate but still gigantic—for the evangelization of the masses. It is true little has been effected if measured by comparison with what remains undone; yet if we literally take into account the work accomplished since 1835, the harvest will appear vast and satisfactory. London is slightly raised above its pitiable condition of forty years ago; and even the question is almost appalling —Into what would the worst districts have lapsed, had no efficient means been used for rescuing their perishing thousands? While handling such topics, who can help wondering that Christian England for so long contentedly rested over the threatening volcano of crime and immorality which have often been the precursors of national ruin to others.

Though the aspect at present continues sufficiently alarming, the cause of social reformation in London does progress. Take, for an example, the improved condition of the streets effected by the Act for closing refreshment houses between the hours of one and four a.m. Prior to the passing of this measure the open profligacy of certain quarters grew so disgracefully bad that a feeling of disgust and indignation was awakened. Some tradesmen in and around the Haymarket, accustomed as they were to scenes of fast life, or something worse, were at last so shocked by the brazen-faced depravity which nightly stalked abroad, that they waited on the Home Secretary to propose government interference in checking the encroaching tide of iniquity. Thus originated the Act of Parliament which afforded grateful relief by abating some nocturnal nuisances. The primary object of the agitators was to promote the enforcing of already existing laws; but on the hardened proprietors of west-end night-houses the penalties exercised no visible effect. Landlords summoned for sheltering improper characters, paid fines in the morning, and at evening continued the business of demoralization. The new Act, however, coming into force in 1864, introduced many well-defined restrictions, which, to certain characters in the world of profligacy, were the occasion of some chagrin and consternation. The scene presenting itself in the most notorious vicinity—the Haymarket—on the 27th of July, was a novel episode in London life. During its passage through Parliament the Bill was only feebly opposed by the publicans in general; and the offenders aimed at by the new statute hardly realised that the obnoxious measure was gradually progressing into law, nor believed its clauses would be enforced though sanctioned by the authority of Lords and Commons. As the specified time drew near, the police served notices at every night-house; and the proprietors not daring to resist what they now perceived would be rigidly enforced, emptied their saloons, exact to time, as prescribed in the Bill. The crowd of pleasure-seekers—some being in a state of semi-intoxication—on their sudden ejectment from the decorated haunts of conviviality, presented a singular appearance. The air was polluted by the muttered curses and loudly-spoken oaths of youths, who, choosing this merry road to perdition, were bringing shame on friends and parents. Besides these, the pavement was thronged by their companions in the paths of riot and lust—the daughters of shame, whose outward finery seemed to mock their heavy hearts and blasted lives. A number of police were ready to quell any disturbance; but these vainly endeavoured to clear the foot-way, many persons refusing to move onward, and avowing their determination to wait until the re-opening of the houses. If any adopted the threatened procedure of waiting, their sensations were not sufficiently pleasant to encourage a repetition of the experiment. From that night the improved aspect of the neighbourhood has been highly satisfactory. A proof has also been afforded that, though people are not made decorous by Act of Parliament, yet legal interference, when judiciously exercised, may repress flagrant vice and smoothen the way for social reform and Christian aggression. This virtual abolition of London night-houses was an important concession to the wishes of working philanthropists. Curious, however, was the defiant resistance of a few obstinate spirits. One proprietor, near Cremorne, was fined £5 forty times in three months for breaking the law. But while such folly was enacted, the comments of those principally affected constituted a tribute to the righteousness of the measure. To many who had long known the Haymarket the change seemed incredible; and aged inhabitants, who remembered the locality for half a lifetime, regarded the transformation as though their eyes deceived them. 'London is turned upside down,' was the expression of some. 'You will starve us all out,' remarked one interested party. Then a cabman observed, 'My wife will have to thank God for closing these houses.' Said another cabman, 'My children now will have a pair of shoes on their feet.' The women also spoke in appreciative tones. 'Many a poor cabman's wife,' cried one, 'will thank Sir George Grey.'

The reform in outward decency, consequent on the closing of night-houses, extended beyond the classes directly affected, fallen women and their associates. The missionaries, who, prior to the passing of the Act, nightly perambulated the streets, literally and even heroically making known the power of Christ in saving to the uttermost, to those most needing the reclaiming hand, were familiar with other phenomena of social life—nocturnal beggars. Always an eyesore to all who encountered them, these prowlers were also an abhorred class. Many of the fraternity were found to be persons reduced from affluence by vice and improvidence. Hither and thither they roamed, shivering in the cold, drawing their rags more closely around them in the rain or snow. The operations of these adventurers consisted in drawing from the pockets of fast livers—perhaps only differing from themselves by being more elegantly attired—certain voluntary offerings, which forthwith contributed to gratify an appetite for low indulgence. Even a missionary himself—perfectly familiar with their tricks and impostures—has had his gullibility sounded by one of these half-drunken reprobates, who, with mock misery, and with turned-up eyes, and clasped hands, has related a cleverly-concocted story. The official besom, while removing other nuisances, aided in clearing the streets of these unsightly characters.

But will it be believed that among such refuse as night beggars a human gem has been found, and found by a London City Missionary while on his errand of mercy? This man, a dark-complexioned native of South America, when first met with, had sank to a degraded and miserable condition. Of good descent and endowed with a liberal education, he once owned a comfortable competency; but having frittered this away in fast living, nothing was left but the husks of misery and despair. When discovered, he possessed no settled abode, and was without any means of obtaining food, his only covering consisting of a few filthy rags. But the truth as spoken to this man effected a mighty reformation. Christianity proved a saviour from death and also from temporal ruin; for the lately ragged mendicant was subsequently found enrolled among the agents of a society which sends the Gospel to foreign lands.

Such instances are necessarily rare; but when occurring they show how surprisingly the Gospel triumphs over inauspicious circumstances. Many-sided is the aspect of the streets at night, as seen by the street missionary. The fallen and the prodigal may demand a word, but there are other objects of commiseration, *e.g.*: 'The frost was very severe, and the wind very cutting. The place (Willis's Rooms) was brilliantly lighted, and the music heard at some distance. There were between three hundred and four hundred arrayed in very gay attire, dancing away the hours, and partaking of the luxuries provided for them; some of them so overpowered with heat that the front door was opened that they might gain a little fresh air, and then return to their enjoyment, for if we may conclude from external appearances, happiness was pictured on their countenances. Contrast the outside, and there is to be seen a number of cabmen shivering with cold, most of them over sixty years of age, sitting on their boxes, very anxiously waiting for a fare. As I went to one cabman after another, giving to each a tract, and saying a few words about Him who for our sakes became poor, I heard the remark from several, "Oh, sir, I am almost froze to death, and I haven't a penny to get a cup of coffee with." I could not refrain from saying, "Here, father, is a penny to get you a cup of coffee;" and the joy which was seen on their wrinkled faces I shall not soon forget, as with great difficulty they would try to move to the nearest coffee-house, with many thanks for the trifle given.'

The experience of those who undertake this itinerancy of Christian charity includes an acquaintance with the weaker traits of the human character. In grossly wicked localities, like Poplar and Shadwell, familiarity with vice seems to beget extraordinary apathy. In such places shopkeepers are largely dependent on seafaring people and customers of loose morals, and thus abandoned characters too frequently associate with those who affect a show of respectability. Hence sin of the darkest dye is often regarded as something to be tolerated rather than abhorred; and mothers and daughters, who converse with fallen companions, or even admit them into their company at home, look on the temporary undoing of a sailor-son or brother with comparative unconcern. In the vicinity of the several docks scenes also occur sufficiently trying to the evangelist, but known to the public only by hearsay: *e.g.*, when a number of seamen, after arriving in port, receive their pay. Then is it that droves of depraved creatures—the scum of their horrible profession—throng the river bank, and seize on their too willing dupes, who, after twenty-four hours of mad convivial glee, sometimes awake to find that the wages of many months have vanished. The shameless iniquity stalking about the river-side is both deplorable and shocking. What makes matters worse, is that numbers of the fallen are discovered to be wives of sailors, who claim licence because their husbands boast of their excesses in foreign climes! Shadwell and Ratcliffe are completely inundated with women who, having sank too low in iniquity to prosecute their calling in other parts of London, retreat hither to complete the last stage of their career before retiring into the hospitals to die. 'Now and then one poisons herself,' we are told, 'and the rest think nothing of it; and so loathsome is the appearance of some, that in conversing with them I am obliged to turn away my head.'

In these fearful districts every species of sin is in such rampant ascendency that probably the missionaries are tried there as they are tried nowhere else. Fallen women abound in surprising numbers, and assume a mien of peculiarly shameless depravity. Frequently, and especially among the Irish, the visitor is exposed to gross insult, or is even threatened with injury. On some occasions he risks being openly attacked, and is pelted with filthy missiles, dirty water, soot, or little bags of floor. But though the field of labour is apparently stony ground, it is not entirely unfruitful; for were it as sterile as it appears the faithful worker would not endure the burden. Encouragement comes in due proportion. 'I am no scholar, sir,' cried one eagerly, 'but I want to know how my soul may be saved.' An episode which occurred in a house in this neighbourhood, shows that the most hardened may retain a heart susceptible of saving truth. The missionary was civilly received in a room occupied by an old woman and her two daughters, the elder of whom was far gone, but the other, seventeen years of age, had only just entered on the course of sin. Some suitable advice was given; and then as the trio listened to the awe-inspiring fifth chapter of Ephesians, the aged sinner quaked with terror, until the girls also trembled and evinced anxiety to begin a life of virtue and industry. The youngest transgressor was rescued, and after passing through an asylum, lived to be grateful to the mission.

In common-place style it is easy to expatiate on the misery occasioned by commercial crises without realising the magnitude of the suffering entailed. Nothing more readily enables one to comprehend the woe springing from loss of property and the failure of large firms than many of the examples coming under the notice of the London City Mission. This will plainly appear in the following narrative:—

Some years ago the cashier of a London bank lost his situation by the collapse of the establishment. While holding this appointment, the gentleman's family, consisting of two daughters and a son, were handsomely maintained, the household being replete with everything to make life comfortable, religion only excepted. When the clerk retired into private life, however, dark days set in, and gathered their sombre clouds around. A business embarked in failed, and left the whole family destitute. Amid these crushing troubles the wife died, and, seized with illness himself, the father entered an infirmary, and thence went into the workhouse, leaving his children to shift for themselves. The missionary found the girls living together in bitter poverty. Repeatedly but vainly he had endeavoured to gain admittance to their lodging; when at last he entered, he did so all unawares. The room was nearly bare of goods—a chair, a box, and a bundle of rags for a bed, making up the inventory of the furniture. 'This is not the conduct of a gentleman to intrude in this manner,' said one of the sisters, rather indignantly. The intruder admitted the justness of the rebuke, but pleaded in excuse the importance of his message; and then the poor girls, instead of being incensed, were visibly affected on hearing: 'I feel assured, from your appearance and manners, that your position in society has been very different.' They were read and prayed with, and to prayer they had long been strangers in the hard and prolonged struggle for existence they had undergone. First they sought to gain a livelihood by needlework, but still harassed by want, they surrendered to temptations which ever attend young girls in poverty. After the elder sister's yielding to the enemy she persuaded her sister to follow her example. The father of these unfortunates was also visited, but he remained unacquainted with the fulness of the calamity which had overtaken his daughters. The youngest transgressor passed into an asylum and was rescued. When taken away by the missionary, she was sorrowfully though willingly parted from by her companion in sin, who confessed that they had 'cleaved to each other in all their guilt and misery.'

How uncharitable is it to suppose that a large proportion of these fallen girls have grown callous to emotions of shame and decency. On the contrary, they appear to retain sufficient sensitiveness of their lost condition to make them continually miserable. 'Sir, I could not read it,' one will say, when offered a tract suitable to her troubles. Another will take the paper and immediately show a face suffused with tears. Others will both listen and read, and prove by their behaviour that they only need an opened door of escape through which to leave their wretched profession.

Sometimes the evangelist is favoured by opportunities of reconciling family differences—which have borne fruit in saddest results—when less potent interposition has broken down. Anon, he may restore a lost child, for whom search has been made and rewards offered unsuccessfully. One day a missionary entered a house in Lambeth known to be inhabited by loose women. The inmates received him with that civility so frequently awarded Christian visitors by abandoned characters. As head of the household reigned an old dame, hardened by years of transgression; but she who especially attracted attention appeared as a fair girl, seventeen years of age, and an object of surprise to her companions. 'Ah,' said they, '*she* has a father and mother, and could leave this, but she won't.' Her history was given. She had lived happily with her parents till a woman, enticing her away with artful words, and providing showy attire, introduced her to a life of iniquity. She left this vile hag, taking with her the finery supplied. Since escaping she had been in the hospital; but now, reduced in health and strength, the end was seemingly approaching. What? and only seven months before she was a parents' pet! As she stood among her associates in sin, and by the side of the crone ruling the establishment, the missionary administered to the girl some faithful advice and warning; and, strange to say, the words spoken were seconded by the bystanders, until 'remorse, shame, fear, all seemed to arise in her mind, and she burst into a flood of tears.' The next step consisted in visiting the young creature's home, the address being procured with difficulty; and it then appeared that the old people had not heard of their daughter since her original disappearance. They inserted advertisements in the various newspapers, and in company with a police officer the father industriously explored the dens of London. The prayed-for discovery, however, came home to the parents at a moment when least expected. Entering the cottage, the missionary observes, 'I am a stranger to you, my friends, but I have some important business.' 'What is it, sir?' the mother inquires. But because he will not break the news abruptly, he looks interestedly at a child present.

'Is this one of yours?' 'Yes, sir; what may be your business?' 'You have another daughter, have you not?' he asks, still parrying the woman's curiosity. 'Yes, sir; but she is not at home.' 'I know she is not,' returned the intruder, significantly. The truth now darting into the mother's mind, she, with quick matronly instinct, ordered the children away, and fearing the worst, listened to the visitor's communication, weeping copiously. No difficulty arose in the way of receiving home the wanderer. She would be forgiven and affectionately welcomed. On the next morning the missionary, accompanied by the father, went forth to complete the work of reclamation, his companion carrying a bundle of clothes, through fear that the child might be destitute of decent raiment. Leaving the parent at a house appointed, the missionary and a woman of good character fetched the girl from the horrible place wherein she was immured. Then the meeting of father and daughter was a never-to-be-forgotten scene by witnessing bystanders, for the emotions of both bathed their faces in tears. The poor old man administered no reproof beyond sobbing in broken accents, 'Oh Mary, how could you do so?' After commending the family to God, the working agent of reclamation looked on the party with delight and satisfaction. Well might he do so, when, as he truly testified, 'Angels might have rejoiced at the scene.'

That young girls should ever be led to ruin by mere decoyers excites intense indignation; and the following incident, belonging to the annals of the mission, may be useful to the unwary. One day a lady, while walking along Oxford-street, was suddenly accosted by an old woman: 'Miss, your boa is on the ground: shall I pick it up?' Then, lapsing into a confidential tone,—'I want to speak with you particularly.' 'With me?' 'Yes,' continued the woman. 'A friend of yours, who knows you well, wants to be introduced to you. Come, I will show you the way.' Fortunately the lady was sufficiently acquainted with London life to discover the snare, and by simply threatening to give her in charge of the police, occasioned the hag to beat a precipitant retreat.

While in such instances a little presence of mind will be all that is required, young women, who go comparatively unprotected into the world, should remember that Christianity is the only trusty safeguard against temptation, as well as the surest support under trial. In the early days of the mission, a visitor found a lady who, by the death of friends and subsequent misfortune, was reduced to penury. Being highly connected, a few pounds were subscribed by friends, on the representations of the missionary, but, notwithstanding, she soon relapsed into painful straits. One day, when not possessing a shilling, a captain, who knew her in the fashionable circles they had both frequented, proposed that she should relieve poverty by the ready means within her command. But want could not conquer the young creature's self-respect, and with a spirit worthy of an imperial nature, she bade the man begone. This noble bearing, in a crisis of anguish, so favourably impressed a lady who heard the relation, that she put the girl in the way of earning an honourable living.

Doing right and trusting in God will not fail to ensure victory.

The examples of 'brands plucked from the burning' are very numerous, and the chronicler can only pick up a case here and another there to serve the purpose of illustration. Yet each fresh success stimulates the earnest labourer to proceed in hope, undismayed at the present ascendency of the evil against which he wars.

In hospital-wards devoted to patients drawn from the various classes of fallen women, it is the custom of the missionary, while addressing individuals, to speak loud enough for others to benefit by what is spoken. One Sabbath evening, in the Royal Free Hospital, a girl occupying one of the beds was observed to be wringing her hands in agony of mind, and calling out, 'Oh, pray sir, do something for me. I don't care what I do or where I go, so long as I can get out of this course of life.' Lying as she did, weakened by physical pain and mental misery, the sufferer could not then receive more than a few words of advice; but when, soon after, her health partially returned, suitable instruction was given, while the girl strongly repeated her desire to escape final ruin by means of an asylum. Of respectable birth, she had also been politely educated, her father having served as a commissioned officer in the army. During girlhood and subsequent early life, this young woman's path in the world, so far as human foresight could discern, was fair and enviable, and her fortune amounted to £2500. When still too young to act independently, she took a fatally imprudent step by encouraging the advances of a Spanish gentleman who professed a warm attachment, and though she returned faithful love for his specious words, and married him, he, as the sequel shows, turned out at heart a villain. In the early days of their married life this couple took a large hotel, and though living happily for a time, the temperament of the husband was changeable, and he moved from house to house until he tried his fortune in five separate establishments consecutively. It was now that calamity overshadowed the wife's chequered path. While lying confined with her seventh child, the attending nurse agitated her mistress by whispering suspicions of her master's infidelity; and her nervous system was so visibly shaken, that she lay for days in the balance between life and death. At length, attaining sufficient strength to leave her bed, and following medical advice, she sought a change at Margate, where, though benefited herself by the sea-air, she lost her babe, and now possessed only two out of seven children. She returned to London, strengthened in body; but what was her horror to find home bare and forsaken, the husband and father having decamped with the barmaid and his two daughters, at mention of whom, especially, the poor mother was greatly affected, having neither seen nor heard of them since their first disappearance! What a picture of real life, exceeding the inventions of fiction—a wife and mother, tenderly nurtured and educated, left alone in the world, in the twenty-seventh year of her age, by a wretched creature calling himself a man! Even while speaking of her wrongs, the woman's agitation baffled all endeavours of the missionary to make her calm and comfortable. She seemed to desire misery while brooding over her troubles. 'I cannot describe my feelings when I found my husband was gone,' were her own words. 'My parents were dead; my only sister was married to a clergyman, and they had left England. I lived upon the little money I had with me and by selling my clothes. But my trouble so overcame me, that I took to drinking in order to drown my sorrow and smother my feelings. In a very little time I spent all my money and sold all my clothes. I was then quite destitute. As I was never happy but when the worse for liquor, my love for drink increased. I had now no prospect before me but the streets. My mind was so distracted that I could not have been happy in a situation.' Poor outcast! How had life's fondest hopes been wrecked by the troubles springing from one false step of youthful impulse. Did she not know that her sinful mode of life cursed the body while ruining the soul? She knew this just as well as do any who are virtuous in their happy homes; but let her finish her narrative. 'No one can tell what I experienced,' she went on. 'I was not a young giddy girl; I knew what was right and what was wrong; but I appeared to be driven to that course of life as a last resource. I have walked about London with scarcely a bit of shoe to my feet or clothes to cover my body, and in this state I have slept in the streets for several nights together. I shall never forget *one* night; it snowed fast for several hours. I knew not where to get a shelter. The snow beat upon my shoulders as I walked about seeking a refuge. No one showed me mercy; every one despised me. It was in this state of wretchedness I came to this hospital seven weeks ago.'

Ah! poor erring woman, even in so desperate a condition as was yours, the world was not so hopelessly dark as it seemed. The enemy was not permitted to have entire dominion over you. In bringing you to the hospital-ward, One *did* have mercy on you. For the body He gave you medicine, necessary nourishment, and tender treatment; for the soul He sent His message of mercy as spoken by the visiting missionary. *You* recognised the blessedness of an agency which rescued and blessed you. May gratitude like yours awaken deeper sympathy, and prompt the Church to contribute substantial means for rescuing thousands more of the straying daughters of sin and misfortune.

III.

'JACK KETCH'S WARREN.'

'*JACK KETCH'S WARREN.*'

HAVING heard much about the special features of the notorious neighbourhood of Clerkenwell-green, we were desirous of testing some conflicting reports; and the shortest, as well as the easiest method of arriving at truth, seemed to be that of visiting the spot to judge of its peculiarities for ourselves, the time chosen for the excursion being a pleasant Sunday afternoon in the early part of October.

Starting with a companion from the west-end of the town, the streets, as we draw near to Clerkenwell, assume a closer and dirtier appearance, till we emerge on to the 'Green' itself, and stand under the shadow of the Sessions' House, which, amid a cluster of rookeries, occupies a position for the punishment of crime, as though by a stately presence it would warn transgressors of the majesty of the law.

We may for a moment look around almost regretfully on Clerkenwell-green, standing as we do on classical ground. Times were when Clerkenwell-green was famous for its spring of clear water, the delight of those martial monks who lodged in the priory of St. John—heroes who, wearing a black habit, were sworn to defend the Church against pagan aggressors. These zealots evincing much bravery in warring against Turks and heathens, their services were acknowledged on the disbanding of the Knights Templars, when the monks of Saint John of Jerusalem inherited their lands. Their great priory was founded in the year 1100 by Jordan Briset and Muriel his wife, whose beneficence also extended to establishing a nunnery at Clerks' Well. In the midst of a dense assemblage of courts and alleys, and close, unhealthy streets, two relics survive of those bygone times—a well and a gate; the one being the modern representative of Clerks' Well; the other claiming attention, not only on account of ancient associations, but because Dr. Johnson looked on it with reverence, and because there Edward Cave worked as a pioneer of periodical literature. The monastery, a costly and curious building, at the time of the Dissolution became 'Imployed as a storehouse for the King's toyles and tents.' The bell-tower, destroyed in the reign of Edward the Sixth, is described by Stowe as 'a most curious piece of workmanship, graven, gilt and inamiled to the great beautifying of the City, and passing all other that I have seen.' The sanctuary of Saint James, once forming a part of this nunnery, became a parish church at the Reformation. In 1623 the ancient steeple tumbled down with a terrific crash, and on being rebuilt it fell again, and with its heavy bells destroyed the greater part of the building.

But dropping archæology, we proceed to view life as it is to-day in Lamb-and-flag-court and its famous neighbours, Bit-alley, Frying-pan-alley, and Broad-yard—the veritable 'Little hell.' Walking down the first-named court we are immediately confronted by the quaintly designated Lamb-and-flag Ragged-school, an establishment occupying the site of another institution, the maintenance of which, thirty years ago, probably cost more than do all the ragged-schools now existing in London. This was no other than 'The Thieves' Kitchen' of 'Jack Ketch's Warren,' where, in the early days of the City Mission, one of its agents broke the ground of reformation by gathering a few scholars.

Entering the room a little before the time for afternoon lessons, there is found to be a boys' prayer-meeting, and affectingly striking are the petitions offered by lads who but for this agency would probably remain ignorant of the nature of faith. Looking over the interesting congregation, a question involuntarily arises, 'Where are the rags?' for though about three hundred learners are here—girls, boys, and infants—you would not find even one subject corresponding to the legitimate type of neglected children, who, ragged, dirty, and shoeless, are supposed to pass their days in the gutter, and their nights on a few shavings in some abominable attic. 'Now you would not take this to be a ragged-school,' says the superintendent, admiringly surveying his flock; 'but the fact is, we are obliged to clothe many of these children.' This remark applies especially to the younger scholars; for the elder ones are mostly employed during the week, so that they only attend the sabbath or night-school. Many of the girls are sempstresses, artificial-flower-makers, book-folders, and such like; and as they now sit around their teachers, clean and clothed in their best, they present a very respectable appearance. The scholars who are supplied with clothes are in many instances the offspring of drunken parents, and would be in deplorable destitution were it not for a rescuing agency. The parents of some of these unfortunate little creatures are their worst enemies, and a poor life's opening would theirs be were there no helpers in the persons of ragged-school teachers. The clothes, when given under these circumstances, are stamped with the name of the school, and so rendered unpawnable.

Yet, while the popular notion of a ragged-school will not be verified by a visit to Lamb-and-flag-court on Sunday afternoon, it should be remembered that we are looking on an improved condition of affairs, effected by the agency of the London City Mission and kindred societies. The work, though still rough, is far from being what it was in 1844, when London ragged-schools were instituted. Faithful, persevering labours are beginning to bring forth fruit in these rookeries. The good seed is yielding a hundred-fold.

In the meantime the children are pouring in, each carrying a ticket with a class number printed thereon, and without this none are allowed to enter. The school is now opened with singing and prayer, conducted by a superintendent; and to a stranger, the lads' singing is somewhat spirited, though pretty good time is kept throughout. The same process is gone through in the girls' room above, where the singing is also satisfactory. This over, the assembly settle down into classes, order is maintained, and all seem interested in the lessons.

The school having begun, we leave the children in care

of their teachers; for another now appearing on the scene in the person of the Cow-cross city missionary, he volunteers to conduct us over his district, familiarly known as 'Jack Ketch's Warren,' and the offer is too tempting to be refused.

Starting on a tour of inspection, the way being led by the missionary, we soon find ourselves groping cautiously up a dark ancient staircase, which, narrow and worn, has done duty since those olden times when a rogue or blackleg, once having gained these purlieus, could carouse in safety by his attic fire, secure from molestation. On reaching the top we enter a small room, our conductor calling out cheerily, 'Well, Mr. ——, how is the child? No better?'

No, the patient is no better. The doctor has been again to see her. Quiet and nourishment are what she needs.

Although her domain is tidy and sweet, the woman, well knowing the bad repute in which this locality is held by the outside world, with delicate consideration, opens a casement overlooking 'the warren.' The room we now stand in, being almost bare of furniture, may in the last age have been just such a retreat as a housebreaker or highwayman may have prized; but lodgers very different from thieves are now in possession. On a poor bed on the floor lies a little girl prostrated by a late fit. She does not appear to be asleep, though neither moving nor uttering a sound; and the bond of sympathy between the sufferer and the mother is plainly shown, for the latter is kneeling by the bed in tears. There is a tea-kettle steaming over a scanty fire—the only sign of there being any provision for eating and drinking. The spectacle, such as it is, appears not a little surprising; for, be it remembered, we are now in a region which is commonly supposed to swarm with thieves,—where children, with not even rags to cover them, scamper to their beds of straw and sacking whenever a stranger shows his head at the door, and where, in the cellars, donkeys are boarded with the family! Our friends of this attic will supply us with no materials for sensational description. Their room is scrupulously clean, the boards being as white as soap and water can render them, though the immates are suffering from bitter, pinching poverty. The worthy man, when *in* work, aspires to nothing higher than stone-breaking; but during several weeks he has not had even that, and, what is worse, some time ago he injured his eyes while at his calling. The Sunday afternoon call of the missionary is visibly appreciated, and his message taken to heart, which consists of some such comfort as this:—'You are poor; but God knows what is best. Had you been well off and free from care, perhaps you would have had less grace in your hearts.'

'Yes, sir, werry likely.'

'Then you are rich in faith. Here you are steeped in adversity; but you have a Saviour who has gone to prepare a place for you—a place in the heavenly mansions. *Not such a place as this, Mr.* ——.'

'Oh no, sir,' says the man in a tone which makes the tears start in one's eyes.

Then the missionary impressively reads those words, 'Let not your heart be troubled,' &c. This over, prayer follows, the scene, meanwhile, being strikingly affecting.

The weeping mother still kneels by the side of her daughter, and it is plain that the visitor himself, as he prays that present adversity may redound to some high end, can scarce restrain his tears.

But what also appears affecting is the manner in which these poor people resent the sensational reports relating to their own and similar neighbourhoods which have become too common.

'It's poor, but it's clean, sir,' said the woman, in a tone betokening the pride which moved her to make the best of her scanty means. By other things spoken we are enlightened as to the hard struggle which has constantly to be maintained in keeping even this, the poorest of homes, intact. The rent—two shillings weekly—is contributed by a daughter in service, and aged fifteen: otherwise the family independence could not be continued. This is at least a brave bearing up beneath the grievous burden of poverty.

Leaving here, we enter a room on the ground-floor of another house, where the master and mistress are out. Though not so faultlessly tidy as the apartment just left, no particular fault can be found, and the signs of prosperity are more abundant. The room is amply furnished, and its present occupants are a lad and lassie—brother and sister—sixteen and seventeen years of age. These are not only clean and clad in their best, but Jenny possesses personal attractions a village belle might envy. In many ways, direct and indirect, the influence of the city missionary is here visible. Jenny's brother cultivates a taste for art, and the maiden's face becomes suffused with smiles or blushes of pride, as she hands us a specimen of his pictures with which the room is plentifully decorated; and the design, though faultless neither in conception nor in perspective, is yet an object to regard with pleasurable surprise. When raised by Christianity, the poorest are found to value the embellishments of home. A lad who will paint a picture is not likely to pick your pocket.

In another room, not badly furnished, a respectable looking middle-aged man assures us he has lately lost a good situation in consequence of the bad repute of his own and the neighbouring alleys. After perusing a description of the locality, this man's employers, on discovering that his home was a den in an abominable rookery, shrank from further intercourse, and sent him about his business, or rather turned him adrift, wanting some business to be about. 'They sent me away when they found out where I lived,' was the artless confession of this poor fellow, who certainly had reason to regret the existence of any popular delusions. Then, notwithstanding the bad odour which in many instances still clings to himself and neighbours, the man, fully conscious of the satisfactory aspect of his own home, silently pays a delicate tribute to his wife's thriftiness by turning down the bed, so that the white sheets shall be exhibited. In common with others, these people in their trouble greet the missionary as a friend, acknowledging his exhortations, words of sympathy and encouragement, by a respectful bearing and many grateful responses.

Why, in connection with the subject of the poor of London, should we be for ever hearing one and the worst side only? Is there no such thing as honesty in the slums?

It would really appear that there is; for as recently as last year a gentleman reported what he was pleased to designate 'an almost unparalleled' instance of that virtue. Why say, 'almost unparalleled?' I would ask. Why should not a poor man enjoy the luxury of a quiet conscience as well as the astonished 'Verax,' who finds his dropped pocket-book restored?

One day, however, a little girl, living with her father in a court of ill-repute, not far from where we are now standing, picked up a pocket-book containing bank-notes of the value of forty-five pounds. The other contents of the packet included the address-card of the owner, and consequently, a day or two after, a very poor looking old man called at the gentleman's office, left his address, and requested Mr. —— to pay him a visit if he had lost anything. On receipt of this welcome news, the owner of the property hastened to the court specified—a place which was seemingly a rendezvous of thieves and loose women. The intruder found himself interrogated by an apparent descendant of 'Bill Sikes,' who in peremptory tones desired to know his business: but mentioning the name of the man wanted, he soon appeared on the scene, and the two made their way into one of the dens of an upper storey, where a brief whispered conversation ensued.

'Are you the gen'lman I called on this mornin'?'

'Yes.'

'Have you lost anything?'

'Yes, I have lost my pocket-book.'

'What was in it?'

'Forty-five pounds.'

'Oh, that's all right,' the man went on. 'Well, I've got it upstairs, under my bed. You go and walk up Holborn, and I'll follow you. Don't say nothing about it to nobody here—they're all thieves: be off as quick as you can, and don't look as if you thought I should follow you, but walk right away.'

Obeying these injunctions to the letter, the gentleman was soon overtaken by the old man, who handed him his property from a bundle of rags.

'There, there it is,' he cried. 'My little girl found it and brought it to me; and as I found your card in it, I came straight off to you about it. You'll find the money all right, and all the rest of the things just as she picked it up. But don't say nothing about it, cos if them fellows knowed I'd done this, they'd make the place too 'ot to 'old me. They are all thieves, and I was afraid that they might smell a rat if you stopped there.'

When he received five pounds reward and five shillings for his daughter, the old man was, if possible, as much dazzled at the liberality of 'Verax,' as the latter was surprised at so uncommon an example of honesty. As regards the finder of the book, no words can express her consternation at the sudden turning up of so grand a personage as the City merchant. She sobbed as though her heart would break, supposing she was about to be imprisoned for the crime of finding so much treasure. The sire even offered an explanation by way of apology: 'She so often hears of her companions being quodded, that she thought it had come to *her* turn.' This is a highly gratifying, but by no means a solitary example of heroic honesty among the very poor. Three hundred and fifty pounds, picked up by a newspaper-seller, have been faithfully returned to the owner. But this is a digression.

An apartment in the house next called at presents a spectacle at once saddening and pleasing. The room, furnished with chairs, table, and bed, is perhaps a trifle less tidy than those previously visited. A man is here found reading his Bible, which exercise, he assures us, is his chief recreation and delight. Though sorely afflicted, his cheery countenance retains no shade of discontent, and he acknowledges to the missionary the peculiar gratification he derived from the last summer excursion, which a few friends arranged for treating the poor of these alleys. Poor fellow! If any might murmur, surely he would be excusable in complaining. A skilled brass-worker, and able in bygone days to earn competent wages, his hands are now crippled by gout, rendering him unable to earn a living. Yet, cheerful in the prospect of reaching a better inheritance, the Bible seems to be the only book he cares to study.

Still proceeding, one more dark crazy staircase has to be ascended, at the top of which we enter a garret, where to remain upright you necessarily stand in the middle of the room. The tenant here lives alone, Sundays excepted, when a lad about fourteen walks from a distance to pay his father a visit. The general aspect of this apartment makes one's heart ache, even though the old fellow's comparative prosperity is shown by his having set up a bedstead since last called on by the missionary. Though not sufficiently dirty to disgust a visitor, the room is nevertheless utterly cheerless and forlorn; and no better proof could be adduced of the present blessing Christianity is to the very poor, than its power to preserve them happy and contented amid such untoward surroundings. In front of a gaunt-looking fireplace is a rough four-legged bench, whereon has been lately spread the Sunday dinner. This, one or two things to sit down upon, and the bed, constitute the total of the furniture and of the old man's wealth; but he gives us to understand that he possesses a hope which money cannot purchase.

In an 'eighteenpenny' room of another house lives a widow, by whom we are enlightened as to the shifts which she, and such as she, are compelled to make while passing through the world. From her words and appearance this woman seems to be an honest, decent creature. Having been short of employment during several weeks, she has fortunately just secured another engagement, but notwithstanding hard work and frugality she tastes meat only once a week. 'My son sends me a bit of dinner on Sundays; and there's what is left of it to-day,' says she, pointing to a rough clothless table by the fireplace. At times, after paying rent, she retains less than two shillings a week for food and firing. A little bread and tea twice a day are her customary fare, and she adds, 'I am thankful for that.' From the agent of the City Mission she had evidently received something better than earth's riches or philosophy.

On some accounts Sunday afternoon is not the most favourable time for visitation in 'Jack Ketch's Warren.' Fatigued by the toils of the week, the people are occasionally found lying down, when it is not advisable to intrude into the rooms, though a less number than might be supposed thus yield to an indulgence excusable enough under the circumstances.

The last room we enter is occupied by a costermonger and his family. Cleanliness reigns here also: the room is crammed with furniture, and it appears that the people make the best of their humble home. Though no scholars, the exaggerated notions of the outside world on these alley-homes have reached their ears to excite their indignation. Here then is a costermonger—and as it would seem a type of many others in Clerkenwell—who, practising cleanliness and sobriety, knows that the self-respect prescribed by Christianity consists not only in presenting a becoming personal appearance, but in well looking after the comfort of dependants. Such, to be properly understood, require to be seen at home on Sunday afternoon. They are then at ease, and ready for any conversation you choose to desire. In the chamber we are now inspecting there exists something more than order and cleanliness; for the furniture has been tastefully selected, so that it becomes a matter of regret that the worthy lodgers are unable to enjoy the comfort of an additional room. As it is, the bedstead monopolising a quarter of the area, the space beneath necessarily serves as a common store. Another considerable portion of the home is occupied by a chest of drawers, which, loaded with ornaments, resembles a stall at a fair; while, to complete the embellishments, the walls are crowded with pictures two and three deep. Apart from the consideration that a family is here housed in too narrow a space to preserve intact the finer sensibilities of human nature, this is not an unpleasant picture. It is at least a striving to maintain an honest independence under difficulties. 'Little Joe,' the son and heir of this costermonger, was singled out of fifty other infants in the Lamb-and-flag school, and brought to the front for inspection, and a chubbier, healthier looking scholar is seldom beheld even in a village street. Thus at every step in these unattractive precincts—a place still calling loudly enough for the interposition of sanitary reformers—a district probably once wholly given up to iniquity, we meet with striking evidences of the beneficial influence exercised by the city missionary and the ragged-school teacher. The missionary, who knows every face in these alleys, declares that 'the greater part of the costers' wives are good-looking, The daughters have the bloom of youth. They are clean, witty, business-like, affectionate, heroic, struggling, and smart. They believe in cleanliness, and despise dirt.' Allowing for a little over colouring in this panegyric, such a witness sufficiently contradicts the sensational descriptions of poor districts, which hinder rather than forward the work of reformation. Undoubtedly many vicious people seek refuge in these alleys. The missionary can point to them as he can also single out many slaves of drink. Here, too, may be found dirty homes—which, unfortunately, are not confined to any district—homes too grossly repulsive to warrant pourtrayal; but even in 'Jack Ketch's Warren' these are the exception, not the rule.

The costermongering class abound in these alleys, and from their friend and visitor, the city missionary, we learn that at certain seasons the distress overtaking them is very severe. The coster of 'Jack Ketch's Warren,' excepting when, as in the cases noticed, he is reached by Christian influence, very much resembles the coster of other places. He has his peculiar traits of character, some of which rank as weaknesses. Unless moved by Christian principle, the coster is not particular about marrying the woman with whom he lives, and he is also addicted to prosecuting his calling on the Sabbath. 'Can't be religious, sir, nohow,' once remarked a member of this brotherhood; 'can't let the barrer be lazy on Sundays.' But let Christianity subdue the hardened nature, and what a different story is told; for, exclaimed another: 'Don't work on Sundays, now sir. A good day for trade, I know; but I likes to trade with heaven on Sundays, and learn a little about my soul then.' Some of these men will scarce be persuaded that religion is intended for any but 'respectable' people. 'I ain't a eddicated person,' observed one gentleman of this description, 'but I knows wot's wot; and I know that God never meant costermongers to be religious. Why, don't yer see it couldn't be done.' Yet, only reclaim such unpolished fellows as these, and their Christian profession becomes very sincere, and their life a zealous service. 'I allus felt ashamed of myself,' once confessed a converted sweep, 'when I seed the people comin' out of church, and I'd been a cursin' and swearin'. Now, mates, you want to get to heaven: I'll tell you how to get there. Trust in Jesus Christ; He'll never forsake you. I, a poor sweep, am glad to wash my face when my day's work is done; but how much better to have Christ to wash your black soul? "How do you know you are going to heaven?" sez my old mates. "Well," sez I, "how do you know whether you've got sugar in your tea?"'

Having seen something of the neighbourhood which the conductors of the Lamb-and-flag schools have selected for their operations, we now return to head-quarters just as the children are being dismissed, and learn from the superintendent the plan of aggression adopted. The Sunday-school is held three times on the Sabbath, besides a children's service at eleven, and one for adults at seven in the evening. The day-schools for girls, boys, and infants open during the week, Saturdays excepted. On Monday and Thursday there are classes for those young persons whose employment does not allow them to embrace any other educational advantages. A gospel-lecture by the city missionary is given every Tuesday evening; and on two afternoons a week there are mothers' meetings and others for prayer, &c. There are also a penny-bank, clothing and sick clubs, a maternity society, a pure literature club, and a free library.

What the religious and moral influence of all these agencies must be in a needy neighbourhood will not be rightly estimated by any who have not inspected the working of the institution. Yet descriptive accounts have repeatedly appeared of London rookeries, apparently composed for readers who love a dish of literary horrors, and no word has been inserted about the ragged-schools which we find crowded—in the present instance with three hundred children, all of whom are instructed in the principles of rectitude and in the truth of the Gospel. When will the English people wholly forbear giving to beggars, and bestow their bounty on the poor, by helping forward the good cause of ragged-schools? I believe the assertion may be ventured, that among the persons visited in their distress this afternoon not one would descend to asking alms in the public street.

The conductors of the school erected in the heart of this cluster of courts and alleys can already point to gratifying results. Religion being the greater containing the less, carries in its train every social reform. Even window-gardening has been encouraged by the Lamb-and-flag flower-shows. But such things are comparatively trivial, one Christian life or triumphant death being of more account than any amount of temporal prosperity. One mother, in a day of dark distress, was asked by her little daughter, 'What ails you?' 'Mother is not well, dear.' The child, divining another reason, looked up in her mother's face and said impressively, 'THE LORD IS MY SHEPHERD, I SHALL NOT WANT,' and that same day an unexpected letter brought timely succour. The infants, moreover, have a testimony of their own. 'Folded in His arms, what have I to fear?' asked one dying child; while another, just before quitting the flesh, inquired, 'Mother, am I an angel?' One little girl, whose mother was a slave to drunkenness, confessed to the superintendent, when visited for the last time, 'I am not afraid to die;' and every text repeated she eagerly caught up while gasping for breath. Then again, a lad instructed in this school rejoiced in

Christian hope while dying on a bed of rags with a basket for a pillow. 'I think He will give me rest soon,' he said, only just before he was taken to another and happier sphere.

Our examples of this affecting and satisfactory kind might be supplemented by stories of the children's gratitude after conversion. There was one little fellow—of another school, however—who, while dying of consumption, delighted in being read to and prayed with when weakness prevented his attending class. As he wasted away, to-day weaker than yesterday, he was seized by a strong desire once more to speak with and look on his companions; and accordingly one morning, unknown to his friends, he left bed and home, and startled the school by suddenly appearing like a pale apparition. Having wasted his strength, he sank on to a form, and there spoke of his safety in Christ and of his approaching departure, till all eyes filled with tears. Soon after, when this lamb of the flock was taken to the upper fold, the expense of a tablet erected to his memory was subscribed in farthings.

The above, taken as a whole, is, it is believed, as fair a description of the environs of Clerkenwell-green as can be given in a limited space. The description might have been made more sensational; but sensational writing about the poor and the districts they inhabit misleads the public, besides hurting the feelings, or even injuring the prospects of many honest people who cannot procure a better home than a rookery supplies. We explored the recesses of one alley after another, including Broad-yard —'Little-hell'—and though, as before remarked, there is room enough for the operations of sanitary reformers, we cannot 'tell of a condition of things so horrible that to exaggerate them would be impossible.' The pavement of the alleys was as clean as that of hundreds of other close streets, where respectable people live or pass through without complaining. The atmosphere of many of the apartments was somewhat close in consequence of ill ventilation, but outside the air could be breathed freely without any disagreeable sensations; and we observed neither heaps of refuse nor stagnant pools which some others preceding us appear to have discovered. It is certainly true that there are persons hereabout who are confirmed drunkards of repulsive habits, and who follow vicious practices; but to infer from this fact that the majority of the inhabitants are of this order, would be to libel numbers of respectable but unfortunate citizens. The missionary can lead the way into rooms where, the senses being shocked, the visitor retreats disgusted; but these, I again repeat, are not a sample of the whole.

On such a theme let us eschew all caricaturing. Years ago the habit of literary exaggeration, or what may be stigmatised as cruel mockery of the indigent under their crosses, was complained of as an obstacle to the progress of the evangelist. We cannot speak and write without the poorest knowing what is spoken and written, and while a feeling of indignation is awakened by false reports, the denizens of places like 'Jack Ketch's Warren' will harbour the idea that, under the circumstances, it is useless for them to reform. 'Of what use is it your coming here,' has been asked, 'if we are constantly to be represented as rogues and vagabonds?' The London City Missionary and the ragged-school teacher have visibly improved this notorious neighbourhood. Should not the Peabody Trustees now follow in their wake, and extend their operations to providing dwellings for the very poor?

IV.

SUNDAY NIGHT IN THE TAVERNS.

SUNDAY NIGHT IN THE TAVERNS.

It is the last Sunday of July. The day has been a stormy one, and as I traverse the fields in the direction of London, the sodden earth bears testimony to the copious showers which have fallen since morning. The brightening sky, however, now promises a fair night; the air is delightfully cool and fresh, and the scene, stretching into the distance, has a quietness resting upon it beautifully in unison with the Sabbath evening. To stay amid these surroundings, and to occupy a place in the rural house of prayer, would be far more congenial than the task prescribed for this evening—viz., to accompany a city missionary into the taverns of Marylebone, for the purpose of witnessing his operations in those places among the thoughtless and the profane.

On arriving at that great centre of metropolitan life, King's Cross, the luxury of quietness can no longer be enjoyed. Not that King's Cross does not assume a Sunday guise; for though publicans are opening their doors for the evening, the shutters of several of the more orderly houses are kept partly up—a mark of respect for the day. The coffee-house keepers stand at their doors washed and prim, more intent on seeing what is doing without than on serving customers within. Others are busy in serving out fruits of the season to passers-by who throng the pavement. Among these you will notice many of that peculiar genus of the hobbledehoy species which delights in shuffling along, to laugh at its own amateur jokes, and too frequently to insult better people. Perambulators are not scarce. Now and again you meet a happy man of the clerk or warehouseman order pushing a little vehicle forward, while Mamma walks leisurely behind, leading one or more of the elder youngsters, who are proud of having arrived at the walking age.

This is what the scene is made up of until arriving at Gower-street, where a few young men outside the mission-station are singing a hymn, to collect a congregation for a service about to be held within. A number of persons are attracted, and among them stand a dozen or more little children, nearly all of a height, who evince great anxiety to obtain the tracts and also the hymn-leaflets which are freely distributed, and not badly sung—the words, rising above the rattle of the Euston-road, doubtless reminding many of Sunday-school days in far away country villages :—

> 'In robes of white, o'er streets of gold,
> Beneath a cloudless sky,
> They walk in the light of the Father's love ;
> Shall you be there, and I ?'

As yet I have not set eyes on my friend the public-house visitor. Our meeting-place is to be in front of Marylebone Church, and the sign of recognition is a black case in which are carried the tracts and periodicals for the publicans and their customers. Arriving shortly before the time appointed—eight o'clock—I have an opportunity of speculating on the kind of functionary with whom I am about to become acquainted. In what respect is the London City Missionary supposed to differ from other people? The 'Amateur Casual' has made his readers familiar with the evangelist of Cow-cross—a hero found to differ essentially from what was expected. Instead of a shabby-genteel, white-neckerchiefed creature of the preacher type, he was found to be a thick-set, determined-looking being, who, with Bible in one pocket and a bundle of tracts in the other, went forth to work among the dens by which he is surrounded in a very matter-of-fact fashion, and commonly humming a hymn to cheer the way. From one or two polite notes received from the public-house missionary, I had formed a good opinion of his urbanity and desire to render an asked-for service; and any notions contracted in regard to his *personnel* were quickly set at rest by the appearance, exact to time, of the gentleman expected. As in the instance above referred to, he did not correspond with the ideal of my imagination. For this rather rough service, one might have looked for a man whose physical strength equalled his moral courage, and whose readiness to speak was matched by his ability to stand on the defensive when threatened with maltreatment in certain of the dens he is required to enter. A man of middle height, well dressed; of ready utterance, and of a quality which proves a fair amount of mental culture; mild features, bespeaking a sensitive, not to say a nervous temperament, and we have all that need be said regarding the person of the missionary.

The clocks are now striking eight, but we are still early for the work in hand. Many of the people we desire to see on this fine summer evening are as yet away in the country, and so a little spare time is improved in listening to my companion's street experience. During fifteen years he worked one of the worst districts of the mission, in the rear of Lisson-grove. In one street pointed out—known in the vicinity by the name of 'Little-hell'—he attended eighty-five cases of typhus fever! As a common visitor among divers diseases, he has never personally suffered inconvenience; but his children have been prostrated more than once by infection carried home. In the infamous rookery alluded to he walked safely at all hours among the haunts of the most vicious of our race—so completely were the respect and the confidence of the inhabitants gained. His experience proved that roughs may contemn religion and yet remain strongly superstitious. One of the first cases visited in 'Little-hell' was a woman of notoriously bad character, on whom Death had set his seal. There were several sons—tall, large-boned, powerful men—dust-collectors by profession, and just the kind of material to interfere with the visits of 'the parson,' had not an hallucination of the mother helped to raise him in their confidence. As the missionary endeavoured to lodge seeds of repentance in the sufferer's soul, she related, with expressions of horror, how, while lying there, SOMETHING—a dark looking being—had approached, and had tried to pull the bed-clothes away! 'But,' she added, 'it has not been since you have visited me.' Though this woman died, the evangelist had won the freedom of that dark community. There was not a ruffian in the entire length of the street who would not, had occasion arisen, have defended 'the parson' by word and hand.

But passing from this digression to the subject of the Christian visitation of public-houses, we find that the work is somewhat different and less easy from what it was a few years ago. The alteration in the laws affecting night-houses has wrought some sweeping changes. One in search for strange histories and the subject-matter of romance in real life, had only to look into a night-house, and he was sure to find something to his taste, and more or less remarkable. Night-houses are now virtually abolished; and the ordinary visitation of public-houses has been rendered more difficult by the prejudice engendered by the late Government Licensing Bill, and also by the prosecution of small Sunday traders by good intentioned but mistaken persons.

But it is now about half-past eight o'clock, and the emptying of the churches and chapels adds to the crowds of the thronged thoroughfares. We have now arrived at the portals of a large establishment, occupying a commanding position at a four-crossed way of leading streets. 'We will go in here,' says the missionary; 'but we must exercise caution, for the landlord is unfavourable.' 'Unfavourable,' in the sense here used, does not mean that the host is violent or abusive, but that he looks coldly on endeavours to promote his own and customers' benefit; and while distantly civil, he would be better pleased were the missionary not to darken his doors.

On entering the bar the work commences by the visitor handing to one or more of the young persons employed a copy of the 'Sunday at Home,' provided for this service. Speaking to these *employés* is foreign to our present purpose; for their evening occupation will only allow of their giving a brief passing civility. The time for addressing landlords and landladies, barmen and barmaids, is morning, and consequently to *their* benefit the missionary devotes more or less of the early part of each day.

Mark well the scene. There may be forty or fifty people in this bar; and the mingling of voices with the clatter of pots and glasses makes up a picture of low life and a din of confusion such as can only be witnessed in one of these places on a Sunday night. But to be fair—and I would avoid over-colouring the picture—the bar and bar-parlour must not be associated with badness exclusively. The chances are against our finding one drunken person in all this company, and loudly-spoken ribaldry or blasphemy would not be tolerated. It is now time for the tracts; and as these are handed round few reject them, and most return a gracious 'Thank you, sir.' Here and there a subject is picked out for conversation. See yonder middle-aged man. He has seen better days, and knowing that he is not what he ought to be, wishes he were a better man. He is sure that what the missionary says is all right, and he hopes to find mercy at last. Close by is a younger clerkly-looking individual, who on taking a tract observes, 'It is not the first by a good many,' and his wife and children always read them. Note, moreover, that respectable-looking mechanic, to whom the missionary is not unknown. His features instantly assume a serious cast as a few searching words are addressed him—words touching repentance and the good old way. He too thinks of getting to heaven in the end; and then, his countenance meanwhile lighting up with the happy thought, he asks, 'Don't you think I shall get there if I have *one* good thought in my heart?' With brevity and pointedness the conditions of reconciliation with God are explained by way of reply, and the man's eyes speak his appreciation of the words spoken. Our chief tracts for to-night, with the exception of books for children, are 'Do you want a Pilot?' and 'The Way to Begin.' Observe the shabby-genteel gentleman standing by that huge barrel: he does not know that he wants 'a pilot.' He has always endeavoured to be honest and to live respectably; and with a small show of triumph he believes that's about the thing required. But listen a minute—and amid this babel of conviviality you must listen intently or you will not catch a word—and you will discover how ruthlessly every fond self-righteous hope is rased, and the man pointed to a sure foundation. Then see that little knot of pleasure-seekers—two youths and two maidens—all arrayed in the smartest wares of the cheap outfitter. Poor girls! After the drudgery of the week they are supposed to be at church or chapel; but each has chosen to take, instead, a stroll with her young man. It is saddening to watch the youngest holding her glass in a manner quite convincing that she is little used to this sort of thing. While they continue merry and talkative, my companion remarks, in an undertone, 'Much discretion is required over interfering with a party like that;' but though fully recognising the peculiar obstacles in the way of a faithful discharge of the work, I decline a good-natured invitation to test the difficulties by turning amateur missionary myself for say half-an-hour. The youthful party just mentioned now number another, the missionary having joined them. They entertain no prejudices against religion. They are even respectful in their chaffing way, and take the tracts with some show of interest, believing the visitor to be 'a good sort,' who wishes them well. Then material for a joke is supplied when the intruder, laying a hand gently on the shoulder of one of the girls, offers her a tract, and remarks that all need 'a Pilot' who would arrive in the right haven at last. 'Holloa there! 'ands off old feller yer know; go and talk to the barmaid if yer want a gal,' cries one of the men. This playful gallant being chief of the party, it was satisfactory to find that his jealousy was altogether of a mock species; for becoming serious, he added, 'But I say, guv'nor, what'll yer take? I'll pay for anything yer like.' These invitations to drink are very numerous, and while invariably declined, are answered by an inculcation of wholesome counsel.

Many women and girls are met in these places who in city mission phraseology are 'respectable.' Passing some of these, and offering them tracts, they hang down their heads in some confusion, as though ashamed of being caught in these questionable precincts, and in some instances the good offices of the missionary are refused. Passing from the bar to the 'parlour' in the first house visited, we enter a room packed with thirty or forty persons, mostly young men of the clerk and shopman class, and all pledged to a fast life. The company is not composed of men entirely, however;

there are a few women, and from their not very happy cast of countenance, we judge them to be wives impatiently waiting for dissipated husbands. Nor are these all. The hot smoky atmosphere is breathed by at least one little girl, who in her Sunday finery, and sitting by her mother's side, is now beguiling the hour with a child's book presented her by the London City Mission. The 'gentlemen,' to whom drinking and smoking, laughing and talking, under rather stifling conditions, constitute enjoyment, little heed our intrusion. Tracts are handed round and received with few remarks, with the exception of one determined objector, who being a thick-set, well-dressed man of or about thirty, discovers in his features abundant evidence of an obstinate spirit. He does not appreciate being followed by religion to this festive haunt, where he would fain reap undisturbed enjoyment; and so incomprehensible does the matter seem, that indignation prompts an argument against Christianity itself. By loudly-spoken words and vehement gestures he would convince the company that the action of the London City Mission curtails the liberty of the subject; and as he assumes the airs of one who has ideas and arguments to exchange, a specimen may be given: 'Suppose I was to foller you into church with a pint of ale and bitters, what would *you* say?' 'If you were to follow me into a place of worship for the purpose of benefiting my soul I should be grateful,' is the reply; 'but no good could arise from acting foolishly.' The thick-set, determined man 'couldn't see it;' yet an onlooker could see that he was somewhat chagrined at having a fancied good thing turned into foolishness before his companions.

The cool street proved a grateful exchange for the hot and noisy scene imperfectly described as a specimen of the large establishments visited. But this is only one department of the work; for in the back streets of this large parish numerous small houses are found where quiet opportunities constantly offer themselves of explaining the Gospel to separate individuals; and having a sad story to relate in connection with a rendezvous of the humbler class, we will tarry a few moments at the —— in —— street.

This house, belonging to the humble order of publicans, is of narrow dimensions. At the end of the bar a door opens into a poor tap-room, which has an interest attached to it on account of its strange connection with the life history of —— ——, a doctor of medicine and graduate of the University of Edinburgh. On entering this bar one day, while on his usual rounds, the missionary observed two men in the little compartment above mentioned, and a remark of one of them, an old gentleman in rags and wearing a white hat, struck him as extraordinary—'If you do not kneel down and ask the blessing of Almighty God, I will not prescribe for you.' On proceeding to question the speaker, he found him to be a reduced physician of highly respectable connections in the various learned professions, and who retained enough of the reverence belonging to better days to prompt his teaching his low and ignorant associates to acknowledge the overruling power of heaven. As this poor man paid great attention to the message of the missionary, it is hoped that some good thing may have found a lodgment in his soul. A short distance from the —— I was shown a cobbler's establishment, where, after relinquishing his mansion and carriage—which until he took to brandy drinking were a part of his every-day existence—the physician found a friend.

To finish this story, I must explain that a day or two afterwards I presented myself at the shoemaker's stall, and was rewarded by finding the good man quite communicative on the theme of the sad fate of his friend the physician. In various ways this poor fellow had striven to soften the lot of his still poorer neighbour. Among other services he acted as the almoner of the Doctor's family, having been entrusted with the weekly allowance —at first one pound and subsequently eight shillings —which the infatuated drunkard regularly received. The money being sent to the shoemaker, was by him, according to instructions, doled out in daily allowances. After this experience it doubtless sounded strange to the honest man to be asked confidentially, 'Did you know Dr. ——, who formerly went about these streets?' for he knowingly answered, 'I should think *I* did.'

I learned that during the last days of his life, or for a period of seven or eight years, the physician spent his time in the public-houses of Marylebone and in the cobbler's stall, sleeping at nights in the lodging-houses of the district, until he became sufficiently unwelcome to be refused admission into any but the least orderly of these common sleeping-places. In this reduced condition he still followed his profession; or, as my informant expressed it, 'he made a good bit by doctorin about' among his miserable associates, and also among more respectable people, who, knowing his history and rare medical skill, sought at a cheap rate the benefit of the poor outcast's advice. It would seem, however, that this advice had to be taken at favourable seasons; for after indulging in spirit drinking, the Doctor's head became affected, and then he was scarcely trustworthy. He would steal, and commit other meannesses, from which, when in his right mind, he shrank with the horror of a refined nature. This wretched existence was prolonged until nature refused any longer to hold out against the strain put upon her; and one afternoon the wanderer was carried from a low lodging establishment to St. Giles's Workhouse, where he died the same night. 'It was the bath did it, it's my belief,' said the old shoemaker. 'I always said that if he ever come to it, the work'us would be the death of him.' If this digression of the life-story of poor Dr. —— supplies a remarkable instance of the ruin engendered by sin, it also shows how grateful an agency, under the saddest circumstances, centres in the London City Mission.

Pursuing our round, the next call is at an 'Irish' house—so named because largely patronised by natives of the Emerald Isle. How you are received in these places will depend on the effect taken by the drink on the various tempers of the drinkers; for, as a class, the Irish Romanists are perhaps the most drunken section of the metropolitan population. In the bar are found a company of repulsive-looking women, bonnetless, dirty, and ragged; and what estimate they form of their individual worth is shown in a passing compliment we receive for venturing in *there* among the roughs. They possess all the garrulous characteristics of their race and sex, and appear to rejoice at the opportunity of having persons better dressed than themselves with whom to converse. One wishes our tracts were of 'the true religion;' another would read them if she could be supplied with spectacles; and while the others are offering individual opinions on Christianity in general, one naïvely insists that all religions are sufficiently alike to come to the same good end. The missionary addressed a few telling words to this rude company; but as all who have tested them know, the Irish, and especially Irishwomen, are impatient listeners. They clustered around their adviser, raising meanwhile a babel of confusion, while I was specially singled out by a stout motherly dame with dishevelled hair, who in a Celtic brogue surpassing comprehension, insisted on relating something with strange vehemence; and the weaker my capacity for understanding her words and gestures, the more violent became her endeavours to enlighten me. This party of amazons conducted us to the street, and dismissed us with shouts of laughter and complimentary farewells— 'Good-night, sir!' 'Good luck to yer!' &c.

But spirit-loving Celtics are not the only gin-slaves we come in contact with to-night. In one bar we found sitting *tête-à-tête* a couple of demure old women, dirty and slatternly, whose quiet, oily English speech made them a marked contrast to their sisters of Ireland. Empty glasses stood beside them, and to judge them by appearances they were thoroughly gin soaked. From their conversation I learned that they were known to the district missionary, and attended his meeting; and this being so, they were partially inclined to apologise for being caught in a public-house on Sunday night. The stock of Christian knowledge possessed by these dames was singularly striking to a stranger; for their familiarity with the work of Christ was strangely out of keeping with their appearance and surroundings. The subject of death was mentioned. 'Well I *shouldn't* like to die in a public-'ouse,' remarked one of the ladies, 'though I 'ave knowed sich a thing to happen.' These characters dishearten the zealous evangelist. They understand the claims of the Gospel, but gin has too strong a hold on them to allow of their responding to the call of Christ. In regard to the pitiable objects before us, nothing more comforting could be drawn from them than, 'I goes to the meetin' sir, and if I 'ad only a pair of specs I could read the tracts.'

But of all characters among whom he moves, perhaps the most dreaded by the city missionary are those hard, unimpressible natures who resist kindly efforts to do them good as though an injury were intended. You cannot go far abroad in the field of Christian work in London without meeting with some of these. In one bar which we entered there sat a man about sixty years of age, who, with the exception of a good coat, was attired as a working man. His countenance bore no traces of sensual indulgence; but as he looked up into the face of the missionary from the bench he occupied, his eyes expressed uncompromising hatred of the Christian agency which had found him out in his Sunday night retreat. The remark he made on receiving a tract it would be an offence to repeat; but from other observations I learned that this class of persons are envious of any who are paid for Christian work. 'You wouldn't come here if you wasn't paid for it,' he cried, half savagely. 'My friend,' replied the missionary, 'I am paid for doing my duty.' 'I thought as much; and then perhaps you go home and get drunk. I expect now you earn a matter of five shillings a day by giving them tracts away.' 'Oh, more than that!' is the half-playful answer. 'But look here, my good sir; you have received benefit at the hospital in your time?' 'Yes I 'ave; several times they did me good, too.' 'Well, then, were you not a very silly fellow to go and seek good at a place where doctors and nurses were all paid for curing you?' This reply told well, but neither cowed nor softened, the old man took further offence at being spoken to of repentance. He never *had* repented, and never meant to repent of anything he had ever done! Repent? why he read the Bible, said his prayers, and was as good as the missionary any day! On such hard stony ground the good seed can only be dropped in by the wayside evangelist, and its fruition left with Him with whom all things are possible. The man above referred to had nothing to oppose to Christianity as such; but classing himself among the righteous, was deaf to reproof and exhortation. Yet how repeatedly, in the annals of the London City Mission, has an unpromising beginning preceded substantial results.

We next came in the way of some soldiers, accompanied by one or two good-looking girls, seemingly servants, supposed by their employers to be at church. A foreigner was also of the party. The latter being the worse for drink, and the first instance of the kind encountered, our fiery English liquors moved him to enunciate his religious views with an air both serious and authoritative, the effect of which, joined to his wearing his tall hat on the crown of his head, was a ludicrous picture. A conversation ensues, and one of the soldiers observes that he does not see how religion could benefit *him;* and he also confessed he never entered a place of worship excepting when forced to do so. These men were good-natured, jovial fellows, and the importunity with which they offered the missionary refreshment strangely contrasted with his earnestness in pressing upon them the claims of Christianity. 'I was in a place of worship this morning,' he said, as he laid a hand on a man with one good-conduct stripe on his arm, 'and I saw a soldier wearing *three* stripes. How does it happen that those of your profession who serve Christ so frequently go about with marks of honour on their uniform?' The worldly benefits of religion are never underrated by these visitors. The missionary cannot afford to lose sight for a moment of the temporal good springing from following Christ. Religion serves the body as well as the soul. The clear, winning, forcible manner in which this truth was exhibited in the public-houses during my brief acquaintance with them, was highly satisfactory.

The missionaries who systematically visit the taverns

of London, pursue an arduous, but not a thankless calling. Some years ago, when the committee of the society requested one of their agents to prove what could be done in a west-end district, the man was overwhelmed with the difficulties of the proposed undertaking, and he spent some time in arranging a plan of action. The office requires a person not only pious and devoted, and possessing gifts specially adapted for the work, but one of a temper not easily provoked. Our friend alluded to went about the then novel occupation with consummate caution. At first he took copies of religious periodicals with tracts enclosed, and these were handed over the bar of each tavern in the district. On calling a second time questions were asked in reference to the papers previously left, when answers, shaped by the circumstances of the minute, were returned, and, if possible, the landlord's sympathy was enlisted. If the gentlemen in authority showed no open signs of opposition, publications were distributed in the bars, and future visits saw the parlours and tap-rooms boldly invaded. Of course the landlords differed in their natural dispositions. Some would have preferred that the Christian visitor should keep away from their doors; some only permitted tract distribution; but others, of a more genial turn, allowed the missionary to do much as he pleased, even showing their good-will by becoming pressingly hospitable. Yet unlike as are the landlords, these men do not differ more widely in character than do the houses they superintend. Many of these houses are closed entirely on the Sabbath; others are respectably conducted, the servants being allowed opportunities of attending public worship; and excess in drinking or in bad language is discouraged by every available means. Unfortunately taverns of this order are few in number; the majority including the gin-palace, the second-class public-house, and the still lower beer-shop, all of which, in too many instances, are hot-beds of immorality and traps for the unwary.

Any considerate person, who during a few minutes has attentively watched the assembly in a common bar, will not expect Christianity to make much visible progress among those whose lot is cast amid such untoward associations. There is a fatal idea abroad—'Religion is out of place in a public-house.' Barmen, barmaids, waiters, and potmen, as servants engaged in a hard service, deserve sympathy, and in the matter of sending them the Gospel, help also. Among these young persons the missionary will frequently find the remains of good seed sown long ago. To-day it will be some sensitive barmaid who is anxious for advice, because she can remember happier days, when in a quiet, provincial retreat, she not only enjoyed a happy home, but appeared week by week as teacher or scholar in the rural Sabbath-school; to-morrow it may perchance be a young man who has heard before of the things pertaining to Christ, and would hear more about the mystery of eternal life. But what time has *he* to think of religion? In common with his fellow-servants, perhaps, he has the afternoon of each alternate Sabbath; or, it may be, he has only two or three hours to call his own once a month. A member of the last class of unfortunates was once encountered; and as he had to clean the bar and engines on Sabbath mornings, he requested the missionary to call round and converse with him while thus employed. Responding to this request, the visitor was found, Sunday after Sunday, imparting religious instruction to a humble inquirer in a place which, but a few hours before, had resounded with the songs and jests of the thoughtless and the oaths of the profane.

We had now arrived at the portals of another large establishment, and of the select class which does not open until eight o'clock on Sabbath evenings. The landlord being 'favourable,' I am given to understand 'It is all smooth work here,' which remark is immediately verified by the warmth of our reception. Here are found several young men, who receive the tracts and the words accompanying them in the usual civil manner. One of them is attended by a large dog, and being of a nervous temperament, my companion casts some suspicious glances at the hungry beast, until a word from its owner showed how completely the shaggy animal was under discipline. The ready evangelist drew hence a moral lesson. 'The very dogs,' he said, 'are obedient, and respond to the word of their master. It is only when we come to man, formed in God's own image, that we find sinful resistance to the will of his Creator.' Finding these Christian sentiments were received with respect, and even with gratitude by those to whom they were offered, it became more than ever evident that the good seed of eternity could not be sown thus abundantly without some good resulting from the labour. Some of these people will go hence, and what they have heard will not immediately bear fruit. But some of them may become encompassed with trial; and will not some of the missionary's words, dropped by the wayside, then spring up and serve the purpose desired? May they not spring up as an oasis of green in some memory crowded with recollections of evil, and in sorrow or sickness yield the harvest of life everlasting?

Thus we have learned something of the manner in which the tavern-missionary goes about his business. On being appointed to a district he gradually becomes known to the landlords and bar-servants, and also to the customers; and the majority of the people treat the visitor in the manner above depicted. The cheerful light and costly fittings of the gin-palace are a splendid and mocking contrast to the rags and misery of those who crowd the fatal precincts; for have not wives and children been stripped of comfort and even of necessaries to provide the gilded cornices, sparkling chandeliers, and showy mirrors? One house might be named, where the bar rejoiced in a musical-box, which, having cost a hundred and twenty guineas, acted like a siren charmer in providing merry airs for those who were hurrying to ruin and an early grave. In this house a missionary one day met an emaciated young man, who, squalid, ragged, and dejected, was a too common sample of the reducing power of drink. As he was conning a tract just given him, this poor drunkard felt a hand laid on his shoulder, while the words, 'We must each give an account of ourselves to God,' were spoken in his ear. 'A pretty account mine will be,' he answered. 'This house has been my ruin.' On hearing this you would have judged the man to be an object of interest. It was so indeed. A life-story, fraught with warning, belonged to those glassy eyes, and to those haggard, sunken features. Once he had enjoyed life with the wife of his youth, and gleeful children surrounded the family board of his happy home. By his profession—wood engraving—he earned good wages and prospered in the world, until a propensity for drink blasted all that makes life worth having. On one memorable evening, after a course of his usual excess, and as he staggered homeward, he came in violent collision with a lamp-post, and this mishap originated the disease which finally hastened him to the grave. His nerves and system became so shaken that he could not keep a hand sufficiently steady for following his employment, and consequently he sank into the degradation of loitering about the bar, over which had passed the greater part of five years' earnings. 'You see,' he said, 'my old pals let me drink out of their pots, and give me a bit of victuals.' Health, happiness, and the welfare of dependants were, in one costly sacrifice, offered to the demon Gin; but even this man had reason to thank God for His mercy in Christ, and for the agency of the London City Mission.

On entering a side bar of the 'favourable' house just mentioned, a fresh-coloured, handsome barmaid, being in a merry mood, gave us to understand that had we postponed our visit we should have missed the pleasure of seeing *her*. The 'gentlemen' were at once interested; and in reply to the inquiry, 'What's up?' the natural answer was, 'A wedding.' A wedding it was probably; but as our fair friend would only convey the news by arch smiles and dark hints, we can only guess at the truth, and in any case wish her life-long happiness.

In the taverns of a genteel district gentlemen's servants are frequently found; and the marvellously important airs they affect will excite your mirth, or move you to commiseration, according to circumstances; for Jeames appears before you in the smoking-room of 'The Green Dragon,' or 'The Crossed Keys,' with just enough of the good breeding pervading his master's dining-room to make him the caricature of a gentleman, and with more than enough pride of his own to render him ridiculous.

A little space must also be devoted to the fast young man of London pseudo-fashionable life, who haunts the private bars of large taverns. A little experience with our itinerant missionary would reveal that, between these gentlemen and the barmaids, there exists a sort of tacit understanding. What the pseudo-fashionable fast young man does for a living it would be hard to say; for he seems to possess no qualifications more marketable than those which shine in a ball-room or gain favour at a pic-nic; and what wealth of intellect he commands would seem to be expended on his costume—short or long coats, tight or peg-top trousers, as the fashion of the passing hour may prescribe. In the street he uses due precaution to impress inferior passengers with the fact of his individual consequence; and if he is not recognised as 'a gentleman,' it is no fault of the tailor's. His gloves appear to be new every morning; his hat is perfection, and perfectly adjusted, and he pursues his way along the street with many an air and gesture learned of the dancing master, and intended to enlist the envy and good opinion of less fortunate beholders. Note with what studied gracefulness he twirls and switches his silver-headed cane. He has a partiality for the theatre, but is still fonder of the music-hall, where he can smoke threepenny cigars and drink sherry-cobbler. He not only receives music for his money at the music-hall; he enjoys an opportunity of exhibiting his good breeding, by addressing the waiters in aristocratic slang, and also by a knack he has of sitting with one ancle resting on the opposite knee. Besides music-halls and theatres, he has divers refreshment-houses by the way-side. These are usually large, showily-fitted up, and brilliant places, known to the initiated as 'fast' houses. The barmaids are fair and handsome girls, whose fine figures, winning graces, and faultless toilets might impress even stoical men under circumstances more propitious. These poor girls understand precisely what their employers expect from them, and in the exercise of their petty feminine arts they also know they are lowering themselves. With the fast young man their occupation brings them in daily contact. They can form a shrewd judgment, for their estimate of his worth might be accepted without hesitation by the moralist or the divine. But, notwithstanding, the fast man himself, poor fool, thinks every barmaid on his beat is captivated by his *personnel* and his gallant conversation. Behold how yonder bewitching siren can suppress the scorn she feels when he ventures beyond prescribed limits in his gross familiarity; and how artistically she can affect injured innocence by a pert toss of her pretty head, and a word or two in keeping, when the 'naughty man,' as she calls him, counterfeits displeasure. Thus the fast youth talks and drinks, imagining in the mean time that these hired servants of the public-house are excellent playthings for toying with when nothing more attractive is at hand. While drinking, chatting, and laughing pleasantly and condescendingly, how little is he aware that they, whom he would fain persuade himself are competitors for such questionable honours as he has to bestow, really regard him with contempt, and behave as they do merely for the sake of turning him into profit by making his weaknesses tell in their employers' favour, like fair deceivers as they are.

But to proceed on our evening round. In one bar we entered an opportunity occurred of witnessing a very common-place difficulty, such as the public-house missionary frequently encounters. I refer to the dogged opposition of ignorant unbelievers. A man sat there of middle age, who, being arrayed in broad-cloth and fine linen, took umbrage at being overtaken by religion in a place whither he had come to seek enjoyment. Both the matter and manner of his conversation showed him to be illiterate and conceited, and not even master of the merest common-place objections to Christianity. Yet his hatred of the Bible and of all pertaining to Christ found vent in stupid remarks and meaningless blasphemy; and the only warrant for giving publicity to this instance is, that it represents a large number of similar cases encountered by the city missionary. The man did not believe in God, for no one had seen Him; nor in heaven, for none had ever returned to witness of its existence; and the manner in which he vented his wrath on that mild production of the Religious Tract Society, 'Do you want a Pilot?' would have given reason for mirth had the occasion been less serious. Indeed, temper well-nigh choked this creature's utterance. 'Them things,' he stammered, alluding to the tracts, 'them things is a-a-a-all very well for *children*—f-f-for Sunday-school children; but I-I-I call it a-a-a insult to cum ear and hoffer 'em to a MAN.' In such an emergency the tact and moderation of the disciplined missionary appear to advantage. An ordinary person would grow contemptuous, and would answer the fool according to his folly. But this is not the procedure of the London city missionary. I have no reason for supposing that my companion's words carried aught of sarcasm when he mildly reasoned with this specimen of low-bred conceit by delicately pointing out the evils arising from intelligent men like his friend not sifting evidence and honestly searching for truth. There is one master obstacle, however, as yet untouched, in the way of conducting these arguments. Mr. Landlord is almost sure to show signs of restlessness, and according to his disposition he will take the infidel side, request the missionary to 'be off,' or otherwise gently hint that religion is out of place in a public-house. Then these low infidels greatly pride themselves on their manliness, even though their lives are a libel on everything which ennobles human nature. They expect also that deference shall be paid to their opinions. 'It's *my* opinion what you say is all humbug,' and 'It's *my* opinion that the Bible has no truth in it,' are fair examples of the state of culture at which these small but noisy fry have arrived. They are slaves of darkness, who imagine that they alone walk in the light. They are poor dupes, and little aware that the best things they are able to vend are merely the scourings of ignorant prejudice.

Good results certainly do follow in the wake of this mission to public-houses, for the current of testimony is too strong to be gainsaid. A woman attended by a little child has been observed to leave her gin untasted after listening to a few words on the way of Christ's receiving little children. 'Please to take this back,' said a medical student, at another time, to a missionary who handed him a tract as he was gaily chattering with some male and female companions. 'Please to take this back. I have just passed my examination, and I am out for a spree. I am afraid I shall turn it into ridicule. I am not in a fit state to have it.'

The good influence of the mission has, on several occasions, extended to the landlords, and for evidence of this we are not solely dependent on the missionaries' reports. The roughs of this Marylebone district have a testimony of their own, which, as impartial judges, we shall pronounce unanswerable. One day some members of the fraternity, who delight in beer and in gossipping in unwashed ease at street corners on Sunday mornings, were observed entering a barber's shop, not far from where we are now walking. Their tempers had been ruffled, and that but recently, by some untoward event. 'He won't serve you now, if you're only a bit tight,' remarks one, in reference to a landlord, who, living hard by, had, according to common report, 'grown more queer than ever.' On what kind of basis this complaint rested appeared from the observation of another gentleman. 'And if you let slip a word (*i.e.*, an oath), he says, "Now then, that won't do in *this* house."' 'Why, he was not always so,' cries another; 'he used to be as good a chap as any, and could swear as well; I've heard him.' 'Ah, but he's not fit to be a publican now,' exclaims a third, with the approval of all the rest. 'What's made him do so? do you know?' 'Know! yes, to be sure I do. Why, them missionary fellows walk bang into the beer-shops now; and one's been in there, taking his religion and tracts with him; and he's so worked on the landlord's mind that he's quite turned it, and now he treats his customers in this way.'

More singular still was the experience of the visitor whose adventures first suggested the organising, into a regular system, of the Christian visitation of public-houses. This is published in a separate form. The narrative tells how, one day, the missionary endeavoured to hinder a miserable woman and her health-shattered husband from entering a large gin-palace. The woman turned on the speaker rather angrily, and said, 'He shan't be without his enjoyment for the like of you.' The woman then explained that she customarily left the invalid in the bar, to be treated by customers, until she finished her daily round. The missionary followed them into the tavern, and was there jeered by the company, who lit their pipes with his tracts, and on his proceeding to speak with the people the landlord violently ejected him into the street. But the invalid was followed home, and, receiving the instruction of the missionary, he became a subject of the mercy of Christ, and died in triumph. Soon after the landlord, hitherto a coarse infidel, ruptured a blood vessel, and, visited by the friend who could return good for evil, he also embraced the faith. People saw the gin-palace transformed into quite a different place from what it had been, and the former eye-sore became a model to the trade, in consequence of the rules enforced for ensuring order. Then, when the proprietor died in Christian hope, the widow relinquished the business.

One cannot go among the taverns of London for Christian purposes without contracting some amount of sympathy for the publicans themselves, who have trials peculiar to their occupation. Many proprietors, in low districts especially, feel their calling to be one of degradation, and some will even send their children to be educated at a distance, so as to separate them from the contamination of home. A high-principled publican will confess: 'A man, to do a trade, must stifle conscience; and as for religion, that is out of the question.' And a certain landlady spoke thus to a missionary: 'I feel my soul is lost, and that I have been training up my children for hell all the years I have been in the beer trade, and now they have grown up they turn round and abuse me; if I talk to them about religion, they call me a maniac!' 'I cannot be religious if I would,' said another innkeeper; 'you come and take *my* place for twelve months, and that will soon knock all religion out of you.' Nevertheless, good is being done; and some in the trade are striving nobly against the stream of adverse circumstances. Some landlords are mean and grasping, and to allure the unsuspecting working man, will even put rum in the coffee served out to him on his way to work of a morning. But these are exceptions, not the rule. As a class they are open-hearted, extremely hospitable, and glad to welcome any who wish them well. The visitor frequently meets with signs that good is progressing among them, and one landlady manifested her appreciation of the mission work by papering her nursery with the sheets of the 'British Workman.'

I now come to the last house we entered on our evening round—a large establishment, in which we were well received. Indeed, the fashionably-attired barmaids welcomed us with smiles and civilities, and one of the two, not having received her periodical on the last call, poutingly expressed her belief that she was not deemed good enough for the customary attentions. As, however, it would be highly injudicious for the London city missionary to single out favourites among his constituency of barmaids, the oversight is instantly and gallantly rectified, while the apology is adroitly made to carry some sterling advice. From the scene of this little episode we emerge into what a late unsophisticated generation would have called 'the tap,' but which is now found softened into 'smoking-room.' As the clock-hands are fast approaching the hour of eleven, the company here is neither large nor select. There are two or three solitary drinkers scattered about, who, sitting alone with pipe, pot, and their own muddled cogitations, seem to be enjoying a sort of sottish contentment. While the tracts are in course of distribution, a wizened-featured man emerges from a corner of the room, and with a touch of his hat begs a pamphlet. He is garrulous, and finds a pleasure in telling his life-story. 'I've served the Queen in my time, sir; twenty-two years ago I was in the Kaffir war. See this mark in my cheek, sir? That's a sword-cut; and this here, sir' (uncovering his ankle and showing the scar of a gun wound), 'is a shot mark. Please to feel it, sir; it's as hard as the bullet as hit it. I'm a kebman now, sir, and you'll find *me* all right if you make inquiries. I never works a Sundays on any account.' And here he forcibly explained that he would not 'put a 'oss in a keb,' even to fetch the doctor to attend the most interesting of domestic crises. But however cruel this strange adherence to principle may make the old cabman appear in the eyes of sensitive readers, I believe he merely intended to insist that doctors should set the example of walking on the Sabbath. He also confessed, in tones of high satisfaction, that he had not sworn for twenty years. 'I can assure *you*, sir, I wouldn't take a oath for a thousand pound, exceptin' afore a magistrate, and that's legal and a different thing like. I tell yer how it come about, sir. Twenty-three year ago I 'ad a mate who swore fearful. Well, one day, after he 'ad bin calling on Almighty God to blind 'im and blast 'im, and all that, sure enough he went blind twenty minutes arterwards, and before wery long he died! I 'ave never took a oath since that day, sir. 'Ave I got a Bible? no, I ain't got one, sir, but I should wery much like one; I always reads the tracts.' The old man's address was taken, and doubtless, ere this, further instruction and the Book he needed have reached him in his own home.

While thus engaged at one end of the 'smoking-room' with the cabman, I was missing the substance of what was occurring elsewhere. The missionary was addressing some five or six men, one of whom evinced his approval by assuming a benign cast of features and declaring, 'I'm not illiterate, yer know.' There had been a meeting during the afternoon in one of the parks—presided over by a man who ought to have known better—to protest against the allowance to a scion of the Royal House. Opinions are consequently vented the reverse of loyal. England is degenerating, the men maintain, and a mechanic's life is fast approaching to a resemblance of the task-work of Egypt, where bricks had to be produced though straw was denied. 'Let each one keep his own kids, I say,' and 'So say I,' are about fair samples of the sentiments expressed. But as the missionary will not tolerate this controversy, he turns the conversation into a quieter channel. The respectful consideration he still meets with as a religious instructor continues to be strikingly satisfactory. One man, who attempts to expatiate on that common-place objection everywhere encountered—'Religion is out of place in a public-house'—is at once silenced by a clamour of opposition; and as we retire from the room some of the inmates rise in our honour, and amid a chorus of 'Come again, sir,' 'You *are* appreciated,' and other well-meant compliments, we pass into the street, and so conclude our Sunday evening inspection of the taverns of Marylebone.

'In all the towns and countries I have seen, I never saw a city or a village yet whose miseries were not in proportion to its public-houses.' Probably Goldsmith was right, for in Marylebone, during service-time on Sunday night, the persons carousing in drinking-shops outnumber those who are found worshipping their Maker in the churches and chapels of the various denominations.

V.

THE SUBJECTS OF MISFORTUNE.

THE SUBJECTS OF MISFORTUNE.

No wise man desires what is evil for its own sake, but when evil is made corrective, or when it teaches some necessary lesson, only the weak or the short-sighted will fail to acknowledge the favour of Him who, from the seeming calamities of time, 'still educes good.' If this great London, with its thousand and one attractions, may be compared to a broad landscape, fair and chaste, commanding the admiration and envy of distant beholders, it has undergrowths possessing no beauty. The wealth and intellectual culture, which to superficial observers make up a vast expanse of green, with varied pretty tints, is merely a gay canopy covering an appalling mass of poverty and suffering. In one direction are met those who accept hard fare and wretchedness as their natural state, and in another those who strive to patch up penury until it wears quite a genteel front. There is also another class, of whom it will be interesting to learn something, those whom our missionaries come upon in obscure garrets and cellars; unfortunates, who having succumbed to poverty, have fallen from a station of affluence, or even from an aristocratic position, to be associates of the vulgar in the purlieus of want. The missionary whose life-work consists in ministering to the needy of all grades is no stranger to such phenomena, and not seldom is he a very friend in need sent by heaven to the children of misfortune.

One Sabbath evening, during the summer of 1860, a certain missionary was conducting an open-air meeting in the broad space of Lincoln's-inn-fields. Only a few minutes prior to the commencement of this service, there emerged from one of the miserable garrets abounding in the neighbourhood, an extremely aged and very forlorn-looking man, whose unsteady gait beneath the burden of ninety years showed he was on the edge of the grave, while in his features, picturing as they did intense abject misery, he more resembled one whose right senses had flown with his strength, than a sane individual. Overwhelmed with melancholy, he had just formed a dark resolution. The world was becoming at last too much for one whose poverty was aggravated by infirmity; and now that the grave had closed over the remains of the partner of a long, long pilgrimage, he would escape from intolerable loneliness and bitter misery by the short though painful road of self-murder; and where could be found a more convenient spot for completing the design than Lincoln's-inn-fields in the quiet of the Sabbath evening? Going determinedly onward with his desperate undertaking in hand, the old man happens to raise his eyes, when in the distance is descried a crowd, which a man appears to be earnestly addressing. There will be no harm, he thinks, in drawing near to discover what it is about, so inquisitive is the soul under the gloomiest circumstances. As the intending suicide approaches the speaker, he hears him read the chapter relating to the Philippian gaoler, and the words, 'Do thyself no harm,' entering the soul of the aged listener as a message from heaven, they are the arrow which opens a way for gospel truth. He returned to his solitary garret, instead of completing his wicked resolve; but having discovered new sources of strength and joy, the lately sterile solitude became a very paradise, gay with opportunities of good. Forsaken by the flatterers of prosperity, the impoverished merchant found a trusty friend in the city missionary, who now constantly visited him, until his happy spirit winged its flight to a better inheritance, and to whom he told his strange, not to say romantic story.

The old gentleman had been born in the east of England, and in humble life, and on coming to London to push his fortune, during the last decade of the eighteenth century, he sought employment as a journeyman tailor. Inheriting a fair amount of business tact and shrewdness, and being of frugal and industrious habits, the workman made rapid progress, and soon found himself in a position to begin business on his own account. The tide of prosperity continued to favour him until he ranked as master of a large west-end establishment, and still increasing in wealth until he amassed £100,000, he kept his town house and country mansion. But at this conjuncture he presented a sad example of infatuation, and of the evil inseparable from hastening to be rich. Had he cultivated contentment, while possessing more than enough, he would have remained in affluence; but the fatal pitfall into which so many have stumbled here presenting itself, he fell into the snare. He rashly speculated in Spanish bonds, and in one venture lost nearly the whole of his fortune. The man who so lately had been able to afford himself every luxury of life was now utterly ruined, and he had to relinquish the appendages of wealth for the shelter of a miserable attic, whither he and his aged wife now removed, the same being the house whence he issued on the memorable evening of being attracted by the missionary's message. In the annals of the Mission, perhaps, the gospel never achieved a more pleasing triumph than in this instance. The good hope now enjoyed by this once sin-hardened and miserable subject more than compensated for lost possessions; and the man of ninety years derived peculiar satisfaction from attending the services in Lincoln's-inn-field's, where he first learned that a human soul was worth more than a hundred thousand pounds. He now took his frugal dinner more thankfully than when faring sumptuously, for mean temporal provision and large eternal prospects were preferred to former abundance. The old man had no means of support, but his extreme age and striking history awakening public sympathy, various friends supplied what little was needed; and, for this manifestation of regard, the recipient returned such gratitude as can only be shown by a Christian gentleman.

Extreme poverty leads to despair, and from despair to suicide is but one short step. On many occasions the missionary has just appeared at the critical moment to prevent disaster or crime.

Some of the worst parts of Bethnal-green, especially a district such as borders on the precincts of Shoreditch church, are no less physically unhealthy than they are moral eyesores. There every form of disease riots in unchecked ascendency, aggravated by circumstances which might be controlled by the sanitary commissioner. In these neighbourhoods during an epidemic the inhabitants fell by myriads; and the experience of the Christian visitor includes much that is heartrending; for there the wretched and the unfortunate crowd the tenements, necessity, not choice, bringing them together.

One day, in the course of visitation, a missionary of the east-end of the town met with an adventure, which would probably have startled a gentleman less accustomed to the novelties of poverty. It is the practice of the City Mission itinerants to begin exploring a house at the upper storey, and work downwards, so that should any disturbance arise, they, by descending, get nearer the street. In the present instance the visitor knocked at a kitchen door—'a damp and loathsome place'—whence, after standing some time, a female voice faintly responded, "Who's there?' 'A friend.' The door is then opened by a woman, who, emaciated and dejected, presents a shocking spectacle. What are her circumstances? In that bare room called a home, a room which has proved less hospitable to her than does a prison to the felon, there is not a particle of food, and such is the woman's destitution of clothes, that she cannot appear in the street, not even to crawl to the workhouse door to seek relief! The appearance of the missionary, for the first time in such a home, is a blessing which can scarcely be over-calculated as regards the poor creatures, the inhabitants. The woman opens her heart to *him;* and will not even disguise her intention—suicide—and that by a great crime she intended to escape her present misery. She could tell of happier days, when, respectable and respected, she regularly attended the Sabbath-school. But, falling low, she had eventually allied herself with a man who sang songs in public, and who, even then, while she whom he had undertaken to protect was literally pining to death, was probably bawling a gleeful ditty at some street corner with the air of a merry fellow.

All may rest assured that, if they will search for them, Bethnal-green will supply some rare curiosities in the department of poverty. In the case of the missionary these things rise to the surface in regular course, till he is scarcely surprised at meeting with what is merely singular. In an attic, the small windows of which peered over the murky housetops, and where the roof's construction interfered with a person standing upright in the room, was once found a being, who may be accounted a subject of misfortune, since an hallucination confined him to the apartment for months together, his seclusion arising from peculiarity of temperament and not from necessity. This man and his wife led a remarkable existence, the woman searching the streets for old shoes and leather, which, after due cobbling and manufacture, were disposed of to such as chose to become purchasers. In the confined attic, amid large heaps of his peculiar merchandise, the man was enthroned, unwashed and unshaved, till any but the missionary would have pronounced him a phenomenon in insanity. Though this man could see no attractions in the outer world, the world itself grew so visibly interested in his grotesque appearance, whenever favoured with a sight of him, that after one appearance at the prayer-meeting, it was not deemed advisable to press his further attendance. The brightest side of such a story is, that these people are never too singular to be saved; but, were it not for Christian visitors who delight in bringing to Christ those who have no other friend, they would remain in ignorance of things pertaining to their best interest. The most heathenish districts, and, humanly speaking, the farthest removed from hope of reclamation, have been proved not impervious to gospel influence. An old woman is found living in a Shoreditch court — a close, dirty, fever-breeding place — who had lived there during seventy years without having received any religious instruction. Ignorant of the gospel, she had not troubled herself about its claims, till, accepting the message of the missionary, she became a Christian herself and strove to Christianise others. Such works should be stimulated by a sympathising public; especially when this Christian invasion of the moral deserts of London needs a sum of moral courage and of physical endurance which it becomes all beholders to admire and honour. It is well sometimes to ask, at what personal sacrifice do the visitors penetrate these hideous localities, where landlords, while growing rich, are content to leave their tenants to battle, as best as they can, with disease and death? The crazy stairs, leading to dirt-encrusted landings, and foul, pestiferous rooms, are frequently only partially supplied with hand-rails and balusters; and through the very steps you would jeopardise a leg, were it not for a friendly piece of oil-cloth, or a barrel stave, on which you tread. In these places the decencies of our nature cannot be observed, and the poor creatures who are compelled to inhabit them rush to gin-drinking as a desperate compromise; but, like a madman who would dash his scalded hand into a bowl of molten lead, they find the cure worse than the pain. What is too often the self-sacrifice of missionaries may be seen in their reports. One will inform his committee that all his children have been prostrated by contagion carried home; another that his wife has died, or that all his offspring have been laid in the grave!

While the London City Mission is pre-eminently an agency for benefiting souls, it should be borne in mind that, though the society does not profess to provide temporal relief, and, as a rule, discourages its agents in extending their operations to mere bodily wants, the temporal good constantly accruing to those coming under its influence is very remarkable. The grateful effects of the working of the Mission are constantly observable, and it has repeatedly been proved impossible for Christianity to extend her reign over the captives of sin and misfortune without socially raising them; and, in many instances, the missionaries have opportunely appeared, at the very crisis of a downward course, to snatch a sufferer from death by starvation.

On a piercingly cold morning, as one of the agents was going through a house in a court of Whitechapel, seemingly left by the authorities in charge of typhus, small-pox, and their attendant terrors, he noticed, in an exposed place beneath the stairs, a huddled-up heap of rags, which his experienced eye detected to be a human being. From the indifference of this as yet still living creature to repeated efforts made to rouse him, the missionary thought that life, which had held its own against pain and disaster, was at length succumbing to the frost. This; however, was a mistake. The sleeper arose, and appeared as a young man, who, notwithstanding the severity of the season, wore only a few rags to cover his emaciated body. The house afforded shelter to six families; and a woman, who rented an apartment, had noticed this outcast, and learning that he possessed neither lodging nor means of procuring any, she told him he could sleep under the stairs, and accordingly that was his only accommodation during three months. Reduced by lack of nourishment and frost-bitten feet, the man appeared well-nigh bent double; and, besides other afflictions, his body swarmed with vermin. Now, this sum of misery originated neither in vice nor in waste, but sprang from what was in itself a virtue—a shrinking from burdening others with his own calamity. The man told the missionary that his rearing had been creditable and even genteel, while he had passed the usual time of apprenticeship to a Clerkenwell watch-jeweller—and he could prove himself a good hand at that delicate profession. Being of an independent turn of mind, he, on the cancelling of his indentures, went into a separate lodging, where, though overtaken by illness and coming to want, he still refused to inform his parents of his necessity. Unable to work, he sold his clothes and other articles, so that on regaining strength, a shabby wardrobe prevented his returning to the work-room among better-dressed companions. In addition to other evils, his landlady—a hard, unfeeling woman—perceiving her lodger's inability to pay the weekly due, resolved on ridding herself of an encumbrance, by sending him on a fool's errand, and quietly locking the door on his back.

Poor fellow! he was, doubtless, an artless simpleton, honest himself, and placing too implicit a confidence in others. In a confidential manner he mentioned to the landlady the fact that a well-to-do uncle of his resided somewhere in London; he did not know the locality, but on finding the address he could obtain temporary assistance. Either suspecting the story to be a fabrication, or concluding that the unfortunate watchmaker would never discover his uncle, this worthless woman resolved on making the man's anxiety a means of ejecting him from her premises. She therefore gladdened him with declaring she had discovered the needed address to be in High-street, Whitechapel; and hither the hoaxed lodger went, with light heart and good hopes, to tell his troubles to a true friend. The journey only resulted in the discovery that the woman had invented an infamous plan of relieving herself of a burden, by turning the burden itself into the street. Alone in Whitechapel, without a home, the man might still have sought refuge in his father's house, but each step downward in the social scale increased his intense nervous dread of confessing his forlorn condition to near kindred. At this crisis he made the acquaintance of the old stall-keeper—the same who proffered the boon of a sleeping place under the stairs. There the missionary crossed the wanderer's path, when, resembling a man of thrice his years, he stood shivering in the frosty air, crouchingly resting on a stick to support his enfeebled frame.

Here, then, was a fellow-creature within a few weeks of death, unless assistance were forthcoming. Is it not gratifying to know that in these instances of emergency the needed help is invariably given? The missionary begged a suit of clothes, and then, accompanying the man to a bath, he saw him washed and clothed and placed in a temporary lodging; and the subject of this solicitude appeared overwhelmed with grateful surprise at the agency which had seized him while hastening to the gates of death, and in a few hours transformed him into a clean, warmly-clothed, and comparatively happy being, supplied with the necessaries of life. The next step was to wait on the parents of the rescued one, who listened with tearful eyes and bleeding hearts to the strange relation. Having lost sight of their son in a mysterious manner, they would have rejoiced in rendering succour had they known of his misfortunes. The work of this case was now finished by fetching and presenting the long lost son to his friends. It happened to be the season just preceding Christmas, when people were beginning to make ready the feast in honour of Him who came to bless His people, whether prosperous or unfortunate. 'Oh, sir,' said the young man, as he walked homewards, 'oh, sir, I did not think I should have seen my father and mother this Christmas. Had it not been for you I am sure I should have *died.*' Then ensued a joyous family gathering, and when, after a short stay in a hospital, for the cure of his feet, injured by the frost, the late vagrant once more resumed business among old associations and at former wages, he indeed realised the goodness of God who had put it into the hearts of His people to originate an agency so benign in its working as the London City Mission.

A case even more remarkable than the above consisted in the reclamation of one who fell into vicious courses from the position of an ordained minister of the gospel. As a result of the missionary's long and forcible pleading, the renegade relinquished drink and evinced true penitence.

From the last instance, it would be impossible to estimate the good effects likely to arise. Equally satisfactory, if less striking, are the more unpretending triumphs of the Mission. One day one of its agents tapped at an attic-door, in a street inhabited by the squalid and the profane, and, within, found a reduced gentleman's family, whose means now afforded them no better shelter. The father, a well-educated person, served as a commissioned officer in the army, and, as it occurs in many similar instances, neither vice nor improvidence was the occasion of present trouble. The mother and daughter, whose bearing was that of ladies, possessed only one shawl between them, and gratefully accepted a ticket for bread and coals. This old soldier, after retiring from the army on compensation allowance, met with misfortune, and, parting with the last of his property, he depended on precarious earnings and even charity. But, as a weeper with those who weep, the visitor now takes a seat among these downcast children of penury, kneeling with them in prayer when they are seemingly abandoned by other friends. Intensely do such persons appreciate this gracious ministry. 'Unsought and unsolicited, you found us out,' cries the father; 'spiritually exhorted us daily and unceasingly to fly to God, our best friend and succour in trouble, and in deep, grinding, and pinching poverty. Through you, many of our wants have been relieved at this inclement season. You have visited us as a friend and counsellor without fee or reward.'

Thus the missionary is often made the means of communicating temporal good, as well as of instructing souls in righteousness. He becomes familiarised with uncommon histories, until the strangest cease to appear remarkable; for, expecting to encounter them, they become merely a part of the daily routine. In the garret of a large house, in a court near Holborn—a tenement which in former days probably sheltered a family of distinction—was once found a person who, being a fitting subject for this chapter, was also a refreshing example of the power of vital Christianity. This man, a plumber and glazier, had long since been laid aside, or reduced by gout in the limbs from a skilful workman to a mere cripple. Yet, forlorn as is his condition, you have only to examine the grounds of his thankfulness, to read a lesson or two worth knowing. First, the landlord, moved by his pitiable state of bitter poverty, allowed the free use of the room occupied. His income from the parish is two shillings a week, and we learn how this sum has to be expended. Fivepence buys twenty-four sheep's trotters, washing cost threepence halfpenny, and the remainder went for bread and potatoes. For weeks and months this coarse fare was thankfully partaken of by one prostrated by weakness and pain! If murmuring were reasonable, it would surely be so under these circumstances; but instead of complaining, the invalid is 'humble, pious, grateful, and contented.' 'Don't you ever take tea and coffee?' 'Oh, no, sir,' he answers; 'then there must be milk and sugar, and I cannot have *them.*' 'Do you never murmur?' 'I do, sir, when my pain makes me so ill that I get sick of my trotters; but I immediately check myself.' He might have entered the workhouse; but he objected to this, chiefly on account of a favourite pastor by whose ministry he profited on the Sabbath. Notwithstanding this beautiful testimony to the supporting power of Christianity under an Egyptian night of trial, unbelief, like a cowardly enemy, approached, and sought to take away from this poor man the pearl of pearls by insinuating doubt. An infidel entered the attic, and suggested difficulties sufficiently tormenting to the unlettered listener, until the missionary became the means of re-establishing the ascendancy of faith.

It is a grateful work to encourage the fainting and sympathise with the afflicted; but the history of the London City Mission further shows that when people lose goods and position, and all that makes the world go pleasantly, a friend in the person of the visiting missionary, finding them out, has, besides teaching them the best of all knowledge, helped them to take the first step upward again. In illustration of this, take the history of a family who, residing at the West-end, were very substantially benefited. The father having been very clever with his pencil, secured a good position as an artist. On one occasion, which was the turning crisis of his career, he designed certain pictures for an exhibition of art in Westminster Hall; but not winning the prize coveted, the disappointment slightly affected his reason, and from a comparatively happy condition he lapsed into a misanthrope, and was thenceforward more burden than help to his family. When knowing him in happier days, the missionary usually met this gentleman on the friendliest of terms; but, under sadder circumstances, he was never encountered but to be assailed with coarse and violent abuse. Not discouraged by this untoward reception, the visitor took especial notice of the eldest son of the family, in whom was discovered a strong genius for music. This boy was characterised by a thoughtful reserve, so that he more resembled a matured student than an uneducated youth. Becoming deeply interested in this young fellow's welfare, the missionary, by the assistance of an influential lady, apprenticed him at a large pianoforte manufactory, where unusual proficiency procured him the payment of wages almost as soon as admitted. Other friends, attracted by the talents of the youth, subscribed enough to purchase a pianoforte; but the morose parent, who, in disgust at the absence of popular appreciation, had cut a number of his own pictures into shreds, threatened to convert into firewood any instrument brought into his rooms, and, consequently, it was placed in the house of the missionary. By daily visiting for practice, the young man continued to progress in musical art, and also in knowledge pertaining to the soul. Finally, he became the chief stay of the family, and of a mother surrounded by afflicting circumstances. It does not belong to man to limit the blessings which may result from an interposition like the above. The missionary, as an agent of good, doubtless exerted an influence which will affect future generations.

In some instances the missionaries find themselves in positions where prompt relief is the only alternative, and frequently, but for these almoners, disastrous results would ensue. A gentleman in a western district, who devoted his time to the reclamation of fallen females, was called on by a woman, who explained that at a house specified, in a neighbouring street, a singular spectacle might be witnessed. She had given shelter to two young girls, whose appearance and bearing told their genteel extraction; and, through their having no home, she still protected them, otherwise they would have starved. These young creatures, having sold their clothes, were terribly conscious of their abject condition, as was shown by their frequently kneeling together to call aloud on God for relief and direction. Possessing the instinct of a true woman, and moved to pity, their protector implored the missionary to interfere ere the enemy, by enticing them to vice, cut off retreat from a vicious course. The man went as requested, and, finding the girls as described, listened to their story.

They had been reared by a God-fearing and tender mother, now long since committed to the grave; and mother and daughters in their happiest days were comfortably provided for by the husband and father, who flourished as a picture dealer, and their home was a tasty suburban villa. The girls were carefully and liberally educated, having received all attentions which parental solicitude can suggest, or money procure. Then came days darkened by misfortune. The mother died, and in an evil day their father married another wife—a mere girl, who, besides despising her husband and slighting her step-daughters, committed other follies and extravagances, according to the bent of her evil passions. Then, as it often happens in social history, decline of business followed on home disorder; and, unhappy with the wife whom he married for the sake of her personal attractions, the old man sought to drown care in the drunkard's cup. The girls, formerly so well loved, were now roughly treated, or even ill-used, and appointed to menial labour. Ruin, complete and irretrievable, followed these disasters. The worthless wife eventually ran off with a paramour when money failed; but, still possessing his daughters, the stricken husband would have been supported by them, had employment been procurable; but where can delicately-nurtured women find work in the hour of pressing necessity? Employment failed, as it has failed in thousands of other similar instances equally heartrending; and, while one article after another of wearing apparel or of household furniture was disposed of for food, the sire sank into hopeless imbecility amid the ruinous calamity his own folly had ensured. The walls of a lunatic asylum now secluded him from the world, and his daughters were left alone and unprotected in the great and wicked city. Under such dark circumstances, probably, no better friend could have strayed across the wanderers' path than the sympathising missionary, whose stock of worldly knowledge is not contemptible because he is mainly concerned about spiritual affairs; and you cannot brighten his path by anything more tempting than an opportunity of snatching innocent maidenhood from the blight of vice, disease, and misery. Heaven heard the cry of the worse than orphaned girls, and sent relief and direction. The missionaries often possess able friends with whom to advise in the persons of their superintendents; and, in this emergency, one of these gentlemen gave the sisters an outfit previous to their installation into respectable situations. The youngest found a Christian lady for a mistress, who acted towards her almost like a second mother, while the elder sister was likewise introduced to a comfortable home. Thus God, doubtless, heard a mother's prayers, and, as it would seem, made the city missionary the medium of His interposition.

Had these girls been of a more romantic temperament, they would probably have sought escape by suicide. Cases of self-poisoning frequently occur among such young creatures, who thus find their way into the hospital-wards, and come under Christian influence. Many will seek to lay violent hands on themselves on account of very trivial grievances. Disappointment in love, or reverse in fortune, affords a sufficient excuse for taking a deadly draught. One infatuated maiden, who though slowly recovering, lay prostrated in extreme weakness in the London hospital, told the missionary that she swallowed poison after disagreeing with her lover. Disappointed of earthly felicity, she took what she imagined to be the nearest road to heaven!

But perhaps the most pitiable subjects of misfortune are the girls attracted to London by itinerant villains, whom the law does not show sufficient vigilance in tracking for condign punishment. Numbers of unfortunates are persuaded to emigrate to England, and are thus enticed into courses of crime after being respectably nurtured in continental homes. This uninviting subject should not be hushed up and hidden from public notice, in deference to our too nice notions of delicacy; for the enormity of the sin demands a strong remedy, and morality must be advanced by promoting detestation of vice. The story of one whom a missionary assisted in regaining a social standing, will illustrate my meaning. The girl was a native of a pleasant village in Belgium; and, while living happily with her parents, there one day appeared at the cottage-door a fellow, in the garb of a gentleman, whose smooth speech was calculated to deceive the unsuspecting. He represented that his business in the vicinity was to search out young ladies of education, whom he required to fill stations as governesses in distinguished English families. The parents perceived the impropriety of their daughter's leaving home with a stranger; but conquered by the 'gentleman's' blandness, they finally consented. The young lady herself suspected nothing wrong, but doubtless rather congratulated herself on the fortune which so opportunely gave her the means of providing an independent income. Alas! on arriving in London, the prospect lost its gay tints, and the horrible truth that she had been entrapped for a vile purpose appeared in its hideous reality; and, as concealment could serve him no longer, the decoyer, a regular trader in this department of infamy, threatened to murder his victim if she exposed him. 'To my shame,' she confessed, 'I have lived a sinful course of life since then, but at last I succeeded in running away.' This girl was subsequently married, and taken to a home worthy of the name; but there are such histories constantly occurring in London, the sequel to which is darkness and death. What punishment is too severe for the unmanly cowards, who for miserable gold can adopt the profession of entrapping unsuspecting maidens? The ruffianly hero of the above story, on having his path crossed by the missionary to whom the victim told her experience, was filled with fear and rage at the dread of detection, conveyed in the threat of being handed over to the police, and he declared he would murder the woman if he ever met her again. Young girls of foreign parentage, of blighted life and happiness, and whose histories nearly correspond to the above relation, abound in London. Is it not intolerable that society in the nineteenth century should be disgraced with such abominable characters as these decoyers? Should not they be hunted from their lairs without mercy, and when captured, visited with heavy and certain retribution? These miscreants cannot bear detection in any form, for having lost all manly instinct, they are abject cowards; and only a slight recognition and exposure by one who knows them and their ways, will cause them to slink into the shade, or to seek safety in ignominious flight.

Thus the phases of suffering with which the missionary has to deal are extremely diversified. Many cases of depravity are too shocking to be detailed, and in these, innocent, unsuspecting ones are too often the victims. Does not the sum of misery arising from iniquity call on the Church to lend her aid in repressing crime and in reclaiming the fallen?

Of all objects whom a kind heart would desire to serve, probably a helpless girl sunk by misfortune to the despair of poverty, and about to take the fatal first step to ruin, is chief. Such abound in London; and not being able to resist the allurements of vice, when vice clothes and feeds them, they are lost to virtue; and when next encountered in the hospital, or in the penitentiary, the missionary can only seek their reclamation from vice.

One evening, while crossing Vauxhall-bridge, a gentleman was accosted by a girl, who, unaware of his profession, related her troublous history. Out of place, and having spent her all, she was in bitter want; and the proposal she made to avoid 'pacing the streets all night,' showed to what a desperate resolution she had arrived. Bidding her follow him home, the friend (as he proved) supplied her immediate wants, and gave her sufficient money for a lodging, and on the following morning accompanied her home. There a scene occurred which is happily rare even among the lowest of the population. The father would not admit his daughter, on account of the expense she would incur. The mother wept; but nothing could be elicited from the sire than that the girl might 'go and hang herself.' Thus, in taking her to a refuge, from which she soon after was removed into a situation, the missionary became a better friend to one in need than even her own father!

Possibly, some who read them, will judge that these examples, one following the other in sad succession, have a monotonous ring, out of harmony with literary taste. The object, however, being to illustrate the working of the Mission in an important department of work, yet another case is ventured wherein the reclaiming agent stepped up just at the right moment to prevent a crime.

One spring morning, the gentleman alluded to observed a girl approaching the Regent's Canal, and her excitable manner aroused fear and suspicion. Being recognised she retired, and on being questioned she declared herself there for no particular intention, but immediately afterwards she confessed that her determination had been to commit suicide; the reason being that, without friends, shelter, or money, she was regarded as belonging to a degraded class, though of unsullied virtue. Subsequently she actually threw herself into the water, and after suffering a week's imprisonment for the offence, she came under the missionary's influence, who saw her received into an asylum.

The depths of misery and of degradation into which persons who once flourished in the world are found to fall, present some of the saddest phenomena of human life. In the byways of London, stragglers of all classes are detected, and when by misfortune they lose their footing, the social vortex engulfs them, and they sink unpitied and unnoticed by the crowd, who have something more engaging to attend to than the alleviation of other people's troubles. Now, in a hidden garret, or loathsome cellar of some uninviting court or lane, is found a subject of misfortune who once commanded an establishment and willing servants. Anon, in the recess of a forbidding looking lodging-house, where the very air is putrid, and where you must not venture without afterwards observing the precaution of burning the clothes worn during the inspection, may be found those who, educated for learned professions, have lost social standing through false steps, unaccountable reverses, or unconquered sins! Among all these, among the reduced as well as those who embrace poverty as theirs by inheritance, the missionary passes on, delivering to all in common the same healing message of grace.

In this itinerancy of mercy, poverty like the following is more frequently met with than is desirable. The scene is a Southwark district, the house being situated in a miserable court, where the windows, bedimmed by the accumulated dirt of years, exclude the light which would afford a yet more unwelcome sight of a more repulsive interior. The stairs being dark and narrow, the first inconvenience encountered is a collision with a beam, which allows none but the initiated to pass unmolested. At length a chamber door is reached, and knocking softly, a voice in screeching tones replies, 'Come in; I know ye.' The visitor is too well seasoned to these pestiferous retreats of the great city to be shocked at trifles, or easily repelled, but the sight now revealed, and the abominable effluvia issuing from the room, produce some sickening and creeping sensations. The contents of the apartment are utterly disgusting. In one corner a heap of the excrement of dogs awaits transition to a neighbouring tannery, and close by is a collection of bones ready for the mill. Besides these, there are pots, kettles, plates, and other minutiæ, a description of which is spared the reader. There is other furniture, however; for beneath the bed are gathered onions, fuel, and other miscellaneous ware. The weather being cold, there is a small fire in the grate, and feebly crouching over the warmth, smoking his pipe, is an old man whose history properly belongs to this chapter of the annals of misfortune. Aged and infirm, he no longer moves downstairs; but a son and daughter conduct the collecting business and share the home described. The old fellow retains no capacity for aught beyond putting on a rag or two and creeping from the bed to the fire, and thence back to bed. But he has a story to tell, piquant enough to whet the curiosity of a social explorer of sufficient daring to invade the precincts of filth and disease to carry away the relation. Long ago, and far away in the country, he served a clergyman in the capacity of gardener during twenty years; and, being now eighty-five, he has married and buried three wives and the greater number of twenty children. Does he ever pray to God? kindly inquires the missionary. 'Oh yes, I always prays to Him when I feels sorrowful.' Does any one ever come to see him? 'No, sir; nobody ever reads to me but you.' Are not such cases those which will repay our help and sympathy? A family of three, each welcoming instruction, is open to Christian influence; for the son and daughter, as well as their sire, hear the gospel faithfully proclaimed, and we are not without reasonable hope that their hearing will not be in vain.

But, to pass onward; for the subjects of misfortune stand, sit, and lie thickly around, and there is only time and space for stopping one minute here and another there, to listen to their strange stories. Follow the missionary as he turns up a close repelling court of five feet wide and sixty long, on the southern side of the river. The door knocked at opens on a landing and an interior no more inviting than the last-mentioned, and the family within, eleven in number, is sunk in forlorn, bitter, hopeless poverty, while from the place they call home emanates a stench 'most disgusting and intolerable.' There are children underfed and scantily clothed. In one direction lies an old man prostrated by disease, and in another corner reclines a woman who has just given birth to one more heir to this appalling misery. The woman's husband is a blind beggar, who contrives to exist by exhibiting a placard in public and soliciting alms. On being addressed he is communicative; and it is no fault of his if the story he tells does not teach a worthy moral lesson to such as have escaped the sands on which the speaker's poor life-barque has stranded. Sitting there in the solitude of blindness, he calls to mind days when, nurtured and trained for a liberal profession by anxious parents, the world stretched far and wide around him, like a gay expanse of pleasant things. Poor fellow! his stumbling-block was bad company, and the evils arising from the vicious examples of worthless confidants. Influenced by these associates, one fatal day he enlisted in the army, and in that service met with the accident which deprived him of sight. But he has long since bitterly repented of these youthful follies, and now listen to his subsequent experience. 'The police, you see, sir, drive me about, so that I am weary of my life.

I seldom get a shilling a day; and sometimes I stand all day in the rain and don't get a penny. I always carry my character in my hand, and my dismissal, so that if any one doubts what I say, I may show them.' Were he able to see he could read, and he is the only member of the household who has attained to that distinction. Then it is affecting to hear him speak of the comforts attending married life as compared with single blessedness, and his remarks carry some compliments, which quickly reach the appreciative ears of the lying-in woman of the corner. 'Yes, sir,' she cries eagerly; 'my husband is a very good man; he does not like swearing and that sort.' Who would not wish an increase to the number of those agents of mercy, who can ignite a spark of comfort or of hope in such abodes as these! These foul retreats are not completely barren ground; for a harvest is surely garnered when from their precincts subjects are gathered for the missionary's meeting.

It is scarcely probable that those who know the sweetness and value of true sympathy in times of sorrow and trial, will under-estimate the blessing these visitors must prove to hundreds of families, who, though neither vicious nor profane, have yet lost ground in the social struggle, and have therefore been deserted by their summer friends. '*You* are always welcome,' said one to the missionary; and the wife of a man who, after having lost the savings of a lifetime, was slowly approaching the border-land of death, remarked, 'It is only God's people we want now. All the others have left us.' Is not the gospel the only cure for the evil of human selfishness?

In one sense, the working classes of London, considered as a body, rank in the social arena as subjects of misfortune. Strictly speaking, the labourer or artisan, like the rest of us, is answerable for his own actions; but, like others, he too is a creature of circumstances; and it not only becomes the affluent to ask themselves, how far they have contributed to the evils he endures, but also to determine what they have done for the amelioration of his condition. What is the life-long condition of many a working man in London? The answer to this question might be found in one house and in one room, selected at random from hundreds of others in any such neighbourhood as Leather-lane. In these days railways and improvements have invaded the localities of the poor, till driven from abodes where they were sufficiently crowded before, they necessarily migrate into other quarters, where for the privilege of adding to their own and others' inconveniences they pay an increased rent. Enter the specimen-house above-mentioned, a description of which, being very general, would suffice for the bulk of its neighbours. The room called 'home' is dirty and bare, the stock of furniture not exceeding in value the amount of the weekly rent-charge. The family consists of young and old, the one bed being appropriated by an elderly couple and the smaller children. The other occupants perhaps include a married pair, and two or three single lodgers of both sexes, who contentedly lie about the floor like animals. It may be very well to turn in disgust from such a spectacle, because the people are victims of drink and improvidence. They have scarcely enjoyed any opportunity of following a different course of life, never having possessed a home worthy of ranking higher than a nightly shelter; and surrounded and depressed by evil influences, they can only by a greater effort than most would care to exert maintain a respectable position. There is not only no comfort at home, the places where thousands of men and women warren by night are just about as repulsive as imagination can conceive, and while man remains what he is, such homes will not successfully compete with the attractions of the gin-palace and the joviality of the tap-room. Warmth, congenial company, and stimulants, all conspire to allure the working-man from the confusion and discomfort of his miserable lodging. Then his wife is by no means a total abstainer; but after passing through such an education as her training has been, how can she, poor creature, be expected to act the heroine; for heroine indeed she would be if, in a squalid room in a disease-stricken neighbourhood, she presented an example of tidiness and prudence. Poor woman! she has many trials peculiar to her station, and these have perfected her in the exercise of many petty arts. On Saturday evenings she makes a point of following her partner from his work to the tavern, so that a due share of the weekly salary may be secured while it remains intact. Observe with what feminine dexterity she pursues her task, till triumph crowns her endeavour by the withholding hand yielding the grudged half-sovereign. She deserves sympathy; for, worn and slatternly, she endeavours after a manner to make the most of things; and would laugh in her sleeve were you to demonstrate what is fairly true, that a little knowledge of domestic economy would be equivalent to an increase of five shillings a week in her means. She is also a regular patron of Mr. Pawnbroker, whose establishment, flourishing at the head of the court, is a necessary adjunct to the carved and gilded gin-palace opposite. Between her and Mr. Pawnbroker, and especially between her and Mr. Pawnbroker's assistant, there exists a long-established understanding; for though they may come to high words over a difference of threepence, more or less, the quarrel is forgotten to-morrow, like 'the falling out of faithful friends.' The woman herself really believes she could not continue paying twenty shillings in the pound, unless she maintained her alliance with the proprietor of the pledging institution. Her best gown, if she possess one; her husband's best coat, should he aspire to that luxury; or even her flat irons and wedding-ring, are as regularly taken in charge by the licensed proprietor of the three balls as Monday's sun rises. Taverns and pawn-shops are two master curses, combining to depress the industrial populace of London. The workman's earnings are too often squandered in drink, but no small portion also enters that musty-looking green-baize door, through the dirty oval panes of which the gas feebly glimmers to make the obliging announcement, 'Money Lent.' The pawn-shop thrives in poor neighbourhoods by becoming a regular tax on improvident families; for by this system, more notably than by any other, will short-sighted ignorance allow itself to be shorn. A man or woman who commands the coveted possession of 'best clothes,' will originally purchase them at an exorbitant rate of the tally-man, and subsequently pays a handsome weekly premium to the pawnbroker for the privilege of wearing them on Sundays. The certain tendency of this mode of living is to sink the subjects of it gradually lower in the social scale, and weekly borrowing becomes a necessity, until a still lower depth is reached in the loan-office, where, as we learn from a prospectus-card in the window, loans are advanced from 'five to five hundred pounds.' Such are the meshes within which poor people hopelessly entangle themselves, and from which Christianity and education would ensure them liberty. One woman was found disposed to periodical fits on account of the worry attending her weekly payments. Nevertheless, there exists a wide-spread love of independence among these classes. What must that poor creature's self-respect have been, who, in dread of burial by the parish, showed a missionary the foresight he had exercised by providing '*A last great coat*,' *i.e.*, a coffin!

The condition of the poor of London being what it is, this chapter is written in the hope that persons of abundance may open their hearts, and do something, by strengthening the City Mission and kindred agencies in their work of raising their less-favoured fellows. As before observed, vice and improvidence are not so invariably the cause of social privation as many are apt to imagine. The trials of numberless families are traceable to causes over which they could have exercised no control, and bravely do they bear up against the tide of adversity. The honest and honourable sufferers, however, often belong to a class who have known better days, and who, in breathing the impure atmosphere of confined courts and lanes, experience a sore affliction.

The hearts of the City Mission visitors often bleed at the sight of poverty they could not relieve, even were it their business to minister to temporal wants. When they come in the way of those who resemble a certain clean and thrifty mother, who was found serving out potatoes and salt for her children's dinner, while the father was seeking work, they are tempted to wish, either that they were rich, or that wealth were entrusted to them for distribution.

While mentioning the various characters whom the missionary encounters, actors must not altogether be omitted. Actors are popularly supposed to be merry people, easy living, and lighthearted; and the following story will illustrate the Christian visitor's influence among them. A missionary in Westminster called on an actor and his wife, whose profession had taken them through the provinces. On speaking to them about the realities of a future state, and the necessity of preparation, the husband, who at ordinary times was of a giddy disposition, significantly shook his head, and remarked gravely, 'Ah, *that* frequently bothers me!' 'What bothers you?' was inquired. The man answered by pointing to a bedstead in the room, and adding, 'When I lie there, after working myself tired, I frequently cannot sleep for hours together; it is that long word EVERLASTING!' This interesting playwright was fairly educated, having been intended for the medical art, but on losing his parents, he married an actress and adopted her profession. Forsaking the path of life for which he was partially trained, he never reached any higher grade than that of a clown, and, until the date of meeting with a friend in the missionary, he lived a loose kind of existence. But now 'Everlasting' took deep root; and, the truth reaching their hearts, he and his wife relinquished a calling which conscience forbade their continuing, and engaged in the less lucrative and more humble employment of writing window-tickets. These actors were striking examples of the transforming power of religion. The late clown in his spare hours became a zealous conductor of a Bible-class.

Romance is always more or less attached to the lives of those who from affluence have fallen to a position which associates them with the low and degraded. Suddenly to come upon one whose mien and conversation discover a polite education, or even an aristocratic rearing, and to find him inhabiting a dirty room in the rookery of a squalid locality, is certain to whet curiosity. How far from uncommon such instances are, the annals of the City Mission have proved, and still they rise to the surface. Some years ago, a missionary in the north-east of the town entered the lodging of one who seemed instinctively to shrink from observation. The visitor, however, was gently pressing in attentions, and read from the first Epistle of Timothy. During the reading the gentleman—for such he was—interrupted. 'I was not aware there was such beautiful language in what people call the Bible.' How should he know? He had not opened the sacred volume for thirty years! 'You will come to my little meeting,' remarked the evangelist. 'Sir, I don't like,' he answered; 'my old companions will laugh at me,'—adding, on second thought—'I certainly will pay you a visit.' After blessing his new friend in no feigned manner, he was observed to be in tears. Indeed, all was breaking and giving way beneath him; and, just as he realised that earthly things are founded on sand, he also discovered the unyielding Rock. The new light had come, but with it came also an obstinate struggle with the Old Adam. 'I did not see you at my meeting,' remarked the missionary on a future occasion. 'Well, sir, I *do* hope you will excuse me for not coming in; but I went and listened outside and heard the whole of your exhortation, and was endeavouring all I could to suppress my feelings, and so pop in; but I could not overcome them; and I have been again and again, but I have never summoned up courage to join you.' Who of us may throw a stone at these weak natures? The speaker was of gentle birth and classical education. His inheritance consisted of an ample fortune, and his proper station in life was that of an independent gentleman. From all this he fell, and would have descended lower in the social scale had not the downward course been arrested by the agency of the London City Mission. Christianity came to the man in extremity; and if it did not restore a lost fortune and forfeited social influence, it made him heir to what he now prized even better—the unsearchable riches of Christ.

Many strange stories are brought from the workhouses, workhouses not being neglected by the Missionary Committee. Nevertheless, space will not allow of an extension of this chapter in the direction named. A missionary once testified that some of the happiest moments of his life were spent in Shoreditch workhouse. Entering spiritedly into the work of visitation, what really were toils became pleasures, and the paupers hailed his appearance with joyful expressions. 'Oh, sir, I am glad you have come to read and pray with us: are you quite well, sir?' and, 'I am glad you have come to talk to us about Jesus Christ,' are samples of the greetings met with in the wards apportioned to those who, in countless instances, are real subjects of misfortune.

But of all the adventures of the missionaries among these classes, none should interest us more than those cases wherein they have been made the means of averting crime or disaster, to which the subjects were hastening through the depression of poverty. One example more is given in illustration. A young woman, falling out with her mother and friends, resolves on supporting herself in a separate lodging. This for a season she was enabled to carry out; but times growing hard and work scarce, she was compelled to relinquish her apartment, and one night she was found about the streets, wandering in homeless wretchedness. It being the summer season, she knocks at the door of a sister's house soon after sunrise; but the only hospitality manifested here is the assurance that the intruder must find another home. Meanwhile a horrible resolution is forming in her mind. After the ensuing night she declares that none shall have cause to complain of her troubling them. A missionary hearing of this case, and judging suicide to be contemplated, had lost no time in appearing on the scene; but his most persuasive words could not prevail on the woman of the house to allow a destitute sister one night's lodging! Heart-sick at this heartlessness, he turns to the outcast herself, who through a flood of tears is crying out that she has not a friend left on earth. 'You are mistaken; for I have come to advise you. Come with me to the workhouse.' This proved to be a turning-point in her career, and her subsequent history showed how 'the darkest hour of night may precede the dawn of day.'

The missionary to the seamen in the London Docks relates some interesting experience; and did space allow, some instances might be given to further illustrate this chapter of the subjects of misfortune. With large numbers the visitor is a favourite, but not unfrequently he encounters coarse treatment and ribald abuse. He was busily employed in giving words of parting advice to the passengers of the ill-fated *London*, just before that fine vessel was engulfed in the Bay of Biscay. Though the work is often apparently thankless, the missionary finds many things to encourage perseverance; and one of his curious cases shall be the last example of this section. A lad was discovered in the docks—a young West Indian slave—whose notions about the inferiority of the coloured races strangely evinced how ignorance can darken the judgment even to ruin. The lad's late master was a wealthy man of the world, and, pursuing pleasure and the bent of an evil nature, he ruined his constitution, and early sank into the grave. This man invariably assured his coloured dependants that they resembled dogs, and that in death they would fare no better than cattle. On losing this amiable employer the young slave was robbed of what little capital he possessed; but, taking to a sailor's life, he met the missionary in London. Once during a service at sea he heard what to him was incredible doctrine, viz., that blacks and whites, as sinners in common, were included in one grand provision, though, when questioned as to whether he believed this truth, he said, 'I don't know; I fear not.' In such examples the gospel frequently exercises its most remarkable power, and in true life-progress they overtake many who, from their infant days, have lived among the privileges of a Christian country.

VI.

THE DRUNKARDS.

THE DRUNKARDS.

VAST as are the philanthropic endeavours made for the benefit of London, they dwindle when compared with the immensity of the evils to be conquered. The utmost the power of man can effect is, atom by atom, to reduce the mountain of misery, and persevering, unceasingly to supplement his puny strength by that of a stronger Arm. And, notwithstanding the doubts of friends and the disparagement of the sceptical, reward does come to the Christian worker, for large successes have been gained. 'Nothing succeeds like success,' is an aphorism not less applicable to the toil of the evangelist than to the common affairs of life; although the evangelist, while encouraged by the manifest fruits of his labour, has sometimes been indebted to intended rebuke. 'You *must* make impressions on their minds,' said a Romanist to a missionary, referring to the Irish in London; 'you *must* make impressions by your constantly visiting and talking with them. If I were to try and pull up a stone firmly fixed in the ground, though I could not succeed at once, yet by picking and picking at it every day, it would be loosened, and at last it would come up.' The agents of the London City Mission continue 'picking and picking,' and the sentiment expressed nearly thirty years ago, at a meeting, is still true: It is a matter for surprise, as well as for gratitude, that so devoted a company can be organized as that of the society's visitors—a band apparently fitted by God for a special calling.

All social reformers now regard excessive drinking as a master curse of the age. Ill-kept public-houses breed disorder, and the drinking customs of the present day are the chief stumbling-blocks of the ignorant and the lowly. Drunkenness is the heaviest drag on moral and religious progress. The ravages occasioned by this sin stretch around like a true moral waste, and though sufficiently unsightly to prompt our turning aside, they have become too familiar to shock or repel in any great degree.

It is only now and again that examples of the profligacy and ruin springing from the curse of drink come under the eyes of casual observers, to excite intensest disgust or to move to action according to circumstances. One day, some years ago, on entering a house—in a low district certainly, but close to the best parts of Islington—the missionary found a woman, whom drink, in her thirty-fourth year, had brought to the last struggle, amid associations calculated to leave a horrible impression on the minds of beholders. Kneeling by the poor creature's death-bed, the visitor explains the plan of salvation, and speaks of a Saviour's readiness to save, but according to human judgment, the message comes too late to bless the ignorant soul of that gin-wrecked body. There is a wretched hag inhabiting the room, who calls the sinking drunkard daughter, and the kindest action her maternal solicitude can suggest, consists in pouring gin down the dying wretch's throat, until sense of life or fear of death is drowned, and she is dreadfully unconscious of her shocking condition. At last the woman dies, and the mother, acting as though the maddening draughts she had swallowed were rising into demon-life within, seizes the corpse, drags it from the bed to the door, and back to the bed, like a wild Amazon, till overpowered by a son-in-law she is turned into the street. Then drinking ensues, until the police appear on the scene, burst open the door, and end the uproar. What deadlier enemy, stalking among its homes, can humanity have than a vice leaving in its trail such appalling evils? We may harbour qualms about touching 'vested interests,' and confiscating aught of the gigantic capital embarked in the liquor traffic; but in the meantime low dram-shops are multiplying, and the majority, like fetid fungi, are centres of poison promoting the decay of man's finest instincts.

That is a false delicacy which would hide and hush up things shocking and repelling in themselves, but valuable in the service of warning others. Not only is drunkenness a master curse of our age, it is hard to imagine how any other sin could yield fruit in a catastrophe like the following scene, which occurred in the neighbourhood of Saffron-hill. A man having expended his resources on a tavern carousal, returned home to procure further funds from his wife, and on her refusing to gratify his passion, she was beaten until her screams brought the interference of some neighbours. Cowed and baffled, the husband stood forth, in gin-inspired frenzy, to strike his arm in token of wishing that both hands might drop off, that he might become blind, deaf, and dumb, and finally sink to perdition! On concluding this mad farrago the speaker fell to the earth a corpse!

One of the chiefest calamities which can overtake a family is embodied in a profligate father, but an object yet more repelling is a drunken wife. Of the social suffering and life-long disaster to children springing from gin-loving mothers, and of their own too late repentance, many dismal stories might be told. The following will show how the Christian visitor may become the means of effecting a timely reformation.

In a narrow, busy thoroughfare, bordering on Wood-street, there dwelt a prosperous bill-sticker, who in business employed several assistants. But industry and tact availed nothing; for, though commanding an ample income, his family yielded no satisfaction and the domestic hearth no comfort, the intemperate habits of the wife counterbalancing all social advantages. When the missionary first called on this citizen he was well received, and soon the man recounted with tears the domestic afflictions he was called to bear. More than once after this the visitor witnessed saddening scenes of home desolation, the wife often lying insensible on the bed. 'There she is, as usual,' said the husband on one occasion; 'I really think I shall immediately sell all I have and go abroad. Last Christmas Day I thought I should like to have a few friends, and I did all I could to encourage her to keep sober, so that we might have a comfortable time. I bought a fine goose, and had everything as good as any tradesman need have; and in order that she should not be fatigued I hired a woman to help.

I went out early in the morning to business, and came home at one o'clock—we were to dine at two. As soon as I entered the kitchen, the first thing I saw was the woman that I had hired, dead drunk on the floor in one corner of the room; and, turning myself round, there lay my wife, quite as drunk, in the other corner. The goose was standing before a large fire, positively burned to a cinder; indeed, the whole dinner was entirely ruined. Now, if such things are not enough to drive a man away from home, I don't know what are.'

Such a housewife was indeed an object needing to come under the reforming power of the gospel. The husband was advised not to act rashly, and then an opportunity was sought of advising with the erring woman. Warned of the folly of her conduct, prayed with and faithfully counselled, she was eventually led to confess her errors with penitence and tears; and yielding to the truth, she refused all contact with the ensnarer, which, in her case, had proved a curse. She even went to extremities in expressing her detestation of drink, for she would throw it under the grate or otherwise dispose of it. Striking as was the transformation to common observers, more grateful were the emotions of the husband, when a home of confusion was changed into an earthly paradise, and the wife who had even sought to murder him became a loving life-companion. Soon after this woman died, rejoicing in Christian hope.

You have only to overcome the drinking habits prevailing in London lanes and courts immediately to improve the condition of the miserable people. A man and wife addicted to gin-drinking sometimes spend as much as twenty shillings a week in liquor, or nearly their entire income. A man has been known to drink a pint of gin a day, besides other things; and what will strike some as even more strange, a woman has cut the hair from her head, and with the proceeds of the sale supplied herself with spirits!

Thus the tendency of this sin is to harden and deprave; and shocking are the results of its ascendency in London, where garrets and cellars are constantly supplying involuntary illustrations of the curse of the drink; while the prevailing misery calls on all who partake of the spirit of Christ to do their share in lessening its widespread desolation. This vice, like an unclean spirit, seems able even to produce a terror of what is pure and good. A Southwark missionary, after groping up a dark staircase, entered a garret, the inmates of which, mistaking him for the doctor, at first received him respectfully. The room sheltered three women, two of whom were crouching over the fire; but on a bed lay another woman, and one of those pitiable objects, a dying drunkard. She no sooner recognised the Christian visitor than she called out in piercing shrieks, bordering on an unearthly yell, '*Leave me! LEAVE ME!*' Reading the Bible, speaking of judgment and repentance, filled the poor creature with terror; and as it was impossible to calm her apprehensions, she was left in the hands of Him who will judge faithfully.

In another room the scene is varied. The only furniture is a broken chair, and a board lying across some bricks serving for a table. Here sits an emaciated woman, who, having just buried her still-born babe, wants the necessaries of life. Her husband is a silversmith, earning forty-five shillings a week; but as he spends nearly the whole of that amount on his depraved appetite, home is left destitute. It is a pleasant transition to step from such a scene into an orderly home made attractive by Christian influence, and to hear the honest confession, 'Bless you, sir, I knew nothing of these things until *you* came.' A reformer of drunkards renders a service to the State no less than to the individuals, who oftentimes from bare poverty are restored to comparative affluence. In this way one comfortable home owed its attractiveness to missionary enterprise. The husband was found by the visitor in a state of suffocation, lying on the stairs, while the wife occupied the bed of an adjoining apartment in a similar condition. When these people were reclaimed, the man confessed, 'When I left off drinking I took to thinking.' Many such cases enliven the missionary's otherwise dismal round. Gin and chaos give place to social order and respectability; and the welcome change, in many instances, by the Divine blessing, originates from wisely spoken words, and from tracts specially adapted to the wants of those concerned. The poor rescued people bless their reclaimers with tears rolling down their faces.

But note that coarse-featured, husky-voiced, shabbily-clothed man, who, swallowing gin as if for very life, has his downward path crossed by the missionary of mercy. His passion for the life-destroyer will only be extinguished in the grave! Yet to him the Bible and religion are quite familiar. As a son of worthy parents, his restrospect of life carries him back from scenes of riot and coarse joking, to days when his best friends, on leaving him a fair inheritance, entertained for him no better wishes than that he should honour the good old way. He went forth into the world, and resolving to be rich, the shortest road to wealth was supposed to lie through a public-house. Committed to this scheme, he pushed the trade by drinking, chatting, and making himself agreeable to customers, until daily habits engendered tastes which ended in ruin. As a drunkard he has spent two thousand pounds in gratifying low propensities; and during the continuance of *delirium tremens*, which occurs periodically, he can only be quieted by the presence, at the bed side, of a revolver and a bull-dog, to ward off the attacking demons, which come and go in his diseased imagination!

From these facts we infer that drink is Satan's master temptation. To the poor it is so, certainly. Like a destroying angel, the tempter stalks abroad, and too plainly visible is the trail of his successes. None are too degraded for his prey, any more than any are too respectable to be passed over. No condition of life ensures immunity from peril, and religious professors, in common with the worldly-minded, fall into the fatal snare. Any who think themselves strong may surely doubt their puny strength in resisting an enemy capable of so easily breaking down barriers erected by arms of flesh. Follow the missionary down a certain unhealthy street, and into an unwholesome room. Though it is midday the remnants of the morning meal are still abroad, adding to the reigning domestic confusion. Two women—wife and daughter of a man sitting at work—

are quarrelling, and the only interference of the third party is to swear at them by turns. But quote Scripture to this unwashed profligate, and he replies to you by counter-quotations. Whence comes this anomaly? Once respected and happy, he laboured as a Sunday-school teacher. How has he fallen from that enviable station, and degenerated into the ragged, dirty, and ill-speaking fellow now beheld? He spends seventy-five per cent. of his earnings in drink!

It is painfully interesting to note how assiduously the tempter goes about his business. On all hands, by various means, is the working-man seduced from paths of rectitude; and publicans invent ingenious ways of transferring his earnings into their own pockets. In times not very far distant 'select concerts' were the usual tavern attraction, but these have been supplanted or supplemented by other methods of alluring too willing dupes into convivial halls. The musical entertainments 'on Monday and Saturday evenings,' have been damaged by coming into competition with licensed music-saloons, which, to do publicans justice, rank far lower in respectability than the common rooms of ordinary taverns. To make up something piquant for attracting idlers, and also to allure the busy during their leisure hours, other means are now resorted to; and these will be represented by giants and dwarfs of both sexes, or phenomena selected from the animal world, such as calves having two heads and sheep with seven legs. Is something even yet stronger required? Then rat-pits and rat-hounds are provided; and these, it appears, the English law does not proscribe. Encompassed by these depressing evils, the missionary would be more than mortal did not his courage sometimes quail, and did not lack of faith threaten to leave him weak and desparing. The moral deadening influence of drink is encountered at every turn. To-day he is concerned with one who, falling down intoxicated, is seriously injured, and on-lookers are saying, 'That, surely, will be a warning to him;' but on recovering, the man again, week after week, spends some thirty-six shillings on the base indulgence, and because his wife ventures a reproof he drives her from home, and then complains of her running away. To-morrow it is the instance of a man who threatens to kill her he has undertaken to protect, since she will not supply, from her own earnings, cash for gin, and starve herself and children. Such are the episodes of every-day life in which the missionary is called on to interfere; and from them he would turn fainting and heart-sick were he not enabled to hold on his way in heaven-borrowed strength.

The missionaries accustomed to kneel by the beds of dying drunkards, and who in miserable homes endeavour to reason with infatuated victims, witness nothing more repelling than the insanity of spirit-drinkers—*delirium tremens.* In this disease, a judgment overtaking the inebriate by means of a disordered brain, imagination assumes whatever form is most terrible to particular individuals. A visitor, for instance, once entered a house at the West End of London, where a work of vandalism was in progress. The table was broken into firewood, and other articles awaited similar treatment. A man, whose face expressed the workings of evil passion, squatted on the floor, like a dishevelled savage, sharpening a knife for further depredations, or even for murder. 'Look here!' he bawls out; and, holding up the blade as the visitor enters, '*This* is for my son; he has taken out a summons for me, and if he appears against me *I'll* do for him!' Presently, however, the weapon being thrown with great violence across the room, sticks fast in the opposite wall, and only just misses the target aimed at—the wife's heart. A number of ragged, affrighted children occupy one corner of the apartment, but do not appear particularly surprised at the proceedings. Undismayed, nevertheless, the missionary seats himself by the raving wretch, and teaches him a lesson in Christian manliness. But the drunkard laughs as only such madmen can laugh; it is a sardonic outburst of mock mirth, and the overflowing of misery within. 'It's no use, you know; I've been like this for twenty years. I can drink twenty pints a day. There is no hope for ME!' Christianity may be presented to such persons; but in our most hopeful moods we seem to realise that it must be carried to them in vain. 'Do come and see my old man,' said the woman who escaped the murderous missile, as above described. 'Do come and see my old man; he is so altered: he brings home his money on Saturday nights, and buys lots of things.' The good seed, borne on sure wings in the missionary's words, having taken root, social comfort and happiness are their 'hundred-fold' return. Only Christianity in its ascendency is equal to stamping out the drinking-fever which is placing such formidable obstacles in the way of all progress, whether of body or of soul.

One following another, the victims appear in monotonous succession. A man who has endeavoured to murder wife and child, after destroying his household furniture, is presently matched by another whose capacities extend to the consumption of a gallon of ale and five shillings' worth of spirits of an evening, till imagination taking fire, he sees demons and reptiles crawling and skipping about him in the street.

The tempter enters the rich man's home, where the sorroundings tell of influence and education, and thence will select his prey from among women, who, from examples of tenderness and goodness, are transformed into common dram-drinkers. The wife of a gentleman of position and fortune, succumbing to drinking propensities, sank low and still lower, and ultimately found herself seized by the police and lodged in a station cell. Intensely realising the degradation of this position, the prisoner attempted suicide by severing some veins with steel taken from her stays. Fainting from loss of blood, her intention was discovered and frustrated, and subsequently the attempt was renewed without success. Crossing her path, the missionary read, prayed, and advised with this fallen one; and, struck by his solicitude, the lady forsook sin, and becoming a changed character, a valued companion, and the adornment of home, the worth of Christianity shone in her countenance.

On the evils arising from love of drink, one might dilate until the narrative repelled by its sombre monotony. Instances could be given, showing how women have won the distinction of being living terrors to the neighbourhoods they have troubled by their presence, and of men destroying their property in drunken frenzy. A woman has been known to carry away a chair and pawn it for gin, while her famishing son stood shivering in the street; and a female crossing-sweeper, supposed by the householders of the vicinity to be eking out a modest living by selling water-cresses morning and evening, has consumed a gallon of rum and thirty pints of other stimulants in a single week!

An illustration of the infatuation of some women gin-drinkers came under the notice of a St. Pancras missionary. He visited a cabman confined by illness, who, though only forty-four years of age, had travelled the streets for thirty-two years. While exceedingly ignorant, this man gladly and gratefully received the instruction offered, and in return, related his own life-experience. His wife was so incorrigible a drunkard, that to shield her from mischief he lodged her in the workhouse. When at home, nothing could be preserved from her dishonest hands, as she pawned and sold every available article to procure gin. All the service she, as a mother, ever rendered her family, was to cause the death of one child and beggar all the others. Such being the woman's character, her husband never ventured on purchasing a suit of Sunday clothes. But notwithstanding precautions taken, feminine subtlety outmatched the power of man. On rising of a morning the cabman would discover that his boots had disappeared, or that his scarf was stolen; and if driven to extremity, the same thief would take the key of the door, sell it for a halfpenny, borrow another, and procure a pennyworth of gin. Akin to this case was another of a gentleman to whom the workhouse would likewise have proved a proper asylum. 'I never go home sober at night now,' he confessed to a missionary in the bar of a Bermondsey tavern. On being reproved for the folly of thus opposing the claims of the gospel, and insulting the dictates of common manliness, the gentleman continued: 'Well, sir, I have not been home sober more than six nights since last Christmas.' The season being summer, it did not clearly appear how so daily muddled a brain could keep accounts correctly, till the speaker became more explicit: 'Well, sir, when I go home sober, I make a notch on the bed-post, and I find I have six notches!'

How true is it, and how worthy of being remembered, that a man's life consisteth not in the abundance of the things he possesseth, for the wise stewardship of a moderate competence yields more satisfaction than wasted plenty. From drunkenness springs more misery than human imagination can picture, and so heavy is the curse, that not unfrequently temperate habits have more than compensated for decay of fortune. In Leadenhall Market there lived a butcher who, ruined by his evil propensities, relinquished business, and sank into penury. Encountering the missionary, he was prevailed on to abandon his wretched habits, when the change at home was no less remarkable than sudden. The wife's face assumed a cast of happiness, children were better provided for, home rejoiced in more attractions, and the whole family evinced more contentment now that the husband and father was a sober porter than when he was an inebriate master salesman.

Who can explain such mysterious infatuation? Into what unfathomable evil might not the salesman have sank, had not a friend seized him before he passed that line in the drunkard's career, from the blackest side of which there would seem to be no retreat, but only a hastening onward to despair and death? Should we not be showing mercy in restraining certain persons by a strong arm, and by placing them in reformatory asylums? What else should be done with a man who, on entering his home—the abode of blank poverty and of ragged children—can coolly confess that drink is the spring of the abounding misery; that drink has cost him £275 in fifteen months; that the master-sin has occasioned his failure in business three times; and that were he to remain sober, he could not only provide a comfortable competence, but save enough in summer for the necessities of the year? While with diligence and patience the missionary seeks to bring such into the church, as mere social economists we might confine a few of the maddest examples, and subject them to a restoring discipline.

Would not kindly restraint have been a merciful interference in an instance like the following? A visitor calling on a family well known to him, was appalled to find the wife had just fallen down dead, after taking more spirits than nature could bear, her throat even being injured by the fiery draughts. Husband and five children stood in terrified amazement, glad to welcome the friend who has a cheering word for seasons of darkest affliction. A case worthy of being coupled with this relates to one who, after three years' admonishing, is found dying, with a vacant stare, bereft of reason, and his tongue hanging from his mouth. The evil of drunkenness in this guise partakes of the nature of insanity, and on the production of proper medical certificates, as insane subjects should its victims be treated.

Worldly trouble frequently leads to drinking, which, only aggravating the disease, produces irremediable ruin. Nor can this be wondered at when we take into account what man is without Christianity. Neglect of sanitary laws also encourages intemperate habits; for could the abominable dens abounding in London be substituted by dwellings wherein the observance of morality were possible, a broad and smooth highway would be prepared for better things to follow. But though the field of labour remains crowded with obstacles, and the prospective harvest is often unpromising, the gospel makes progress; and the more appalling the ruin whence they are rescued, the more lovely are the trophies of its power. A missionary in Horsleydown once interfered in a case of extraordinary ruin. He became acquainted with a blind woman whose drunken habits and abandoned ways were so abominable, that even the rough neighbours remonstrated when good things were abused, as they imagined, by being carried into her presence. Now this woman lost her sight during a confinement some years previously, and soon after this calamity her three children died. On a subsequent day, her husband, meeting with an accident, was carried home from his daily work a corpse. An only son now provided for the household, yet strange to say, he was scalded to death. The poor creature's mother still remained, to whom affection now clung closely; but as though a fatality were blighting the family, she too was soon laid in the grave beside the others. Then came the usual temptation to drink, and the afflicted one, listening to the allurement, habituated herself to the poisoned draught. Thus from respectability she progressed in transgression, until she shocked her associates by her bold wickedness. But not heeding the well-meant warning advice to let such a subject alone, the missionary passed on, and delivering to the blind drunkard the gospel message, her character became completely changed, and the woman herself rejoiced in Christian hope.

In these unremitting endeavours, not to say self-denying labours, the city missionary rejoices when he becomes a means of blessing to the perishing masses around—a means of blessing merely—but he must feel peculiarly gratified when converts in turn themselves progress into evangelists. Happily this has not unfrequently happened, though seldom have results proved more encouraging than in the following example.

One night in early winter, when the missionary of a western district was just closing the usual meeting, a woman, weeping and manifesting considerable agitation of mind, desired he would immediately minister religious consolation to her sick husband. Not accustomed to slight such calls, the wish was at once complied with, and the visitor found the patient prostrated by fever, but troubled more in mind than body. Seemingly overwhelmed with misery, the man desires that prayer should be offered, and meanwhile confesses, 'I have been one of the greatest of sinners; I have sinned against light and knowledge.' Ah, as he lay in the narrow room of a London back street, with brow burning and sick at heart, how fast memory became crowded with scenes of a rural home in Scotland! There were the preceptors of his youth, the parents who prayed for him and instructed him in the path of virtue. This man left Scotland to push his fortune at twenty years of age, and at the date of meeting the missionary he had been running a career of vanity for sixteen years; and now, as it seemed, was about to be engulfed in the vortex of ruin in London. With the example of the Prodigal Son in memory, he has yet ran a Prodigal's course; and as a slave of sin and drink, has wasted his life substance. He knew the good way; and now, laid low by fever, it distracts him to remember, that instead of enjoying home comforts with a young wife, he squandered time and money in public-houses; and while conscience prescribed his acting a worthy example before dependants, he preferred rioting with low companions. During those melancholy years, truth learned too well in far-away Scotland to be easily forgotten, rose up at times, like an insulted monitor, to assert its authority. Then, one memorable Sabbath evening, he stepped within the precincts of a chapel at service time, and heard what remained fast in the memory. While the teaching of better days rose up to condemn, remorse haunted him like a spectre refusing to be exorcised. The man grew wretched by day and wakeful by night; and when he became more fevered and restless, occurred a still more trying crisis. During the stillness of night he imagined he saw his aged father, long since dead, come, and in a spirit form rebuke the erring wanderer. 'Oh, my son!' said the apparition, 'must I stand at the right hand, and hear that awful sentence pronounced against you, "Depart from Me ye cursed," and confess that it is just?' Awakened by fright, the man more than ever realised his misery—the misery of one who would have prayed and yet dare not venture. Then came the dawn of brighter days. The missionary's word was blessed until the late drunkard relinquished evil habits, and returned to the good old way learned at the parental hearth. Gradually darkness and horror departed, and for a look of agonizing terror when judgment and repentance were mentioned, he showed a countenance beaming with satisfaction or even with rapture. Physical disease succumbed to the surgeon's art; but how small an affair was convalescence when compared with the spiritual victory won so completely! 'You have led me to the Saviour, and my future life shall thank you,' he cried out to his friend the evangelist. But the triumph did not end here. The convert would express gratitude through the medium of a society, which coming to him in the person of its agent, while he lay in a woful condition, had held out a rescuing hand. He founded a ragged school in St. Giles's, and established a working man's auxiliary in aid of the mission. To crown all, he became the first London City Missionary selected from the ranks of those who ascribe their conversion to the Society's operations.

If 'all's well that ends well,' the above is a good story. Had the man persevered in his infatuation; had he really succeeded in stifling conscience, and in hardening himself against the remembrance of a father's precepts and a mother's first lessons, he might have sank as low as did one who spoke of his children as 'cats and brats,' since they deducted from the means of self-indulgence. Drunkenness can annihilate parental solicitude, and it can also inspire children with contempt or loathing for their parents. 'I say, Jack, what sort of a woman is your mother? Does she get drunk?' asked one street Arab of another. 'No, my mother don't get drunk,' replied the urchin interrogated. 'Mine do,' went on the first speaker, 'and that's how I get plenty of money. I takes it out of her pocket when she's drunk, and she never knows, and I goes to the Vic any night I likes.' There is little doubt that a similar procedure is adopted by numbers of other sons of drunken mothers.

Many curious and instructive facts occur in the experience of missionaries specially appointed to the visitation of public-houses. 'A nice parlour on the right, sir; walk in. What will you take?' is the salutation, or something approaching it, which on his first call greets the visitor; and 'Will you take a "British Workman," sir?' will be about the substance of the reply. Of course the publican will take the paper; for his class are too well disciplined in their school to forego politeness. Possibly he may manifest something more than civility, and exclaim, 'I shall be glad to see you as often as you pass this way. Your object no doubt is good, and must do good.' Then you would see, as the missionary proceeds to the parlour, to place a periodical on the table, one or another look up from paper and glass, meanwhile interposing a comment, 'Well, this *is* a new thing indeed, to see these papers on public-house tables!'

Sometimes the surprise of onlookers at these evangelistic operations are more singularly expressed. 'My stars!' observed one gentleman. 'A public-house is a rum crib for spoutin' in. Forty year I've been in and out of these cribs, and never heard a spouter before. What next, I wonder, after this?' At first persons even favourable to missionary enterprise thought the visitation of public-houses an extreme measure. 'When we first heard of it,' said one London newspaper, 'it struck us forcibly as casting pearls before swine, and as exposing the men who are employed in this particular department to unnecessary insult and to certain failure. But we were soon convinced to the contrary. In these dens of iniquity the agents seek out the very refuse—the dregs of humanity—and with the good old Book in hand, carry to them the news of a divine hope, even for the vilest of mankind. It may seem almost beyond belief, but such is the tact, the courage, and efficiency of the agents employed in this particular work, that when they become known to the habitual frequenters of any house, insult or attempted injury would instantly be hooted down by the company; and, more strange still, the publicans themselves often welcome the society's agents to their doors, and do all that lies in their power to obtain a quiet hearing for them. We have highly commended the benevolence which formed and maintained the "Halls for Working Men," and which invites men to come where no intoxicating drink is provided for their destruction; but we must estimate far beyond this the courage which can attack the wild beast in his own den, and by the mere force of tender persuasion can draw away the drunkard from his haunts, and restore him to his wife and children. He is a bold, good man, who in the excitement of battle, with the eyes of the world upon him, and with the hope of the Victoria Cross before him, rushes into the ranks of the enemy to rescue a comrade from death; but he is a bolder and nobler man who, without excitement, and with no human rewards provided for him, can appear amid the reeking orgies of a low London tap-room, and speak not only of wasted health, scattered wages, and deserted homes; but of souls lost, and to be redeemed by the most costly offering that Bounty could bestow for their salvation.'

Public-houses have long since changed their original use, and if we except clubs, loan-office business, and other small matters, have degenerated in too many instances into mere drink-selling establishments. The landlords contract a sort of congeniality of which they are somewhat proud; and in business transactions they are commonly liberal and straightforward; and except it arise from pure misfortune, few have to complain of loss by publicans. In regard to the difficult work of carrying the gospel into bars and tap-rooms, these men do not as a rule usually offer any obstacles, though strange human phenomena appear in their midst as well as among other classes. Thus, one will insist on the missionary's either drinking like a jolly fellow, or leaving the premises; another, unable to spell out a police report in the paper supplied to customers, yet consoles himself with the aphorism, 'Men know too much already.' Among publicans are found all kinds of tempers: while one makes a show of high principle, his neighbour grasps greedily at any money offered. The more respectable of the fraternity decline serving persons the worse for liquor, and discountenance abandoned women. Not seldom a spirit friendly to the diffusion of Christianity shows itself behind the bar. 'Those are good things you give away,' exclaimed one landlord, referring to the tracts. 'Come here as often as you like.' Some, misapprehending the nature of the mission, will naturally inquire, 'Are you a teetotaller, governor?' But the visitor, being simply a Christian instructor, will not engage in controversy, even though he be an abstainer on principle, further than testifying against the bad effects of spirit-drinking—an opinion not a few publicans themselves subscribe. Working men, who during dinner hours and evening leisure lounge about tavern doors, are commonly shrewd enough to recognise in others any honest solicitude for their welfare, and in their homely way they yield back honour and encouragement. 'Hear, hear;' and 'This man wants to do us good,' are the kind of plaudits frequently awarded.

The itinerant missionary carries a supply of periodicals, *e. g.*, the 'Sunday at Home,' the 'Leisure Hour,' and 'British Workman.' Follow him into a large establishment, the fittings and company of which are too familiar to need description. He knows something of the character of that fashionably attired barmaid, and that apart from present associations she is respectable and well-connected. She receives a paper—a 'Sunday at Home'—with the rather mournful acknowledgment, 'Ah, I wish I could spend *my* Sundays at home, instead of being always here like a slave.' A youth standing by, imagining the conversation is taking a teetotal or Sabbatarian drift, remarks: 'I suppose you would like to shut public-houses on Sundays, the only day we have with our sweet-hearts.' But the objection is shortsighted and selfish. 'Would you like *your* sweetheart to be here the whole of Sunday?' is a question putting the evil in its proper aspect. Thus, while the work of evangelisation proceeds, doubtless a day of triumph is in store for the earnest toilers who carry light into dark places, and the gospel into unlikely homes—into the highways and hedges—thereby winning trophies for Christ where respectability dare not venture.

It certainly requires sharp wits, as well as devotion to the missionary cause, successfully to prosecute the task of visiting public-houses. In general, tavern associations are so directly contrary to the spirit of the Bible, that the work might have been considered Utopian if undertaken by any less potent agency than that of the London City Mission. Enter one other large house, and you will learn something more of the difficulties the missionary has to encounter. It is evening; the space in front of the bar is crowded with idlers, and the landlord being of the civil, though unbelieving class, calls out: 'Come this way and give an account of your Bible. You know that it is only a history, like the history of England or any other, only there is more about battle and crime in it.' 'Hear, hear!' 'Bravo!' and other complimentary cheers respond to this speech, while one, pluming himself on his literary discernment, submits what his class call 'a poser.' 'How about the Canaanites?' 'Yes, yes, landlord, you are right,' says the missionary, untying a striped necktie. 'The Bible is a history, but God's mercy to man is plain throughout. It is like my handkerchief; the ground work is dark, but the line of silk is prominent. It is so with the Bible. God wove it in the loom of time, that the bright line of man's redemption might be prominent and clear.' This is intelligent to the meanest comprehension, and Mr. Landlord offers no objection. Even the intelligent mechanic who ventured 'the poser' is silent; and thus encouraged, the visitor further explains the line from Adam to Christ. 'Thank you, master,' cries one. 'That's plain and reasonable,' says another. 'Come again when you like,' echoes Mr. Landlord. Enter another house, where in the smoking-room a number of men are gathered. One, being deeply engrossed over the Sunday paper, is offered a tract, but he shakes his head disapprovingly—'I have something better than that here.' 'Have you. Your news will get stale; but I have a newspaper—producing a Bible—which never grows old.' The good news, and its connection with Christ, salvation, the turning of sadness into joy, and of bad men into good, is explained. This strikes the listeners as being worthy of heeding, and they instinctively feel that a man would not act and speak thus unless he unselfishly desired their good. 'Thank you, Sir,' they cry, in a tone leading the speaker to hope the lesson is not thrown away. In future years, may be, when earthly stays are failing, some of these stragglers will remember hearing long ago, in a certain tavern, of the good news abounding in God's newspaper.

We still follow the missionary, for though it is Sabbath

evening, the sacred season brings him no rest beyond what an extension of his Master's kingdom includes. Here is another bar, where the costly fittings, rich carving, and glasses, rather ludicrously contrast with a company of weather-beaten cabmen from the stand opposite, and who, to-night, are scarcely so well-behaved as usual. They know the intruder well. 'He is the parson's man, who goes about to make people religious.' The present want of good humour of these honest fellows is perhaps accounted for by its being Sunday night, when other people are comfortable in their parlours and churches, but when they are, no less than on week-days, exposed to the damp and cold. Clustering around their instructor, some jeer at his words, or laugh vociferously at the idea of cabmen being religious and all that sort of thing; and some, observing less decorum, take to swearing. But see, there is a hush now; they are listening to a strange story about the disasters which befel a youngster who presumed to pilot a public vehicle before attaining a competent knowledge of the town. Of course a novice like this was destined to run through a long catalogue of mishaps. Perhaps he would drive a 'fare' to Shoreditch, instead of going, as desired, to the Great Western Railway; and he would doubtless hunt long for the Bank of England in the vicinity of Whitechapel Church. Cabmen quickly appreciate this kind of teaching; and unanimously vote the young fellow a fool or worse for driving wrong when he might have gone right by asking. This is just what is being aimed at; for, taking advantage of the occasion and of the impression made, the speaker cries, 'NOW YOU ARE ALL

DRIVING WRONG! and therefore be civil to a man who knows the road, and would set you right. Here is God's road-book—opening the Bible. Let me tell you how sinners may drive straight to heaven.' As it does not come within the compass of a cabman's intellect to gainsay all this, the majority give attention, and on the missionary's leaving, thank him; and afterwards, among themselves, they will vote him 'a good sort of fellow.'

But the duties of the itinerant evangelist lie in a wide radius. With a ready gentle tongue he must answer chartists and republicans, and quash the arguments of Socialistic Infidels. He must keep an open eye to detect small means of effecting good; and strengthened by exercise, his resources seldom fail. See yonder is the Tempter. A young woman with enticing words is drawing a youthful simpleton into her meshes of evil. A quick eye discovering the opportunity, a hand is presently laid on the man's shoulder, and some words are spoken in his ear—'*One day the judgment throne will be set up, and secret things brought to light!*' The young man leaves the house as if ashamed, but not yet ends the episode; for see, the woman is in tears. A word must be spoken to her also. 'If you really repent of sin, come and see me at my house,' says the same kind voice. That woman has enjoyed the privilege of Christian nurture, and as she stands in front of the bar, where only a short time before she would not have ventured, she appears before you as a widow, who, after striving hard against adversity, succumbed and fell. Now she is prevailed on to relinquish sin, and giving evidence of sincerity in her professions, she is subsequently placed in service. Indeed, the Gospel produces so marked a transformation, that her very countenance is observed to alter. Thus the Mission wins its victories in bars and tavern parlours.

Though they may not presently discover it, people spoken to in public-houses have often proved the lasting nature of the impression produced. Persons who take a fiendish pleasure in making little children drink, are open to rebuke, and it is even possible the words spoken may live in the memories of the children themselves. One barman, who rudely opposed the visitor, immediately after became impressed by what he had heard, and burned several volumes of infidel books. In one house at the West-end, the landlord, though never more than civil, did not hinder the missionary from persevering in speaking with those who congregated about the bar. One night a company were carousing with a man who treated them by means of three pounds, lately saved by total abstinence towards establishing a trade, but a relapse occurring, the treasure was now being quickly dissipated. On another day the landlord appeared extremely affable. 'You cut me up the other day while you were talking to those men,' he said, 'and I wish I were out of the trade.' A little later, workmen were observed transforming the dram-shop into a grocery establishment, and the friend whose endeavour resulted in this almost miracle, was gratified at hearing the grocer confess, '*Now* I feel comfortable.' But, sometimes, though not forgotten, words seem only remembered to the hardening of the heart.' 'Old C—— says, "In the midst of life we are in death,"' cried a woman, mockingly, in a gin-palace of the

Cow-cross district, during the prevalence of cholera. Before leaving her glass, the fatal pains occurred, and in a few hours the mocker was a corpse!

Some other examples of the good effects of the Mission are to be picked up. Here, in one bar, the agent is coarsely assailed by one who, on seeing how little his bravado is appreciated, slinks into the back-ground, listening meanwhile to what is spoken; and, anon, he follows the subject of his late abuse into the street, and confesses, 'I know I am a vagabond, or I should not have treated a gent like you as I did. I don't know how to read or write: if I did, I should not be a vagabond. 'You shall not be a vagabond any longer. I'll teach you.' The man was so overwhelmed by this offer, that he vented his delight by crying out, 'Do you mean it? As soon as I get into work I'll treat you to a day in the country, and pay all expenses.' Taught to read, the late rough continued a rough no longer. In another crowded bar, after an appropriate address to the people, an Irishman pushes his way to the front, exclaiming, 'Sure it's myself that needs such a Saviour.' An endless variety of character makes up the scene. Now a young woman, contemplating suicide, finds the missionary a friend in need, and is enabled, with a little assistance, to re-enter service. Then a landlady, remembering the quietness of better days, rejoices in opportunities of religious instruction; or a landlord, who lately mocked about 'the lies of the Bible,' is found rejoicing in the good hope.

As all acquainted with London are aware, separate orders of mechanics have their houses of call, and these places receive due attention. Then other establishments command the equivocal patronage of certain distinct classes. In one retreat dog-fanciers love to congregate; another is the favoured haunt of racing men; and in this or that low-browed, villanous-looking rendezvous, pugilists and admirers of the 'noble art,' as they call it, sit at the feet of the champion of England. Even dustmen have a chosen place wherein to share honourably among themselves daily gratuities or 'dust-luck.' In the parlours of some high-class taverns youths are also found, who are in course of preparation for divers learned professions; and these inexperienced gentlemen deal in high-flown objections against religion, which are commonly a poor reproduction of ancient infidel arguments. Frequently long conversations ensue, and possibly with good effects, for the visitor will be thanked for his patience and pains.

Some time ago, when the advent of a great comet was talked of, tavern frequenters manifested an interest in the subject; the timid-minded even heeding a report about the possibility of our world being encompassed with destruction by the flaming train. Our missionary entered a bar where the absorbing topic was engrossing the company. 'I'll bet yer sixpence the comet won't come,' cried one gentleman, with an eagerness that discovered his anxiety for a prolonged continuance of the present economy. 'What would become of your bet if it should come, and do as some have prophesied?' inquired the visitor, who secured attention by explaining the theory and nature of the mysterious nocturnal phenomena, and by expressing a conviction that the earth would be preserved until the final Day of Judgment. An interested listener approached the tap-room door to communicate the welcome news—'Here's a chap that knows all about the comet.' The company, immediately bustling from their seats and joining those in the bar, were in turn instructed in the history of comets, and in something better; and when the speaker left, a small crowd followed him to the next house, for the sake of further profiting by his astronomical observations.

If we inquire what are the fruits of public-house visitation in the reclamation of drunkards, the testimony of the missionary tends to show that the inebriate are not easily restored. Their emotions are soon excited, and they are readily moved to tears; but their morning resolutions scarcely last till the evening sun. It is therefore in prevention more than in cure that the work of mercy consists. 'You are right, sir; and God helping me, I will never be a drunkard,' exclaimed a youth, accepting a tract and walking to the street, leaving some liquor, for which he had just paid, untasted on the bar. But if drunkards are hardly won to virtue, their lives are fraught with warning to those who are as yet unensnared, and various tragical occurrences supply material for pointing the moral of the public-house teacher. One missionary had only just stepped aside to avoid a brawling drunkard, when the man stabbed a barman. Then, on a Sabbath evening, in a crowded house, one man hitting another in a freak, and breaking his neck, caused him to fall dead on the floor.

But from what has been said it need not be inferred that the Mission is not largely instrumental in reclaiming slaves of intemperance. Some years ago one of its agents, on leaving the bar of a large house where, as usual, he had discharged his duty, observed a woman hastening up, who, breathless and agitated, cried out, 'Do take me home to my husband, sir!' 'Why do you wish me to do so? cannot you go yourself?' 'I dare not, and serve me right, too,' answered the stranger. Her troubles originated as follows. On the preceding Saturday, this now repenting wife received a good supply of cash, her husband having worked overtime, bringing home forty shillings. She was tempted by certain gossiping, gin-loving neighbours, to go out, when all the party became intoxicated; and now, after being lodged in the police-station cell, and staying out three nights, she had spent all the hard-won earnings of the family. Persons in these straits, regarding the missionary as a peace-maker, do not fail to beg his services. The offender now remained trembling in the street, while the interceder entered the husband's room to talk matters over, and make an amicable arrangement. Though troubled and vexed, the injured man received back his weeping wife, and she promised better things for the future. She signed the total abstinence pledge; then the trio knelt in prayer, and the home once more assumed a happy aspect.

As will be inferred, from some things given above, the Mission in a slight degree encourages pure literature, by gratuitously circulating certain healthy periodicals. It is a matter for regret that the rage for light reading in public rooms has increased in the last few years. In many coffee-houses, where the quarterly reviews were formerly taken, a worse article is now provided. 'The desire for light reading is so much increased, that the reviews are seldom asked for,' was the testimony of one proprietor. 'You would not believe the change that has come over people, and what very different magazines they ask for from what they used to,' was the evidence of another. Only in a small measure is this lapsing into vicious tastes checked by the circulation of periodicals like those the Mission provides. Nevertheless, the foul current is counteracted, and were the hands of the committee in Red-lion-square strengthened by more liberal support, larger results would follow. It is understood that the Life and Death of Lady Jane Grey' is the barmaids' favourite, and it is circulated on account of the Romanising tendencies of many churches of the Establishment. There is one other section of the public-house visitor's wide constituency it would be cruel to ignore. He carries appropriate picture-books for poor little creatures who come into public bars, and standing tip-toe, present a jug for beer or a medicine-bottle for gin.

The above, relating to public-house visitation, will supplement what has been said on the same topic in another chapter; while the following will show how varied in character are the cases coming under the notice of the missionary. It fell to the lot of the agent in Paddington to search for a certain lady in a workhouse, who from a high position in life fell to the depths of poverty. Besides her advantages of birth and education, she possessed 'more than ordinary subtlety of mind.' 'It fell to my lot,' says the agent, 'to track her steps, and at last I discovered her, an object for much deeper commiseration than any one at first was aware. Penury and neglect had been doing their work undetected, but with fearful reality. I was hailed as a deliverer, and though a subordinate instrument, the responsibility seemed to rest with me. By some manœuvring, the bottom of which I have not yet fully gauged, authority was soon given me to provide a home for my new charge. The rail did its work anonymously, and brought parcels of clothes, which were left at my door free of cost or inquiry. A nobleman responded to the echo of an appeal, and readily placed forty pounds annually within the reach of my fingers.' Such strange episodes are stintingly reported, caution being doubly necessary when the characters of persons in high life are affected.

The depths from which the gospel can raise the degraded bespeaks its divine origin. In the last case, where friendly solicitude aided in restoring a fallen creature, the gospel still had its opportunity; but its triumphs are more marked when it goes alone to restore the debased and morally lost to virtue and usefulness. A tailor and his wife, living in Shoreditch, became so completely depressed by the tyranny of drunkenness, that they pawned or sold dress and furniture, even to the scissors required in their labour. Their household furniture consisted of a piece of tarpauling for a bed-covering, and a saucepan, from which they fed like animals. Humanity could scarcely fall lower; but listening to the gospel message, they were raised to decency and comfort.

Thus mournfully can intemperance change prosperity to penury, and convert the happiest home into a social desert. A case illustrative of its blighting action, and of the restoring power of Christianity, occurring in the St. Pancras district, shall be the last example of this chapter. A man and wife were found, whose history to the date of their meeting the missionary constituted a narrative of warning and instruction. In a provincial town they formed a strong mutual attachment, and were married. Commencing business under favourable circumstances, they prospered rapidly, employing a number of hands in a manufacturing business. All progressed comfortably until the husband, captivated by pleasure, spent away from home hours needed in the warehouse, and sought gay company, till the neglected trade dwindled; and unable to meet pecuniary engagements, the trader left the town in debt and disgrace. Once committed to a downward course, descent became easy and more rapid, and complicity in a smuggling venture occasioned his imprisonment. The next step consisted in removing to London, where, with a capital of four shillings and sixpence, she who should have been a comparative lady now made an endeavour to improve the condition of the family by setting up a fish-stall in the street. Still descending, husband and wife took to drinking to drown care, and the disorder and filthiness of their home soon rivalled the misery of an Irish cabin. The children, 'destitute of clothes, shoes, and often food,' associated with thieves and beggars. In this condition they were discovered by the missionary when he first prayed by the dying bed of the father of the family. Bitterly now did the man repent of follies, false steps, and errors, and as it is hoped, in an evangelical sense, also repented of his sins altogether. 'Eliza,' said he, with his last breath, 'as soon as the breath is out of my body, send the children to school, and go to some place of worship. I want you to go to heaven when you die.' Though the condition of these people, during the life of the father, continued wretched in the extreme, their resources, had they been soberly and properly husbanded, were abundant. Intemperate habits sapped all social enjoyment and outward prosperity. They possessed forty barrows, each yielding its weekly rental of a shilling; and in addition, they carried on a considerable trade. But the death of the man and the first visitation of the missionary marked a new era in the family's chequered history. At the mission-station prayer-meeting the woman found lasting peace. Then followed trial. Persons only accustomed to respectable associations cannot realise how hard it is for these converts to stand forward, and, by embracing Christianity, dare to be singular among their companions. When the denizen of a low street turns 'religious,' the change supplies occasion for many a joke and sneer. 'Oh, she has sixpence a day for going to meeting,' said one. 'I get more than that; I wish you would come with me,' the woman answered. 'Ah, you have turned good to get another husband,' cried another, derisively. 'I have got another by going,' still replied the woman.' 'Glad of it; hope he is a good one.' 'He is.' 'Ah! who is he.' ''Tis God I have for my husband.' Not apprehending the sacred meaning of this confession, the unlettered listeners judge it to partake of profanity, and greet the words with a depreciative laugh, while one remarks, 'Don't be a fool. Why, to hear you talk since you have taken to religion, people would think you were mad.' Nevertheless, these coarse people are shrewd observers. They can quickly detect and respect honesty, and if converts only evince that they are in earnest, the good opinion of the neighbours, however depraved, is sure to follow.

VII.

LONDON THIEVES.

LONDON THIEVES.

In a population so vast as that of London, the thieves alone form a large class; and their hand being against every man, they imagine every man's hand is against them. Earnest philanthropic efforts have long been made on behalf of thieves; and we learn from those labouring among them, that their natures are not so obdurate as at first sight would appear. Vicious and profligate as they frequently are, the good seed sown among them falls into ground yielding sufficient return to encourage the persevering evangelist. Christian visitors move among them, not only without molestation, but commanding a share of respect. The missionary who presses the gospel upon their acceptance, and warns them of the ruin entailed by unholy courses, is frequently rewarded by ingathering precious sheaves for the harvest of the Lord.

Robbers have been abhorred in all ages, and wondrous devices were formerly resorted to for their extermination. In London, during the last century, when the criminal code was heartlessly severe, thieves abounded in strange numbers, undismayed by the weekly slaughterings at Tyburn. Our forefathers, in aiming too high, often missed their mark; for among the characters who flourished in the olden time, perhaps none were more abominable than the professional thief-taker, who was the creature and product of the system of police which was then popular. The government, in its well-nigh frenzied endeavours to repress crime, supported a fraternity of real criminals. Large rewards were offered for offenders caught and convicted, so that robber-hunting became a lucrative profession. Thieves were entrapped, consequent on secret information gathered by traitor accomplices, the unsuspecting were allured into crime, and innocent persons were boldly accused, and even hanged, merely for the sake of a miserable premium!

To give the reader an insight into thief-life a hundred and fifty years ago—the golden era of the art—much might be told about thief-takers themselves, as they lived undisturbed in dark lanes and alleys before modern encroachments and improvements swept away their own or their victims' lairs. Successfully to complete their vile designs, thief-catchers worked in gangs of five or six persons, and were characters more degraded than the wretches they betrayed. Men, whose own sons were pickpockets, easily obtained the necessary information, and when needing funds, they commonly selected one or more persons, and hanged them for the sake of the reward; and, when a supply of real offenders failed, the informers did not scruple to seize innocent citizens—often mere youths—and to forswear them into an untimely grave.

As the reward of capture was so many pounds per head, two victims served the purpose better than one. The gangs selected these victims from the markets and the streets. The agent appointed to allure the unhappy simpletons would assume the guise of a thief, and then patronisingly ask them to join in looking out for profitable opportunities. The person to be robbed being another accomplice, would be sure to turn up at the right moment. Then, as by appointment, another of the party purchased the stolen goods, while a fourth seized the robbers, taking care that his comrade escaped. A fifth confederate played the part of false witness at the trial. All this actually occurred in 1755, as appears from the copious details of contemporary journals. A man, supplied with money for treating, walked into the Fleet Market, and pouncing on two likely lads, gave them drink, and said he knew of something worth securing a few miles down the country. As planned, the man to be plundered appeared on the road near Guildford, and was robbed of his pack. Another confederate bought the stolen cloth, and another seized the robbers in a public-house. These dupes would have been hanged, but for the timely intervention of one who suspected foul play. Being mostly successful, it was thus that the thief-taker brought his prey to the gallows, and many unsuspecting youths were thus murdered to replenish a rascal's stores.

Thieves in London are of several varieties, and the higher grades refuse to associate with the lower. Boys, whose unskilful hands deal only in pocket-handkerchiefs, have nothing in common with those who contemn even second-rate transactions, and only engage in jewel or plate robberies; or, if they pick a pocket, only care for valuable pocket-books or well-filled purses. Expert swell-mobsmen are aristrocrats in thieves' society, and, leaving their art out of the question, live much after the manner of affluent gentlemen. The swell-mobsman does not always correspond with popular notions about his character and appearance. He is not a coarse nor even a villanous-looking gent, wearing fine linen, and displaying flash jewellery to disguise coarse features, while affecting gentle extraction. On the contrary, he is not distinguishable from a gentleman by ordinary eyes. He probably lives stylishly in good lodgings, his landlord, meanwhile, being unconscious of the character of his tenant. The chief aim of his life is to live unrecognised by the police; but in this he is not always successful, the practised eyes of detective officers peering through the most artful disguise, as will appear from the following story, told in the *Quarterly Review* for 1856.

'One of the detective police, present at the laying of the foundation-stone of the Duke of Wellington's College, thus explained to us the capture of a gentlemanly-looking person who was present on that occasion. "If you ask me to give my reason why I thought this person a thief the moment I saw him, I could not tell you; I did not even know myself. There was something about him, as about all swell-mobsmen, that immediately attracted my attention, and led me to bend my eye upon him. He did not appear to notice my watching him, but passed on into the thick of the crowd, and then he turned and looke dtowards the spot in which I was. This was enough for me, although I had never seen him before, and he had not, to my knowledge, attempted any pocket. I immediately made my way towards him, and tapping him on the shoulder, asked him abruptly, 'What do *you* want here?' Without any hesitation he said, in an undertone, 'I should not have come if I had known I should meet any of you.'"'

From the same authority we learn that ordinary thieves do not employ nippers in taking jewellery from the person; so that if watch-handles turned on a swivel, the chances of losing them would be much diminished. Even pickpockets are divided into classes. The common street thieves are men and women, who, accompanied with boys, push against passengers, and relieve them of whatever is available. There are also people who 'work' omnibuses, and the men, if their features favour the deception, will even affect the clerical character. Next come many grades of house-breakers, of varying proficiency in the art; for house-robberies of magnitude are planned beforehand, the servants occasionally being conscious, and, as often, unconscious abettors of the robbers. One of the conspirators will become violently attached to a pretty housemaid, and the girl's innocent tongue is sure to reveal whatever information is wanting. Otherwise the cracksman will call for his sweetheart, when she is alone on Sunday evening keeping house; and while the pair enjoy a quiet stroll, expatiating on the happy future, the family plate is appropriated by some active members of the gang. The house-breaker is often a man of ill-directed genius; and singular among 'put up,' or deeply-planned robberies, was one narrated in the number of the *Quarterly Review* already quoted.

'A gang of first-rate cracksmen having heard that a banker in a country town was in the habit of keeping large sums of money in the strong box of the banking house in which he himself dwelt, determined to carry it off. For this purpose, the most acute and respectable looking middle-aged man of the gang was despatched to the town to reconnoitre the premises and get an insight into the character of the victim. The banker, he ascertained, belonged to the sect of Primitive Methodists, and held what is termed love-feasts. The cracksman accordingly got himself up as a preacher, studied the peculiar method of holding forth in favour with the sect, wore a white neckerchief, assumed the nasal whine, and laid in a powerful stock of scriptural phrases. Thus armed, he took occasion to hold forth, and that so "movingly," that the rumour of his "discourses" soon came to the ears of the banker, and he was admitted as a guest. His foot once inside the doors, he rapidly "improved the occasion," and in his own peculiar manner. The intimacy grew, and he was speedily on such terms of intimacy with every one in the house, that he came and went without notice. He acquainted himself with the position of the strong box, and took impressions in wax of the wards of the locks. These he sent up to his pals in town, and in due course was supplied with false keys. With these he opened the strong box, made exact notes of the value of and nature of its contents, and replaced everything as he found it. A plan of the street, the house, and of the particular chamber in which the treasure was kept, was then prepared and forwarded to the confederates in London. He persuaded his kind friend, the banker, to hold a love-feast on the evening fixed for the final stroke. A few minutes before the time appointed for the robbery he proposed that the whole assembly should join with him in raising their voices to the glory of the Lord. The cracksman laboured long and hard to keep up the hymn, and noise enough was made to cover the designs of less adroit confederates than his own. The pseudo-preacher, to disarm suspicion, remained with his friend for a fortnight after the theft; and on his departure, all the women of the persuasion wept that so good a man should go away from among them.'

But in now turning to my more immediate subject—the work of the City Mission among the thieves of London—it may be observed that the missionary, as well as the detective officer, can readily detect what is not palpable to common eyes. Since the whole life of thieves is a lie, it is not easy to bring them to a due appreciation of truth; not even when they profess to be seeking escape from dishonest courses. In the case of young thieves the tendency to prevaricate is so strong that their native dialect is a language of lies!

We are informed by a missionary of experience in this department that by certain signs thieves may be as readily detected as a soldier may be known by his drill, and, in proof, the following has occurred.

A lad, thirteen years of age, once expressed a desire to be put in a way of reformation. From the appearance and behaviour of the applicant, he was supposed to be a thief of some experience, both in the art of pilfering and in the imprisonment which is its result. 'Have you ever been in prison, my lad?' asked the missionary. 'Never in my life, sir,' he immediately replied. 'Hold out your arm,' continued the examiner, certain that what he heard was deliberate falsehood. A trained pick-pocket, when suddenly called on to stretch forth his hand, will, if he suspect no motive, act quite differently from an untrained person. For instance, our missionary says: 'If a boy is a pickpocket, on being told to put out his hand he does so quickly, with his fingers straight, and generally with his first two fingers together; but if he is not a pickpocket, he raises his hand clumsily, close to his body, with his fingers bent.' Thus the manner of this boy discovered him to be a practical thief. 'Turn round, my lad,' being the next order, the young sinner's movements betrayed his acquaintance with prison drill. This last piece of evidence was perfectly conclusive. 'You *have* been in prison,' cried the missionary. 'Upon my honour, I have never seen the inside of a prison in my life,' still protested the boy. How can truth be drawn from such strongholds of deceit? This is a question which few can properly answer. A lady happened to be present, having called to inquire about the work among thieves. 'You may be wrong, sir,' said this visitor, pitying the boy. 'I dare venture anything I am correct,' answered the other. 'Still I shall have pleasure in leaving him in your hands, and perhaps he will confess to you the truth.' The lady tried every winning feminine art to elicit the truth, and still came protestations of never having entered a prison. But the evangelist knew of a potent plan as yet untried. 'My boy,' he said, 'I have children of my own; kneel down, I will pray for you.' The three went down on their knees, and a prayer followed, faithful and earnest. The boy was conquered. On rising he was observed to be in tears, as he cried out, 'Sir, I'll tell you the truth; I've been in twice, and I am a pickpocket.' The young culprit was subsequently reformed, and he entered on a respectable course of life.

Though, on the whole, it is difficult and discouraging to evangelise among London thieves, the last day will show that many of this miserable class have been rescued through the agency of the London City Mission. Most of them respect their instructors, and in times of sickness and trial value Christian counsel.

In a poor room in a bad part of Westminster, a young thief lay dying of consumption. 'Well, my friend,' said the missionary visitor, 'you appear to be drawing near the end of life; what provision have you made for another state?' 'Don't mention death to me,' he cried, 'I cannot bear the thought of it. What a madman I have been to spend such a life!' 'Do you know, my poor man, how a sinner can find peace with God?' 'I don't know, sir; but will you tell me?' By this time the man wept copiously and seemed a likely subject for the working of divine grace. He had not been born to this degradation, but had lapsed into it. In youth he assisted his father in a profitable bakery business, to which he himself ultimately succeeded; and he might have risen into comparative affluence had he not forsaken paths of rectitude to become a mournful example of the ruin of body and soul which results from keeping evil company. In the first place he cultivated the acquaintance of questionable characters, and associating with these of an evening in tavern parlours, and neglecting business for pleasure, his downward descent was rapid, for at length the worst of characters congregated in his house, and the man became completely entangled in their meshes. After sinking thus far, complete ruin quickly followed; for he who had been trained for a respectable station became the paramour of an expert thief, a woman famous for her agility in appropriating publicans' pewter for conversion into base coin. Such had been the career, the last stage of which the victim had arrived at, when, weak and faint, the Christian visitor first discovered him. But the man at least discovered one happy sign, he realised his degradation and baseness. While reviewing the past he felt as though his reason would fail him; to look into the future was intolerable. The missionary spoke to him of the thief on the cross, and day by day read and prayed until the welcome dawning of heavenly light. The patient lay several months, and at last, instead of showing terror at the approach of death, he cried out in joy whenever visited, and while speaking of his possession of a peace inexpressible, he also declared his astonishment at the forbearance of God. When called on for the last time, when weakness scarce allowed of his speaking above a whisper, he could yet say, with beaming countenance, 'None but Christ! God bless you, sir!'

Of the blasting effects of evil company on the life and prospects of the young and inexperienced, the annals of the Mission supply many deplorable instances. Moreover, the broad stream of impure literature, together with plays of an immoral tendency like 'Jack Sheppard,' and many others, act like a deadly blight, of which human eyes cannot trace the extent. Loudly do such cases as the following call for the counteracting efforts of the philanthropist and the Christian teacher.

A missionary of Broad-street district entered a house in one of the courts, where a woman appeared to be in extreme grief and agitation. What could be the cause of her anguish and sorrow? Not long before she and her husband were householders in fair circumstances, having reared six children respectably. Becoming reduced, they were in their old age compelled to resort to the commonest employment, but this trouble was now overshadowed by a greater. Thrown among low associates, one of their sons made a friend of another lad of loose morals and dishonest habits, and making the most of his ascendency, this young thief enticed his companion into theatres and other questionable places, a mother's solicitations to the contrary being vainly uttered. One day, while in the country between London and Maidstone, and while professing to be seeking work, the friends met, and coming to a certain residence, and wanting water, the worst of the two proposed they should scale the wall. The people of the house were away; but the tempter, who in the meantime entered the premises, presently appeared at the window, whence he threw a bundle to his comrade below. At this moment, three men passing by, seized the tempted youth, while the real thief escaped. Being sent for trial, this wretched son of now wretched parents was awarded fifteen years' penal servitude, and the missionary happened to call in upon the family immediately after news of this punishment arrived. It was a doleful scene; for after a terrible ordeal of anxiety, and parting with their scanty possessions to pay counsel's fees, bitter ruin had come. The son, who had been a large contributor to his parents' support, was lost to them for ever! Having hoped against hope, the poor old couple now seemed partially bereft of reason. Their son had been enticed away by the syren voice of evil, and wrecked upon the rocks of evil company!

The above is a sad history, and it will not be recited in vain, if any, tempted to turn aside into crooked ways, are timely warned to avoid what is invariably the path to destruction. Even those who are brought up respectably, are no longer safe from the danger of lapsing into dishonest habits if principle be once surrendered. But, leaving this story and its moral lessons, let us see what can be done by the bedside of the repentant professional thief.

One day a missionary was told that a man who lay dying in a certain attic needed Christian counsel. Going immediately as directed, one not more than forty years of age was found in a dirty room, on a miserable bed, and in a deep consumption. 'You have sent for me,' said the visitor, approaching the bed. 'Yes, sir,' replied the patient, 'I have much to do, and little time to do it in. I am about to hop the twig.' 'Spare your jokes,' interrupted the man of God, 'they are out of place now. You are a dying man, if that is what you mean, and it is a serious thing to die.' 'Why, sir,' the thief went on, in more serious tones, 'I want things made a little straight. I don't want to die like a dog. Can you sit on that stool? Don't sit on the bed.' Opening a small casement to improve the atmosphere, the missionary sat down and listened to the man's recital of his life-history; for confessing his crimes seemed to afford the man a kind of satisfaction. And what a catalogue of crimes was that, though not worse than thousands of others which remain untold! Robberies were recounted, a number of women with whom the speaker had lived in adultery were named, while drunken freaks and scenes of lustful riot were spoken of with graphic garrulousness. In the meantime there was heard a knock at the door, and two accomplices entered. 'Halloa, Tom, what are you at now?' cried one intruder. 'Never say die, man.' The poor consumptive, by way of reply, pointed to the missionary—'This gentleman has been kind enough to come and make things square, so mizzle.' On hearing this, the men with due reverence at once removed their hats, offered ana pology, and even expressed penitence for their roughness; though on being invited to kneel in prayer they objected, one declaring he would never mock God with 'a solemn sound upon a thoughtless tongue.' The thieves retired, and reflecting on the confession just made, the patient exclaimed, 'Thank God, that is done!' The agent of the Mission might have been seen tenderly ministering to this prostrate robber; now offering refreshment, then speaking of prayer, of repentance, and of Christ's atonement. So horrible did the review of his life appear, that the man supposed hell to be an accusing conscience. 'If I can judge from your manner, that were enough if it lasted for eternity,' said his friend. 'Sir,' returned the poor creature, with as much earnestness as his little remaining strength would allow, 'you are a stranger to me; but if anybody was to offer me a hundred pounds that you should pass such a night as I did last night, I would not take it.' Long and fervent prayer was offered for this outcast; for the evangelist lingers by the bedside of such with longing solicitude, in the true spirit of his Master. But alas, what can he do other than was done in the present instance—commend the dying sinner to Him 'who forgave Manasseh, Saul of Tarsus, Mary Magdalene, and the thief upon the cross.'

Soon after the death of this man, one of his 'pals' was met in Drury-lane. 'Where did you learn about "mocking God with a solemn sound upon a thoughtless tongue,"' was inquired? The suddenness of the appeal quite unnerved the man, and tears rolled down his cheeks as he answered: 'I learned *that*, sir, in a Sunday-school, when I was nine years of age; and all the bad company I have kept, and all the sins I have committed, have not made me forget that hymn nor those times. Sometimes I think of these things in the night, and they won't let me sleep!' A direct and valuable testimony this of the beneficial influence of Sunday-schools.

But notwithstanding a few redeeming traits of character to encourage mission work among them, the thieves of London are exceedingly sin-hardened; and did we regard them as thieves merely, and not as sinners possessing immortal souls, they would deserve no sympathy. People who do as many of them do, combine the beggar and the thief in one person, are surely of the lowest types of humanity; yet when rescued and brought into the gospel-fold, the gratitude of such is in proportion to former degradation. Repeatedly have testimonials been presented by converts, and extraordinary instances have also occurred of the restitution of stolen property taken by inadvertence from Christian instructors. A hat and a sovereign were taken from a table while their owner, a missionary, went upstairs to conduct a meeting; but a day or two after, while the same visitor was from home, a strange man, whose name was not discovered, brought a parcel and a note, and handing them in at the street-door, disappeared in the darkness. 'I hope you'll forgive me for stealing your sovereign and hat; I came into your parlour and took them off the table. I can't keep the hat any longer, and when I get the money you shall have it. When I entered the house I did not know *you* lived there, or I would not have robbed our missionary. I was coming out of the house, when I thought I heard your voice upstairs saying, "The door is open," and I cut off. And since, I have watched you home, and seen you in your room many times. I have not worn your hat, nor has any one. You preached from, "Will a man rob God?" I have had the words in my ears ever since, "And you have robbed our missionary." I should like to come to your house, but I feel ashamed, though I know you would not hurt me.'

The above is, doubtless, one of those phases of 'honour among thieves,' of which we have been accustomed to hear from childhood. It is not, however, a solitary example.

A missionary of Westminster, who held special meetings for thieves, had a friend who desired to witness the proceedings, but was desired to stay away on account of the uneasiness his presence might occasion. The gentleman came, nevertheless, and while satisfying his curiosity lost a handkerchief. When this petty theft was complained of before the company it awakened great indignation; and the 'captain' of the gang questioned the men and ordered the restoration of the article. The handkerchief soon appeared, but the purloiner was impeached: and though in repentant mood he strove to regain favour, he was excluded the meeting, even the advocacy of the missionary himself not sufficing to redeem a character thus wantonly sacrificed. He had forfeited 'honour,' and it was unbecoming 'gentlemen' to associate with so loose and unprincipled a fellow.

The lowest class of professional thieves have ever shown a tendency to congregate in slums, apparently supposing that the further they remove from orderly people the greater their immunity from danger. In old London several districts were wholly appropriated by the lawless. While still sufficiently infested by the worst of characters, strongholds of crime, as such, could not exist under present-day police regulations. Besides this, many notorious haunts have been totally or partially cleared for modern improvements.

A vile district formerly covered the ground north of the Holborn Viaduct—a neighbourhood which of old could boast its possession of the celebrated 'Thieves' houses.' The curious tenements going by this name were situate in Old Chick-lane, having been removed in 1844, in clearing the ground for the extension of Farringdon-street.

On coming into possession of the authorities, the houses Nos. 2 and 3, West-street, were opened for public inspection, and were visited by thousands of people, from members of the Royal Family downwards. The premises, planned and built as a thieves' rendezvous by one MacWelland—a man high in rank among the gipsies—were known in the past by the name of the 'Red Lion' Tavern, and as such, the place achieved notoriety as a home for law-breakers in general. Many celebrated highwaymen of the eighteenth century caroused in this hostelry, and in its great room planned their depredations. Here, among others, Dick Turpin, Jonathan Wild, and Jack Sheppard, when in town found shelter and protection. In those days, when English law was severe to a fault, it was not worth while turning robber without possessing a genius for the business, nor without a ready tact for taking advantage of any means invented by the ingenuity of others for eluding the public prosecutor. When the 'Red Lion' Tavern rose to the zenith of its fame, it was in many respects an institution replete with appliances at once interesting and curious, if viewed apart from the knavish service in which they were used. In the last century, when highwaymen flourished on the road, the host of the 'Red Lion' kept a stud of skilfully trained horses, able to gallop to York at a minute's notice, in true Turpin style, with any of his customers, who through ill luck needed so speedy a transit. Besides its internal conveniences, the site of the premises was artfully chosen. The Fleet-ditch poured its muddy current beneath; and when anything needed suddenly to be put out of sight, this was a ready channel to the Thames. Within were also 'dark closets, trap-doors, sliding panels, and means of escape,' making the premises 'among the most secure erections for robbery and murder.' In its last days, No. 3 was transformed into a shop; but few adventurers, previously acquainted with its villanous contrivances, would unnecessarily have risked themselves within its precincts. Here was a trap-door down which stolen goods could be instantly plunged and hidden beyond fear of detection; and a few feet distant, another aperture enabled a pursued thief to escape into a cellar, and thence across the Fleet into a neighbouring alley, pulling up the bridge as he stepped on the opposite shore of the ditch. The lower part of the premises was not less singular, as showing the inventive powers of the gipsy architect. The sombre and dirty basement was bounded by the sewer, and had been the last hiding-place of many a murderer or desperate ruffian, whom justice pursued too hotly to allow of his enjoying a less secluded lodging. In one corner was a cell, which none but the initiated would have suspected to be there, so artfully was it screened, the food of the fugitive immured within its recesses having been passed through a hole made by removing a brick. Here also, in less perilous times, the inmates worked an illicit still. This place continued a thieves' retreat until the time of its removal, and as such was entered at least one hundred aud fifty times by the missionary of the district. The evangelist fearlessly entered the houses at all times, and has been known to proclaim the gospel while unconsciously standing on trap-doors, whence he could have been instantly precipitated into the gulf beneath! 'The most extraordinary and ingenious part of the premises,' wrote this visitor at the time, 'I consider to be the means of escape. If a prisoner once got within the walls, it was almost an impossibility for his pursuers to take him, in consequence of the various outlets and communications. There was scarcely a chance for the most active officer to take a thief who was but a few yards in advance of him. He had four ways of escape. The staircase was very peculiar, scarcely to be described; for though the pursuer and pursued might only be a few yards distant, the one would escape to the roof of the house, while the other would be descending steps, and in a moment or two would find himself in the room he had just left, by another door. This was managed by a pivoted panel being turned between the two. A large room on the first floor back is said to be the place where the abandoned inmates held their nightly orgies, and planned their future robberies. From the upper room there were means of escape by an aperture being made in the wall leading to the house No. 2, containing no less than twenty-four rooms, with four distinct staircases. Here also, level with the floor, was a shoot or spout (which remained covered except when required), about two feet in breadth, and three feet in length, by which goods could be conveyed to the cellar in an instant. Thus, even the diary of a city missionary may supply us with facts curiously valuable and illustrative of life in the eighteenth century.

The experience of the Mission has shown that there are numbers of thieves in London who only want an opportunity, and they would gladly turn to honourable courses. One declared he would live on bread and water if he were able to obtain it honestly, and when taken to a reformatory he proved his sincerity. Many reformed thieves, assisted to emigrate to America, have led useful lives; but without such an agency as the City Mission they could not have amended. Indeed, those who earnestly desire to reform find in this agency a last resource.

A poor lad called on a Westminster missionary, and in craving assistance, explained that he had already used all available means to help himself. He had sought out members of his own family—mother, sister, and brother—but they refused him countenance, and would not even see him. 'I have been three days without food, rather than steal,' he said; 'I have been thrice taken off the street insensible, and placed in the hospital through want. I cannot describe what my sufferings have been. I wish to be honest. Do something, for my soul's sake.' This boy, after passing a season in a reformatory, prospered in America; and when writing home described himself as 'one saved from ruin.'

The following example of grateful reformation also comes from Westminster, a locality notorious for the shelter it has afforded to professional thieves.

In a low lodging-house a lad was met with who began thieving at nine years of age, and thus early he also tasted prison discipline. The father being a disreputable character, sons and daughters were trained in crime or shame. This boy's earliest recollections were of ill usage; for unless he procured money or money's worth, he was refused even the shelter of his miserable home, and turned into the street. On this account he forsook the parental roof and slept in the lodging-house, where he was first spoken to by the missionary and taken into a reformatory. News of his son's amendment reached the worthless father, who called on the missionary and said he wished to take his son away to work; but well knowing the bad character of his parent, the lad refused to see him till otherwise advised, and then what he uttered might have been the complaint of hundreds ot other Westminster youths. 'You know that I have been obliged to steal for my living for months, and during that time you had never looked after me; but now that you have heard I have got into this institution to try and do better, you want me out again. When I was at work you took my wages on Saturday night, went to a public-house and sat down, and did not leave until you had spent all; and then during the week I might get lodgings how I could. No! I am admitted here. I want some education, and if the missionary will allow me to remain I will not leave. You want me to go back to my crimes and get transported. I will remain.' On hearing this speech the man stormed and swore, but to no purpose. The boy, after landing in America, found himself in a brighter world, and soon obtained a desirable situation. His letters sent home abounded with expressions of gratitude; for words, he said, could not express the affection felt for the London City Mission, and he prayed daily for the agent who had been instrumental in reclaiming him from the dominion of sin. Were Christians more active, such triumphs might oftener be achieved; for the society whose agents thus bear the burden and heat of the day merits the support of the universal Church.

There are numbers of public-houses specially used by thieves, where they meet as in a common home. A separate room is occupied, where, undisturbed, they hold what are called 'secret jaws,' or private meetings. Sometimes they assemble in small companies at houses comparatively respectable; but, in such cases, Mr. Landlord is carefully kept in ignorance of his customers' profession. A public-house missionary has taken part in a thieves 'jaw,' and one such adventure will be worth recording.

Early one evening, while passing along the street, he met a youthful thief, and entering into conversation, learned that several fellows were going 'to have a little jaw together' at a house specified. Such an opportunity of carrying the gospel to lost characters was by no means novel—for this kind of work had frequently been done before—but the present promised to be a more than ordinarily choice occasion. Something stirring or exciting was in the wind, and was about to be discussed, so that perhaps more eagerly than usual the evangelist walked straight to the place of meeting, an apartment in a low beer-shop. Entering the bar, now nearly deserted, he passed through a forbidding-looking passage, leading to the tap-room; but the landlord, fearful of evil consequences, and perhaps ill-pleased at the bold intrusion, called out peremptorily, 'Don't go there!' Though well comprehended, this warning was not heeded, and with an object to attain, the intruder proceeded immediately to place himself in the midst of a company of ordinary and extraordinary thieves, or as they would have called themselves, sneaks and magsmen. It appeared that some special grievance brought them together, it being just about the time when public indignation prevailed on account of the atrocities connected with garotte robberies, and because of the increase of garotting in general. On that same day a severe article graced the *Times*, approving a more than usually heavy sentence passed on certain of the thieves' fraternity. When the missionary entered, suddenly and unbidden, a start of surprise or apprehension was observable, and some to whom he was unknown desired he would retreat, in rather disrespectful tones, while others, seeing no fear, gave a friendly nod of recognition. It was a critical conjuncture, needing much discretion. 'Pretty fellows, indeed, to hold a secret meeting,' cried the missionary. 'I could not come down the Marylebone-road without hearing about you.' There was a brief silence. Who could have turned traitor? How could their movements be thus blazed abroad? But none spake until the speaker again continued: 'Well, you know I am safe; and I have come to do you a good turn—the best that one man can do another.' Prejudice was now overcome, and the conversation proceeded, the grievance of the hour being freely discussed, while on the beer-stained table lay the current number of the *Times*, containing the obnoxious article. Was not England deeply disgraced by judges, who, in the name of justice, were obviously oppressing unfortunates, and treating men as though they were savages?

Of course, in company like this, the wisest policy is to avoid giving opinions; and, if possible, it is well ingeniously to direct the conversation into another channel. The missionary, therefore, told his auditors of a certain French gaol, where there lived a smith, whose daily business consisted in riveting fetters on the limbs of prisoners. They were surely unfortunate creatures who entered that prison, for once there, there was no escaping the shackles.

But there were others, such as those before him, who wore fetters of their *own* forging, and were so lending themselves to the service of sin, that misery would follow. 'Seven hundred years before Jesus Christ was born,' continued the speaker, 'a prophet wrote of Him as the great fetter-breaker, that He should proclaim liberty to the captives, and the opening of the prison to them that are bound.' These things, and the exhortation to repent and believe, were listened to in silent attention, till the conversation touched on the hard experience of thieves who abandon evil courses and strive to live respectably. In showing his appreciation of the work of the missionary, one present named a late comrade who became a real convert under his friend's instrumentality; and this afforded an opportunity to the visitor of recounting the events of 'Rattling Bill's' conversion and of his triumphant death. After thus spending an hour in a meeting arranged to abuse the authorities, and to devise means of protection in lawlessness, some of the men followed the missionary to the street for further conversation, and three afterwards called at his house for Christian advice. Thus the gospel may profitably be taken into the lowest dens. The darker their surroundings the greater the need of reformation.

But adventures in public-houses among dishonest characters are not always propitious; for though most publicans receive the missionary with courtesy, some will treat him very roughly. One agent, on being appointed to tavern visiting in an east-end district, like his compeers under similar circumstances, trembled at undertaking the task. When he commenced the round he was well received in a number of places, and probably began to regard former fears as phantoms, until walking into a certain bar, Mr. Landlord, on accepting a copy of the *Sunday at Home*, dipped it in beer and threw it in his face. This was soon compensated for, however. Two or three hours afterwards there came encouragement. The city missionary, more than any other toiler, should accustom himself to forget what is unpleasant, and gratefully to welcome what is genial. But even public-houses are not always forbidding, for some landlords close on the Sabbath, and will allow nothing improper to run riot on their premises, their procedure arising from Christian feeling. What is perhaps a little more common is to find the Christian wife of an unbelieving husband gratefully welcoming the missionary's message, and sending his tracts to relatives abroad. But what has this to do with thieves? Nothing more than this: places good, bad, and indifferent, are frequented by thieves; and there the missionary must follow them.

Speaking of tracts, how varied are the adventures of those little messengers among loose characters in public-houses. Once, in a crowded bar, an old man who refused one, directly after, as if repenting, held out his hand, and then converted the paper into a pipe-light. 'That's not the best use to make of a nice little tract,' quietly said the missionary. 'Now I want no talk, so just be off,' said the man in reply. But the on-lookers were not satisfied. 'What behaviour,' one called out. 'Is it not time you were beginning to think of your soul?' The offender knew he was wrong, but rather excited sympathy by confessing, 'I am downright hungry, and I know none of you fellows will give me a penny.' 'How do you know that?' replied the missionary. 'There's a penny; go and buy a loaf, and may the Lord bless you.'

But the agency of the London City Mission extends much farther than merely seeking the dishonest and the depraved in their homes and chosen haunts: it follows sinners even to the bar of justice, to the ante-rooms of police-courts. Alas, those who invade these dismal precincts for Christian purposes, have many stories to relate of the ruin following on the wake of transgression.

In the ante-rooms of a court like that at Bow-street, the missionary finds a miserable company congregated, each awaiting his turn to appear before the magistrate. The scenes in such a place are heart-rending to a Christian mind. From one direction come noisy and profane words, and from another, what, under the circumstances, are dismal jokes. All here do not belong to the degraded class. Had one looked round the ante-room at Bow-street, on a certain morning some time ago, he would have seen in one corner a crouching figure, with shame and remorse written on her countenance. He could have told by a glance that her present trouble was a first acquaintance with the magistrate, for the clouded brow reflected honest shame. One thoughtless act of indiscretion brought her there. Going out with some companions, she drank too freely, to find herself when sober in charge of the police. Now, in answer to what is said to her, she promises to reform her ways, to relinquish drink, and lead a new life. Beside this unfortunate culprit is another offender of a far prouder spirit. She reads the Bible, and knows quite as much about it as the parson can tell her. Even a cautious body may be overcome; but once bitten twice shy; that demon drunkenness caught her in his meshes, but not again will she be a ninny and listen to the tempter. Among such companions the professional thief will also hear a word of exhortation. There, too, stand the trained beggar, the begging-letter writer, and the would-be suicide, all awaiting punishment, or at least rebuke, at the hands of the representatives of law and order. Besides these, behold that pseudo-gentleman, who, with folded arms, consequentially strides up and down the inner court, conversing with a comrade in misfortune. His features express rather forcibly that only by inadvertence did *he* get into a place like this. Those abominable policemen interfered as he, merely for diversion's sake, reeled brawling homeward at three in the morning, and thinking to do both the neighbourhood and him a kindness, they lodged him in a cell of the court, and by their pains aroused his indignation. It is a morally dark and unattractive place; 'for here,' says the visitor, are met 'the married and the single; the fallen, and the female of generally pretty good repute; the servant and the mechanic; persons occupying respectable positions, and others in the lowest scale of society; the shrewd sceptic, and the dull thick-headed animal kind of being; the bigoted Romanist and the reckless Protestant; the swearer, the thief, the murderer, the embryo gambler, who spends his Sabbath in "pitch and toss," instead of going to school, or to public worship; the mother with the innocent babe in her arms, and the woman who has lost all sense of shame. Here they come, week after week, in ceaseless succession, to pay the penalty of their folly or their crimes, and to each a word in season has to be spoken.'

The constituency of the police-court is largely composed of women. There is seen the unyielding countenance of the crone hardened in sin, and there also appears the wretched unfortunate, summoned by some shameless profligate for a petty robbery. These are commonly willing listeners to a friend, who having attended the death-beds of many such, can point to their untimely graves. Then, yonder, is an old one-armed man, with a gaudily-coloured picture of the battle in which, while fighting for his country, he became maimed for life; but as begging is illegal, he has presently to answer for the offence. All classes of offenders crowd the police-courts. Side by side stand the fallen woman and the 'respectable' wife, who, scared and trembling, can scarce tell how the fit of intoxication originated which brought her to this disagreeable place. Many other sin-deluded creatures are here visible; for the syren they have followed leads to destruction! On one seat is a specimen of the saddest spectacles which even police-courts can present—a young man with a countenance expressive of anxious pain, who, just after starting in trade, has too soon arrived at ruin. He might have prospered, but he walked with the foolish; and to support expensive gaieties forged a draft, which brought him within the grasp of the law, and now he awaits committal for trial. Not far away is another forger, whose appearance bespeaks the man of education and of social position. 'Ah,' he says, 'I know all about it.' Yes, he knew better; but mere knowledge could not shield him from 'drink and bad company.'

The above is a slight picture of what may be daily witnessed in a London police-court. One prisoner will turn an indifferent ear to what is spoken, because lost to a sense of shame; another in a freak of drunkenness has lost character—his all. Yet the whole assembly will, if pressed to do so, confess to the missionary, 'If we were to take *your* advice we should not come here.'

Step from the police-court into a district like St. Giles's, and you are on the criminals' acre. The judge punishes while the vicinity of his court is a school of iniquity. The embryo housebreaker practises his art within bow-shot of the hall of justice, and young pickpockets are converted into expert hands on the same training ground. These have to find shelter in districts where the inhabitants are huddled together without regard to decency; and, therefore, we may remember that sanitary reformers are the proper pioneers of city missionaries. Crime must be rampant where life's highest enjoyment is gin-drinking, and its sweetest music tavern brawling. Were it not for our itinerant missionaries, who would direct these sin-blinded people to present peace and an eternal refuge?

It is surely a work partaking of the spirit of Christ to seek the criminal in his haunt, and to transform contaminators of others into exemplary citizens. Such is the work of the City Mission; but so widespread is its influence for good among thieves, that a difficulty of selection naturally arises.

A critical time with a thief, and especially with a young member of the fraternity, on being discharged from prison, is the first few days of liberty. Without friends, or prospect of honest employment, he is sure to find sympathy among old companions, who clustering around, will reintroduce him to their abandoned ways. One youth of this class had the fortune to meet with a missionary before he could be again inveigled by vicious comrades. His position was as low and deplorable as any to which human beings can descend. Being without money, and with a wardrobe only extending to a scanty suit, he in the course of conversation expressed a longing to escape from the thraldom of sin which had sunk him into degradation; yet he saw no alternative but that of returning to thieving until offered refuge in a reformatory. Here he staid about half a year, and only left it through a singular adventure. His family were comparatively well-to-do, but had lost sight of him about four years previously, and inquiries and searches in various directions had been alike in vain. One day, when out walking, the lad met his sister, and she manifested no less surprise than emotion at the sudden appearance of the prodigal. One strange part of the story was that, when this sinner, after voluntarily forsaking the parental roof, would have returned, he could not recover the address. Thus he had been 'lost;' but now 'the gladdened father received him as one risen from the dead.' Leaving the reformatory, the late convict laboured for the support of his parents; and all hearts concerned overflowed with gratitude for the blessing conferred upon them by the Mission. When such are led back to honesty, they regard themselves as counterparts of the Prodigal Son; and happy indeed are the results springing from their reclamation. Instead of contaminating others, a youth becomes an example of industry and rectitude; instead of preying on others, he assists those who require assistance. Multiform are the benign fruits of Christianity.

The evangelist among the thieves is frequently cheered by hearing of good springing from tract distribution; for thousands of tracts are speaking in places where the voice cannot follow; and when one dropped by the wayside brings forth a holy harvest, there is reason to believe others also bear fruits unseen. The following has been often told, but the facts are sufficiently striking to bear repeating.

A missionary once observed a man standing in the street in that hulking manner which betrays the idler who cares not for honest labour. 'Have you no work, my friend?' he asked. 'I am out of work,' replied the man. This answer appeared to be an evasion of the truth, and while expressing a belief that he was living disreputably, the evangelist solemnly asked whether such a course was a happy one. The man confessed he was not easy, but would gladly become respectable. 'To tell the truth, I am not happy,' he went on, drawing from his pocket a dirty little pamphlet. 'That makes me unhappy.' The cause of disquietude was a tract given by an unknown itinerant some time before, and the word had made a sure lodgment. This man, being originally a thief, had become so familiar to the police that he dared not practise in the profession; all he now did was to sneak out at night and train boys for pickpockets. No less than five hundred youths, he considered, had passed through his curriculum! 'But I can never keep the young 'uns long,' he said, 'for as soon as I have made them clever at the business, if they are not taken by the police, they leave me and start for themselves; so that I am obliged to look out for new hands.'

This character, who must have cost the public annually the entire cost of twenty missionaries, was taken into a reformatory, where the care bestowed on him excited his gratitude, and he soon gave evidence of having experienced a change of life. So much for the influence of one tract!

The action ot the missionaries among thieves is the divinest form of charity, and is often a lasting blessing. Some young persons at the crisis of taking the first step in a downward course are stopped; others who have just committed their first indiscretion are helped to regain a respectable standing.

An affecting incident under the last head was once witnessed at the Central Criminal Court, where a poor girl was going through her trial for stealing. Knowing it to be a first theft and a yielding to sudden temptation, the missionary stood by the prisoner at the police-court examination, where she begged him to write to her father and crave his forgiveness. Exposed in open court upon a disgraceful charge, the culprit indeed seemed to be friendless and despised; but one friend would not forsake her in the ordeal of facing judge and jury. The missionary went to the prosecutor, and persuaded him not to press the case too hard; and when the question was asked, 'Does any one appear on behalf of the prisoner?' the same advocate stepped forward and said, 'I do.' This action produced surprise in court, if not something better; for the judge passed an encomium on a philanthropic society whose agents showed this sleepless assiduity.

Professional beggars are thieves also. What shall be done with our swarms of mendicants whose numbers are annually augmenting?—is a question which social reformers would be thankful to have satisfactorily answered. It is time the public relinquished indiscriminate almsgiving; for nothing is more certain than that the majority—and all but a very small minority—of persons practising street begging are impostors. A charitably-disposed gentleman one morning offered a comfortable meal to an apparently famishing wretch who craved money for a breakfast. The conditions were easy and reasonable. A heap of manure being in process of removal from the road to the garden, the supplicant was required to take a few loads to their destination, and earn relief like an independent man. Not liking directly to refuse, the fellow seized a load, but presently retaliated for the insult offered by overturning the barrow and its contents, prior to running away!

Then there was another mendicant, who, affecting lameness, was wheeled about by two companions, pretending to be in a very pitiable condition, and the scheme was doubtless profitable in proportion to the misery affected. One day, while out on a pleasant ramble, the party were crossing a field, where they were unluckily espied by a vindictive bull. The animal made straight for the travellers, irrespective of maimed or whole, and notwithstanding the agility of the beggar's attendants, which enabled them to run and scale the nearest fence almost in a twinkling, the 'lame' man himself was even still readier for the crisis. Springing to his feet, he distanced his companions, and was first out of the meadow!

These shameless impostors crowd the rookeries of London and other large towns, emerging thence into country lanes and villages to drain those sources of charity which should flow for worthier objects. The more clearly to show what kind of thing is sanctioned by indiscriminate almsgiving, a passage from the life-experience of an inmate of Sherborne workhouse may be given.

When young, George Atkins Brine attended the charity school of Sherborne, and at the guardians' expense was apprenticed to a butcher; but early discovering that restlessness or repugnance to regular labour characteristic of vagrants in general, he relinquished industrial pursuits and adopted a roving life. Dorchester gaol he called his town-house, and so well were the prisoners treated, that George would occasionally break a window, or maim a street lamp to secure the hospitality of the prison. He always retained a partiality for his native air, and the master of Sherborne poorhouse stood high in his favour. The freedom of a vagabond life soon came to be highly relished; for he attended fairs and races, and as much as possible associated with the higher classes on the ground. What is surprising in the instance of such a character is the fact of his being endowed with good mental gifts, and a tolerably liberal education. He made a leading figure in a Blue Book on vagrancy, presented to Parliament in 1848. Even now, though in his sixty-third year, he is rather unsettled; for the late master of Sherborne Union having found another sphere, George, at the date of writing the subjoined letter, was anticipating one more ramble. The document was prepared at the request of the Secretary of the Charity Organisation Society :—

July 3, 1871.

HONOURED SIR,—Apologising for not having replied to your courteous note earlier, I beg to answer some of Mr. R. T.'s inquiries respecting me. In the first place, Mr. R. T. desires to know what induced me to adopt such a mode of livelihood ; 2ndly, how I have supported myself in my wanderings ; 3rdly, the casual wards I have visited, and my opinion of them ; and 4thly, the gaols in which I have been incarcerated, with the cause of these incarcerations. Now in reply to the first question, I left Sherborne to seek employment at my trade (that of a butcher), and not succeeding for a time, I soon discovered that more money could be got without work than with it. What knowledge I lacked was soon instilled into my mind by professional vagrants.

2ndly. How I have supported myself during my wanderings. Now, I mean to make a clean breast of it ; I will candidly declare that I have stuck at nothing. I have worked (but very little) at my trade ; I have been a cattle drover ; I have been salesman with three different cheap-Jacks ; I have been a pot hawker ; I have been a vendor of pens, paper, razors (Peter Pindar's), spectacles, laces, &c. ; I have been a distributor of religious tracts ; I have been in the employ (for two years together) of manslaughtering quack doctors—four different ones (I am more ashamed of this than of any other of my follies, for the majority of them are not robbers only, but homicides). I have sold cards at all the principal races in England. I also attended for many years all the principal prize-fights. I have been a 'shallow cove' (*i.e.*, a member of the land navy) ; also a 'highflyer' (*i.e.*, a begging-letter impostor) ; a 'lurker,' one who is forty different trades, and master of none. My favourite 'lurk' was butcher, tallow chandler, or currier ; and to crown all, I have been a preacher ! This game pays well in remote village streets on Sunday evenings, provided you are well stocked with tracts ; but I was not fit for it ; my risibility is too easily tickled ; and once when I was invited to 'hold forth' in a small chapel, I was in no little danger of grinning in the pulpit at my own roguery. This was at Rothbury, Northumberland. I must also tell you, in short, I have been a rogue, impostor, and vagabond of each and every denomination. I say this because it is true, and because I am now heartily ashamed of it.

3rdly. Mr. R. T. wants to know my opinion of the casual wards I have visited. Now I have visited but very few—I think I could swear that I was never in twenty different ones during the twenty-two years

I was rambling—but I am fully convinced that they all tend to foster vagrancy. Even such places as Oxford, Cambridge, Bath, Rochester, Norwich, and Hastings, do more harm than good; for out of every ten tramps there are nine impostors, or professional tramps. You may think this is saying too much, but I am sure it is the truth. If there was no relief to be had, there would be no vagrants. The difficulty lies in distinguishing between the honest working man and the rogue. Now, the distributors of Watts's Charity in Rochester seem to pride themselves upon their own sagacity on this point. I have been a recipient of Watts's no less than eight times, so I leave you to guess whether they relieved a deserving customer in me, or otherwise. In Norwich, at St. Andrew's-hall, it is the same. I once gave my ticket, which I had obtained there, to a poor blacksmith who had been refused one. The reason he had been refused was because he was not so consummate a liar as I was. This is truth. If he had been a trading liar he would have gotten his bread, cheese, beer, and bed, valued at eightpence.

Again, Mr. R. T. and his colleagues will never deal effectually with vagrancy unless they begin at the right end. Let them, or the Legislature, suppress two-thirds of the common 'padding kens,' or low lodging-houses. These are the great receptacles of vice in its most repulsive aspect. It is there the supply of vagrants is manufactured, ay, in the very womb; it is there they dispose of their ill-gotten gains, for great numbers of them are regular 'fencing cribs;' and great numbers of them will not lodge a working man at all, if they know it, lest he should divulge their secrets. And all lodging-houses ought to be under stricter police surveillance. Again, sir, you know, or ought to know, that the greater the villain the more plausible is his tale, and the more assured, invincible impudence he possesses, the likelier is he to attain his ends, at least with people who are little acquainted with these mysteries, for rogues don't care to deal with rogues—in truth they will never trust each other; and I assure you, sir, the gullibility of the British public is so great, and their hearts so finely susceptible to what they believe to be a tale of genuine distress, that their generous benevolence is unbounded. They don't like to be imposed upon; but, as I said before, the rogue, liar, and impostor, practised as he is, soon convinces them that he, at least, does not belong to the cadging fraternity.

And now, fourthly, how many gaols? This is a poser. Well, here goes. I have been in gaol more than one hundred different times! There are but two counties in England that I have escaped 'limbo.' I have also been in several in Scotland and Wales. In the great majority of cases drunkenness has been the cause. I have never been convicted of felony or larceny, but I have for obtaining money under false pretences, and several times for hawking without a licence, many times for smashing windows, and other offences, for the whole of which I richly deserve hanging. To this, I presume, sir, you will say Amen.—I am, honoured sir, your unworthy servant, G. A. B.

Though the above extraordinary document speaks for itself, the following comments of the *Daily News* are worthy of quotation :—

The obvious moral to be deduced from this narrative is, that no piecemeal legislation will ever extirpate vagrancy. The conditions under which relief is given in casual wards must be rendered more stringent. Vagrants are for the most part, if not criminals, at least on the verge of crime—deserters from the army, runaway apprentices, and idle vagabonds, who prefer any form of life, no matter how debasing, to any form of work. On the lowest possible calculation more than forty per cent. of our vagrants actually belong to the criminal classes ; fifty-eight per cent. at least are only waiting for some opportunity to commit crime without detection ; and only two per cent. can be fairly estimated as being really poor, honest men in search of employment. That there are occasional *bonâ fide* wayfarers, we do not deny ; but they are so rare that, as a general rule, it is safer for the lymphatico-benevolent almsgiver to hold his hand instead of putting it into his pocket. If, however, the benevolent man be at the same time active and anxious to assist deserving cases of distress, let him send or take his *protégé* to the nearest workhouse, and obtain food and lodging for him, whilst he sets on foot inquiries regarding him. But let him above all things take care that any poor man or woman in whom he may be interested is not lodged in the casual ward. Next to the common lodging-houses, the casual wards attached to workhouses are the most fruitful forcing-houses of our criminally-inclined population. In them begging is taught as a profession, and many a man or woman who has without evil intention entered one of these hot-beds of vice and sloth has left it hopelessly demoralised.

But to turn from professional beggars and trained thieves, this chapter may be closed with a brief reference to another branch of Christian labour among the criminal classes.

Statistics reveal the disagreeable if not startling fact

of there being some four thousand discharged or ticket-of-leave female convicts abroad, most of whom reside in London. Of late years, since the authorities have discountenanced the execution of women, a murderess occasionally appears among the number—being at large, with a ticket-of-leave, after serving about twelve years of the awarded punishment. The valuable society which seeks to benefit and morally to reclaim this vicious multitude by inculcating Christian principles is called the Discharged Female Prisoners' Aid, the chief establishment of which has been described by a morning journal:—

Near to the Nine Elms Station, and adjoining a bridge over the South Western Railway, is a brick house, standing within an enclosure, which has evidently seen better days. On one of the gateposts are inscribed the words, 'Registry for Servants.' Over what had been the entrance to the kitchen are painted these letters—'D. F. P. A.' The interior of the house is rather dreary and uninviting. There is no trace of luxury in the appointments. On the left-hand of the entrance-hall is an uncarpeted room, in which several wooden chairs are placed in rows, giving to it the look of a school-house in a poor neighbourhood. Here instruction, chiefly of an elementary-religious kind, is imparted to adult women, by ladies who eschew preaching or lecturing, and confine themselves to imparting religious truths to those of their sex who are not only degraded in character and appearance, but are morally no better than heathens. On the right is the office. This is the apartment of Miss Lloyd, the zealous and indefatigable Lady Superintendent. It contains two small writing tables, a few wooden chairs, and cupboards filled with printed forms, tracts, tickets-of-leave, and prison photographs of female convicts, these photographs being affixed to documents like passports, and containing particulars of the names, ages, personal traits of the faces represented on the margins. Appropriate texts of Scripture, written in large letters on strips of paper, are pasted on the walls of these two rooms. In the office is a placard with the heading, 'Nine Elms Laundry,' and underneath it are the following rules:—'The inmates of this house are women who have undergone penal servitude, and on discharge from convict prisons are received here to earn a character. Inmates must do all the work required of them in order to earn their food. No intoxicating drink allowed. Inmates can have no money in their possession. Purchases can be made to the extent of each woman's allowance, at the discretion of the Superintendent. Inmates are only to go out and come in by leave of the Superintendent. Any women coming in intoxicated, or refusing to obey the rules, will be summarily dismissed.'

At the back of this house, in what had formerly been a good-sized garden, are long iron sheds, in which clothes are disinfected, washed, mangled, and ironed. In the space left vacant the wet clothes are dried when the weather is fine; when rain falls they are dried in artificially heated chambers. The clothes of families suffering from infectious disease are washed in a shed set apart for the purpose. The washerwomen are female convicts who have been discharged from prison. Some of the women reside in the Home, but the majority of the workers come at eight o'clock in the morning and go away at six in the evening, bringing their dinners with them. Tea is provided in addition to their wages. These women earn, on an average, 1s. 6d. a day. A lodging can be obtained for them at a place in connection with the Home, at the cost of fourpence. Thus they are able, if they please, to maintain themselves, with the prospect of improving their condition should they conduct themselves well and give promise of continued amendment. The work performed is of a twofold character. On the one hand, regular and not unhealthy employment is provided for the women who, on leaving prison, cannot easily find any means for gaining an honest livelihood. On the other, the difficulty which the poor experience in getting washing done at home is overcome. It is not enough to provide public wash-houses for the poorer classes, inasmuch as the majority cannot always leave their homes in order to do the washing at the public establishment. When forced to do it in their own small rooms, they have many obvious difficulties to contend against. A working man, living in a narrow street, pithily stated the case when he said that he 'dreaded a clean shirt, because he had to go into bed to give it to his wife to wash, and she was generally knocked up by the exertion; while he never escaped a severe cold, for it had to be hung over his head to dry.' Visitors to the poorest neighbourhoods know that it is not uncommon for women to be seen sitting up in their sick beds ironing clothes, and that such a spectacle as a room twelve or fourteen feet square, occupied night and day by seven or eight persons, hung round with wet clothes, is no unusual one. When disease attacks the stronger members of a poor family, and wholly incapacitates them for labouring with their hands, the suffering is intensified. The ravages of infectious diseases are increased in virulence and duration by the impossibility of the infected clothing being properly purified and washed on the spot. For the small sum of sixpence the dozen articles, the soiled clothes of the poor are here disinfected, if necessary, are washed, mangled, ironed, and made ready for being worn again. In other districts the same work is being performed through means of the same agency. It is highly appreciated by the poor. They readily purchase washing tickets, and thankfully accept them as gifts.

These women, who are the chosen constituents of a band of devoted ladies, present a type of the human genus which is quite repulsive. Specially designed by her Creator to be winning and attractive, woman, when she sinks into degradation, becomes the most repugnant object in creation. Too often unacquainted even with the rudiments of knowledge, and reared from infancy in criminal courses, the subjects of the society retain only dim notions of right and wrong, and frequently no conception at all of Christianity. It is difficult for ordinary persons to realise into what a low condition the soul may lapse when deprived from childhood upward of all knowledge but the learning of wrong-doing. On their first hearing it read, the Bible will be listened to as a book of stories to interest, instead of being reverenced as a rule of life, and childish or heathenish comments will be made. The young hands are often found peculiarly obdurate and insensible to good impressions; and well may they be so when 'planning and performing a robbery are as exciting and agreeable to these women as a pic-nic party or a ball is to fashionable young ladies.' It were well could Christian agencies become more aggressive, instead of being cramped in their operations for want of funds. The benevolent ladies who undertake to reclaim, or rather, perhaps, to civilise these outcasts, no less than the missionaries who go wider afield, deserve the countenance and gratitude of all who desire to see the safeguards of society preserved and strengthened.

VII.

PATIENT ENDURING UNDER DIFFICULTIES.

PATIENT ENDURING UNDER DIFFICULTIES.

In this chapter it is intended to reflect in a small space something about that honourable living so often exemplified in the byways of London—the heroism which preserves honesty and self-respect untarnished amid daily contact with extreme poverty. The battle with privation is a more serious warfare than sentimentalism pictures, and they who, bearing its burdens, remain still unconquered, deserve to have honour mingled with our commiseration; and, in yielding honour to whom honour is due, we shall not overlook Patient Endurers.

Some extraordinary examples of this heroism are discovered by the missionaries. Some years ago, two or three gentlemen visited Field-lane for the purpose of making observations such as could be turned to practical account in Christian work. Though vice and degradation reigned unchecked, even that forbidding desert preserved an oasis encouragingly refreshing. In the garret of one house lived a shoemaker between eighty and ninety years of age, happy in the exercise of Christian faith, and still able to pursue a calling by which about a shilling a-day could be earned. Having arrived in London when four years of age, he remembered Whitefield, and could describe the scene presented during the great preacher's open-air ministrations, as viewed from a seat on the back of an adult spectactor, somewhat after the manner of Samuel Johnson's listening to Sacheveral's diatribes in Lichfield Cathedral, while perched on his father's shoulder. Though eagerly anticipating a day when he should be translated to a fairer inheritance, the aged shoemaker greatly appreciated the prolonged health and strength which enabled him to provide necessaries without burdening the parish.

Venerating the memory of Whitefield, he remained a member of the Tabernacle in Moorfields, where he first derived religious benefit. Had he no private resources? Nothing. Is he not too feeble to walk even so far as to the house of God? 'I still go as often as I can,' he answers. He shrank from the idea of accepting charity, and preserved high standard notions of independence. He subscribed the customary pew-rent regularly, and would have been rendered unhappy by an inability to add a silver coin to the communion collection; and on the establishing of a ragged-school in the district he subscribed half-a-crown to the general fund. Surprised at such sacrifices, the visitors ventured some further questions, and discovered that the happy old fellow, thinking it was his duty to set an example of Christian charity, put away a penny a-day for these subscriptions. Anything nobler than this in self-denial, as found in the arena of London poverty and suffering, it would be difficult to produce, and not easy to imagine. Only a divinely-appointed gospel could command such disciples. A heavenly philosophy alone can account for the wide difference between this aged but self-helping mechanic and the subjects of wickedness whose homes surrounded his own.

Though strikingly noble when found in so humble a person, this God-fearing self-reliance is equally attractive in youth, and is especially commendable when found in young women.

Near Saffron Hill there once lived an old couple, inhabiting a back room, and possessing a daughter who supported herself and parents by boot-binding. To the girl the Christian visitor proved a welcome friend, for he taught her to read, besides imparting the truth of Christianity. The present article, therefore, may well plead the cause of those who find the present a difficult and bitter world. Numbers are hidden away in the rookeries of London who are more than poor simply. Their temporal circumstances are so extremely depressed that they only leave their miserable haunt when favoured by darkness; and among such are women whose ceaseless toil does not provide a tolerable lodging, nor enough for the coarsest food properly to prolong existence.

Nevertheless, the procedure has proved useful and profitable which discourages missionaries observing the rule of dispensing temporal relief. Confining itself exclusively to spiritual affairs, there is no misapprehension on the part of the people as to the nature of the Mission; and if the missionary be valued at all, he is valued for his work's sake. That he is prized and respected is seen in the fact of his sometimes becoming the recognised peacemaker of a district; for it is no unusual thing for these evangelists to relieve the burden of police magistrates by kindly interfering in family quarrels which would otherwise entail fines and imprisonment; and their awards have an advantage over those of legal courts,—they are mostly in unison with the sentiments of all concerned. Knowing them so well, the missionary makes full allowance for his poor constituents, who are encompassed with the many trials attending grinding poverty. 'We have one friend we can look to; we must consult the missionary,' one in perplexity will say; while another told a missionary himself: 'I don't know whatever we should do, either for this world or the next, were it not for you.'

But while the visitor may not lapse into a mere alms-distributor, lest a high office should be affected by meaner things, he does, in urgent cases, necessarily supply food and stimulants; for were they not reached by some such helping hand, numbers would succumb to starvation in their hard lot of patient endurance. Take the following as an illustration. The household called on reside in Spitalfields, and, as a man of feeling, the visitor is deeply sensitive of their uncomplaining suffering; and more so, because of the family's anxiety to profit by the gospel message. Once, on hearing that the father continued unemployed, the missionary called specially to inquire of their welfare and of the extent of their necessities. The home scene was indeed deplorable, but was one of a class to which the itinerant London philanthropist becomes too soon familiarised. Pinching, painful poverty was in full possession. The weather being bitterly cold, the mother was confined to her bed through starvation; she, in common with others of the family, having eaten nothing for two days, and the last meal had consisted of potatoes.

Yet this could not be accounted for in any extraordinary manner. All sprang from what, for want of a better name, we call misfortune. No special failing could be detected, such as sloth, waste, or drunkenness. Regarded from a human standpoint, the condition of the family was one of utter misery, but the wisdom they have learned is reflected in the anxiety manifested at the little prayer-meeting for their souls' salvation. Then their experience also illustrates how the Mission in its operations can interpose to relieve privation. A gentleman, hearing of the case, supplied sufficient capital for purchasing a loom; and this, added to the wife's industry in preparing articles for Rag-fair, brought a return of comparative plenty. No charity is more judicious than that which enables the poor to help themselves; and only they who will make an exertion, need or deserve our sympathy. The truly deserving commonly refuse to show themselves begging in the streets, or at gentlemen's doors, with well-learned piteous tales and haggard faces. Properly to know want and misery you must seek them out in people's own homes; for the suffering of noble natures is too shrinking to intrude itself on the notice of the fortunate and the happy.

Another instance of the benefit springing from the Mission to one who patiently endured the evils of poverty may also be narrated. In Spitalfields lived a man and woman of the lowest class. The man sunk in degradation, and, associating with the utterly depraved, acted in a cruel and cowardly manner to her whom he professed to protect. One of the children died of starvation, while its father was squandering money in riotous drinking. When this wretched fellow at length died in an hospital, his last words had reference to a chastisement reserved for the woman on account of her expending a certain sixpence instead of yielding it to him her master. When first found by the missionary, this poor victim was in a condition of extreme suffering—starving and shivering in the cold, and making up slop-shop garments, for which she received a pittance. But, meek and teachable, she listened to the gospel message, and truth reaching her heart, she soon possessed the good hope.

Now, there are individuals in London who cannot hear of honest struggling against the tide of adversity without lending a helping hand; and, not unfrequently, the missionaries' superintendents thus prove themselves the true friends of their poor constituents. The woman referred to received what to her was a large loan—a sovereign, or a capital which promised to make her happy for the remainder of life. The money was placed as security at the slop-shop; and joy overflowed in the now fortunate creature's heart, as she showed the receipt for the cash, and a bundle of work received in consequence of the deposit.

The patient enduring of children must not be omitted from this chapter. Children are the members of a family who chiefly suffer from habits of vice and improvidence in those above them; and, unfortunate in their rearing, they too often in turn inherit their parents' degradation. According to our usual way of thinking, a more hopeless task could scarcely be undertaken than that of morally and spiritually raising the ragged little creatures whose infant lessons of life have been learned in a drunkard's home. But superficial observers do not elicit truth; and, while inexperienced in the work, any adverse opinions we may form are likely to be far removed from truth. 'Seldom a week passes,' a missionary once remarked, 'but some youths are met with by me who were the first of our ragged-school children, who have risen up in life, and have become honest and industrious members of society.' Not only is a general harvest of good results garnered by carrying the gospel to children, reward comes from unexpected quarters, and sometimes a truly royal nature surprises the visitor among our London rookeries.

The facts of the following striking history have been several times published.

In one of the horrible dens abounding in the byways of London, was once discovered a lad who appeared to be endowed with many commendable qualities. The parents were hopeless slaves of gin, and paid little heed to anything in life beyond drinking and providing the means of gratifying their low propensities. Their home contained nothing of value, nor had it done so since the last available article was exchanged for drink. The household goods consisted of an old kettle, two cups and saucers, and a heap of shavings which served for a bed. The family numbered three sons and one daughter, and two of the former were undergoing a term of imprisonment. The third son, the hero of this narrative, as yet untouched by the law, came under the notice and influence of the district missionary, and on being taken to the ragged-school, evinced a surprising eagerness after knowledge for one of his station and associations. In study, as

20

the teachers expected, this lad achieved a marked success; and, because ragged-school rewards are necessarily articles of utility, his first prize was a pair of shoes and a pair of stockings—the first articles of the kind he ever possessed. Though shoes and stockings are valued by the scholars, and are especially prized when bestowed as academic distinctions, they are not such indispensable adjuncts to civilisation as the over-fastidious may imagine. One day, when a freezing northerly wind was abroad, and when frost and snow lay upon the ground, the late prize-taker appeared in school with bare feet, and carrying what few would have voluntarily dispensed with on a cold morning—his shoes and stockings. In reply to some inquiring looks and words, the little fellow explained: 'You see, sir, my feet are all chilblains. I could not bear them on, and I would not leave them at home, because I should not be likely to see them again. Mother would take them to my uncle's, and drink the money. You know, sir, mother would have drank me if I would go up the spout.' That was a sad speech, sad in its truthfulness, if we consider that the boy's case corresponded with a myriad of others, who, not so favourably endowed as he, are less easily raised from the depths of moral degradation. The good effects of ragged-school teaching soon began to appear; for, on attaining to clearer views of right and wrong, the boy declared he would never do as his brothers had done. He would be honest, and eschew the experience of prison discipline. But what an example of the pursuit of knowledge under difficulties did the lad present while mastering the school lessons under crushing social disadvantages. He would leave the nakedness of home and enter the school-house pinched with hunger and cold; and the prospect of evening was still misery and desolation. He was just sheltered like an animal, nothing more. While in this condition, as he industriously strove to master the subjects of study, a happy idea gladdened his heart. He would commence business on his own responsibility, by devoting the evening hours to commercial pursuits; in other words, he resolved on engaging in trade as a lucifer-match seller. Then a master difficulty arose — a perplexity not unknown to other would-be traders whose ambition exceeds their means. The young aspirant needed the necessary capital; and as, at the least, a sum of threepence was required, that consideration became both serious and baffling. Yet there appeared to be one possible way out of the dilemma. On proper representations being made, and acceptable personal security offered, the missionary might consent to lend the money; and in this surmise the enterprising Arab showed himself no false prophet. Being now a competent capitalist, the lucifer-match venture was boldly embarked in; and the first night's receipts showed a profit equal to the cash employed. This mode of living—studying by day, and selling matches by night, continued through two years, the pence gained each evening sufficing to supply his needs. 'You know that I can always manage to make threepence, and sometimes more. I spend one penny for breakfast, another for dinner, and another for supper: that's better than my brothers did; and when I can read and write well I will get a situation.' Scanty as were these resources, his sister, who also attended school, sometimes shared her brother's meals. Then came the day when all these patient endeavours were to be crowned with due reward. The scholar could read and write, and thus prepared, he went abroad in the world to seek his fortune. Taking a place as errand-boy, he rose from that lowly station into confidential servant. In the meantime, affairs at home reached a crisis. The mother sank into a drunkard's grave, and the shocking occurrence impressing the husband produced a short-lived reformation. He forsook the den which had sheltered him for years, and set up a comfortable home; but this promise was no more lasting than April sunshine. The craving for drink returned, home and furniture were sacrificed, and the daughter was even turned into the street. The fruits of ragged-school teaching were manifest when brother and sister, as respectable Christians, were now seen making their way through the world together.

As something akin to the above, may be related the story of a little girl, who, born and reared in a yard inhabited by profligate and profane persons, learned to live a Christian life prior to being taken from the evil to come, at the age of eleven years. Though her mother was a swearer and loose liver, the child progressed into a rejoicing believer by means of the missionary. It was commonly a delightful pastime of this young creature to follow her instructor from floor to floor, to listen to the words spoken and to join in the prayers offered; besides which she would ask divers questions on faith, repentance, and kindred topics. She sent up to heaven many earnest petitions on the missionary's behalf, and ardently desired that the neighbours might become subjects of Christ. The hours immediately preceding dissolution were employed in praying for all she knew, and with her last words she advised her mother: 'Go to the missionary meeting, and leave off swearing, and prepare to meet me in heaven.' Strongly does God denounce sin by raising up in sinful haunts this juvenile nobleness. Let us not forget that this little rose-bud was tenderly nurtured by the London City Mission.

They who cannot lighten it by substantial charity should at least yield a tribute of honour to this patient enduring of the poor of London. Many whom Providence calls on to undergo the pains and penalties of poverty, are chosen vessels of heaven; and it is some satisfaction to know that a Christian agency is abroad, but for which relief would sometimes come too late. The missionary is able to tell of women whose clothing, or want of clothing, preventing their attending ordinary public worship, have nevertheless appeared at his own meeting, on piercingly cold winter evenings, with no warmer covering than a single cotton gown. In numbers of cases the missionaries have stepped up as deliverers where want seemed to be driving its subjects into the grave, the calamity not springing from wilful transgression. They can tell of little children worn to skeletons by being insufficiently nourished, and of a father, in a season of depression, leaving the room because unable to bear the cries of his starving dependants for a morsel of food! Considering the Mission apart from the obligations of Christian charity, as mere social economists, it behoves us to strengthen the hands of those good

Samaritans who relieve the pressure of anguish and poverty; for without such messengers of mercy the wastes of crime and wretchedness in London would be desolate indeed!

Yet it is sad to reflect that, notwithstanding the many philanthropic schemes already in existence, persons may lie and die of starvation in this great and rich London. A missionary has even opened the door of a room only just in time to afford life-restoring succour. A house in Spitalfields was once entered, wherein, supported on chairs, lay a woman nigh unto death, the cause of her weakness being lack of food. By the side of the exhausted creature might have been seen the mission-agent administering bread, brandy, and sugar. To the same agency, as a worthy subject, the woman was afterwards indirectly indebted for substantial relief.

But, in the wide world of London, there is another kind of patient enduring, differing from the cases mentioned by having its spring in former errors, while it is borne as a just retribution of youthful folly or of subsequent false steps in life. An afflicting instance of this kind occurred in the history of a cobbler living in the vicinity of Surrey Chapel. In early days he enjoyed a measure of prosperity, till contracting drinking habits the cupboard became bare, his clothes ragged, and temporal circumstances bad and still worse, until the man was discovered in the woeful condition to be described. His home was a half underground room, furnished with a few broken pieces of board, a chair, and a coffee kettle, besides a battered tea tray, serving as a stall whereon were exhibited the 'translations,' or cobbled boots and shoes prepared for sale. Begrimed with smoke and dirt, the man appeared as though his skin were tanned to match the sombre filthiness of the den he occupied. He had not slept in a bed for ten years, and during a great part of that time had worn no linen! His sleeping accommodation was an ordinary chair, in which he sat resting his head in his hand. Now, here was one sunk low in degradation; and, from information elicited, it appeared how keenly he realised the misery of his position. But he silently bore the stings of conscience, and, never speaking of them, desired neither to provoke sympathy nor to murmur at a hard lot, till the subject of his condition becoming a topic of conversation between himself and the missionary, he candidly confessed that what he suffered was a consequence of former mistakes. The claims of the gospel were urged upon him, and an invitation given to attend the prayer-meeting. The man, however, was in a deplorable state for want of clothes, and could scarcely appear at public worship without exciting attention; but when, in a suit begged by the visitor, he showed a better appearance, the cobbler manifested great delight, and occupied his place at church three times every Sabbath. Rejoicing now in improved circumstances, he still maintained that his troubles represented the Divine judgment on sin. This transformation astonished all who knew its subject, and probably the subject also. 'I used to be very diligent in the service of Satan,' he said; 'I think I ought to be much more so in the service of God.'

To be old and friendless in a workhouse is supposed to be as forlorn a condition of life as any into which humanity can lapse. To destitution, and the humiliation of accepting parish bounty, add loss of sight, and the cup of misfortune would seem to overflow. Let the well-to-do, who are addicted to complaining of imaginary troubles, take to heart the following:—In a certain workhouse lived an old lady called Blind Sally, whose worldly poverty was matched by her mental darkness. On being spoken to on the advisability of learning to read, she supposed the attainment to rank among impossibilities, but consented to make the trial. Being introduced to the system adopted by teachers of the blind—the guardians, meanwhile, making a grant of ten shillings for necessary materials—the old pauper's delight rose high when she could completely read 'the blessed Book,' as she called the Bible. Her gratitude to the society whose agent brought the saving light also very visibly appeared. The workhouse changed into a very paradise, all burdens being relieved by the expectation of better things in future. Then came the last hours of mortality, and Blind Sally expressed her hope in the words, 'Thy rod and thy staff, they comfort me.'

Now, these examples are specimens selected almost at random from the crowded journals of the missionaries. How largely must such instances of patient endurance abound in each squalid district—*e.g.*, one like that of St. Matthias, Bethnal-green, the incumbent of which, when examined before a Parliamentary Committee, not only stated he could not reside in his parish, and would not have accepted the cure had personal residence been made a condition; but that he could not raise five pounds by house to house visitation among ten thousand people, while not more than half-a-dozen domestic servants were employed in the whole area! Such facts supply materials for answering the question, What is London? A fine and great city is the common-place notion; but, of what is the lower stratum composed? Why do plague-spots like St. Giles's and the worst parts of Whitechapel still exist, not as places where outward decency has lapsed into disuetude, but where to the majority of the inhabitants it was never known. What must be the patient endurance of those respectably-reared persons whose hard lot it is to have to retreat into those neighbourhoods—haunts apparently abandoned to uncleanness and dishonesty, where the houses are nests of infamy, and the streets a convenient practising ground for sharpers and thieves.

Regard each city missionary, then, as a high class social reformer. While we, from our comfortable standpoint, take in a general view of their operations, and pronounce the general harvest of the Mission to be encouragingly gratifying, we need not forget that the obstacles encountered by individual visitors are often of a nature to cow stout hearts and depress persevering spirits. Some persons, though they bear up nobly amid misfortune, never ceasing to strive against the adverse current, still object even to a friendly recognition. Years ago one such was waited on, her home being situated in a murky lane in a depraved district. The house, begrimed with smoke, had probably in better days been a rendezvous where wit and fashion were entertained. Proceeding up the broad staircase, with its faded and shattered balusters, the missionary reached a door on the second floor. 'Who's there?' When the door is partially opened, the question is quickly asked, 'Have you any children you would like to send to a Sabbath-school?' 'No! and now I'll thank you to go.' 'Have you the Word of God in your house?' is still perseveringly inquired. 'Yes, and now go about your business, and never come again.' 'Woman,' exclaims the missionary, 'I have a message to thee before I go; you have a soul that must shortly stand at the bar of God.' This is well aimed. The woman is in trouble, and the mention of better things reminds her of happier scenes—the days of childhood and of youth. Instead of reviling she bursts into tears, hangs down her head, and cries out, 'I am not worthy to receive you under my roof. I am a great sinner.' Here perseverance triumphed. Scripture is read and prayer offered; and not only is the woman herself benefited, she sends two scholars to the Sunday-school. How much lighter must be the load of earthly care after so brave a surrender to righteousness; how strengthened must the toiling evangelist feel after so signal a conquest!

But the scene varies. The path to success in Christian work does not always lie through difficulties making the heart sick and faint. Rebuff and insult do not always oppose the progress of good. Physical pain, poverty, and ignorance not unfrequently exist with a yearning after better things. At a certain door, a poor, but not an ill-looking man is observed. 'Will you take a tract, my good friend?' 'If you please, sir,' he replies. But listen! a slight noise issues from within, and it resembles a moan of pain. Can any be in suffering? Enter, and judge for yourself. On a scanty bed lies an emaciated woman, needing many comforts and strong nourishment; but her condition is that of abject destitution. It is just the kind of picture in social life which brings an aching to the feeling heart. Then, see further: on the table lie a number of loose printed leaves—portions of the Book of Job, whose high example of God-trusting patience is bearing fruit in this seeming abode of misery. Poor man! He, too, unconsciously sets a noble example. Though too impoverished to purchase a Bible, he would, nevertheless, borrow these leaves; and, accordingly, it has been a Saturday evening custom of his to walk some distance, for the purpose of borrowing from one, as needy as himself, these precious fragments of the everlasting Word.

But there is yet another kind of patient enduring—the pain of Christian parents on account of renegade sons. In a low public-house in one district, the rendezvous of thieves and loose characters, there lived a landlord who, though seventy-three years of age, had a mother living in the country, a devout Christian, whose only anxiety was concerned for the conversion of her child. 'I am waiting,—how is it with *you?*' the old lady would exclaim, whenever a meeting occurred between them. The publican, though tolerably well educated, seemed determined to sin against knowledge by committing many enormities. He would even carry the Bible into his taproom, to revile its truths among the ribald company there assembled. But he knew better, as all saw, when he was overtaken by a season of sickness. Two members of the family were taken, and while he himself lay prostrated by weakness, none ever evinced more joy than did he in ever welcoming the lately despised city missionary. He looked for repeated visits, and for repeated opportunities of prayer. Then, when the light of conversion dawned, he determined on relinquishing the now hated business of tavern-keeping.

Now, in concluding this section, let the patient endurers of this chapter be contrasted with a singular instance of feminine *im*patience. A woman dreamed a dream which troubled her, and, being eager to possess the interpretation, she looked for satisfaction to the London City Missionary. In the vision she saw two men, dressed in black, who endeavoured to carry away her husband—a loose-living man and unfit to die. He evaded the grasp of the would-be captors, and pointing to his wife, cried out 'Take her, *she* is ready.' Then, straightway the messengers looked on her, and one, holding an open Bible, pointed to the words, 'Thou shalt die and not live.' Though no dreamer, and not usually attaching great importance to nocturnal imaginings, the missionary can turn this rather striking occurrence into a medium of producing a deep impression for good. In the broad fields of Christian labour, all available material must be utilised. Thankful for what is good in itself, the worker must learn to draw telling lessons from dark events.

Having spoken of the patient enduring of a class whom the missionaries visit, we may now turn to the patience exemplified by the visitors themselves under ordinary and exceptionable circumstances.

The working of the London City Mission has shown that on the whole the agents are faithful to their profession. It might have been supposed that the chief difficulty in organising such a society would consist in finding suitable men to carry on its operations. To ordinary persons, possessed of home and family, there can be nothing very attractive in the duty of an obscure Christian visitor, whose wages do not exceed those of a second-rate mechanic, and therefore we are not surprised to find numbers choosing the work from motives of genuine devotion. At any rate it does seem unlikely that men would risk their lives in localities notorious as the lurking-places of deadly diseases; constantly be found in lairs where policemen singly dare not enter; speak of Christ to outcasts in apartments where the effluvia can be tasted, and where the vermin are visible—merely for a poor living. It does not seen feasible that anything so low as mere earthly considerations could sustain men under heavy self-denying duty, such as is the common experience of faithful visitors in low districts.

But if on ordinary occasions the work be trying, what must be the pressure on a missionary's nervous system in seasons of peculiar danger, such as cholera epidemics? Throughout the history of the society, we do not find that its servants have ever proved unfaithful, even in the severest times; and the devotion of individuals has frequently shone out in actions of real heroism.

In the cholera visitation in 1854, probably no part of London suffered heavier calamities than portions of the parish of St. James, Piccadilly, and the scenes which were there witnessed showed how intensely the poor appreciate a beneficent agency when overwhelmed by an appalling tide of physical suffering, sorrow, and death. In one street every house, with only a single exception, could tell of loss, and in one court thirty-two persons were swept away in a few days, while certain houses of the same neighbourhood averaged eight deaths in each! At the height of the crisis, the terrors of the old plague-time, as described by Defoe, seemed to be hovering near. The dead-cart went its nightly round to collect corpses for which coffins could not be provided. Black flags warned passengers not to venture into infected streets; but lest all other precautions should prove ineffective, policemen hindered the daring from passing over proscribed limits. In the presence of the destroying angel, love of gain gave place to terror; thrifty persons closed their shops, and those who were able hurried away. As the disease increased its havoc, the type it assumed became more malignant. Surgeons who ministered to patients one day sickened and died the next; so that despair began to seize the people.

In the midst of these harrowing scenes, the agents did not shirk their work, though apart from the danger of infection, their duties were largely increased. While on the way to one pressing case, the missionary would be accosted by importunities from friends of other sufferers who desired to see his face. 'If I had been the most eminent physician I could not have been more beset,' one confessed, and one who with his brethren found the excessive strain almost more than humanity could bear. The nervous system became reduced and shaken. They found themselves liable to faintness, and even to slight attacks of the disease itself. In that terrible summer some of the fixed rules of the Mission—excellent in themselves—were wisely superseded by others more suited to the requirements of the moment. In some cases it became necessary for missionaries to concern themselves with the worldly affairs of the stricken people. Not only would they have to fetch a surgeon, appoint a nurse, or order a coffin, but when relatives kept at a safe distance, the visitor from Red-lion-square has been chief and only mourner at the funeral of some forsaken sufferer!

From the above it appears that none are more directly exposed to inconveniences attending epidemics than the agents of the City Mission. Should the missionary be appointed to hospital work, he becomes cognizant of the abounding distress both by the influx of sufferers, and by the alarm of patients, who become painfully affected in consequence of the common calamity, and their own increased exposure to danger. But, depressing as is the aspect of the hospital at such times, it is not so appalling as the misery without, for in damp earthy cellars and in squalid attics the distemper at least appears to assume a more terrible form. It were vain to attempt a description of the varied experience of Christian itinerants through such seasons—which is certain to undermine health by promoting nervous debility—though a few stray pictures may be given.

During the epidemic of 1866, the adventures of a public-house visitor in an eastern district illustrated the endurance of which I write. The general dread of the malady was very marked, and what seemed as strange as shocking, some imitated the conduct of those reprobates of 1665, who in their frenzy launched into excess of wickedness. They sought 'to drown their thoughts in blasphemy and drunkenness,' says the missionary. There were others who, terrified by apprehensions of impending death, lapsed into mental derangement, and while in that state cut short their lives before the disease could affect them. The streets and bars shared in the reigning excitement; and it was saddening to see strong men swallow brandy, as though that could ensue immunity from danger.

On one of those summer days one stood talking with the landlord of a tavern in Ratcliffe Highway, a place such as respectable people would be careful to shun. A man entered, painfully excited, and began taking glasses of brandy as though his immediate object were to extinguish reason. He was addressed in gentle tones. 'Don't talk to me about religion,' he answered roughly, with an oath; 'everybody is dying, and I'm queer, if I don't die.' 'A sparrow falls not to the ground without God,' said the missionary, while more spirits were ordered. Then other words were spoken, until completely conquered, tears ran down the man's cheeks, and he cried, 'I am afraid to die! There are six dead in our court now, and I am afraid to go home.' 'I have read in history, what Oliver Cromwell said to his soldiers,' replied the other,—'"Pray to God and keep your powder dry."' Soon something better than fear beamed out of the stranger's eyes. 'I do think God sent you to speak to me,' he said, with tears of gratitude.

In this manner the seed by the wayside was sown, and many were spoken with to advantage. In another tavern of the same district, the missionary, as in the former instance, was standing at the bar, when a powerful man hurriedly entered and called for the supposed universal panacea—brandy. After drinking the spirit, and retiring to another part of the house, a loud scream was heard, and hurrying to see what had occurred, the missionary found the stranger prostrated by virulent cholera. He lay, 'crying out most bitterly to God to have mercy upon him, and promising, if God would spare him, what a different life he would lead.' The sufferer was carried to a hospital, where he did recover, but soon returned to his drink and vanity. Yet at such times many receive the truth, never to turn back. In one house, where the barmaid was carried off, and near which a surgeon also lay dead, a barman was melted to tears at the heavenly message, and forthwith resolved on relinquishing an occupation which seemed to be associated with the worst vices of human nature. In one public-house a bride-elect and her father both lay dead; in another the landlady and her daughter were cut down; while in yet another the son expired while a low concert with dancing was proceeding!

To itinerate under such circumstances is patient endurance of a high order, and a risk of contagion is incurred by the self-sacrifice. Indeed, the wonder is not that some fall, but that so many missionaries work on unscathed. Doubtless God often spares those who honour Him by self-denying labours; and believing that they have found their work, the visitors proceed, leaving all results to Heaven. Yet it is affecting to read how their ranks are sometimes thinned by what looks like disaster. One has been known to die of small-pox shortly after appointment to a district. Another has gone from a fever hospital, which he had bravely visited for a length of time, to die at last of the poison. 'No one but you dare come here,' has been the language of the patients in an infirmary. In the plague-charged atmosphere, surgeons and nurses frequently succumb to death, but no terrors exclude the city missionary.

From all this it must not be inferred that the missionaries are all equal in devotion and efficiency; for the committee confess that had they a Victoria Cross to bestow in recognition of exceptional heroism, it would belong to the man who spends his days in the fever hospital. One who lately exchanged this noble service for a heavenly mansion, went through a strange experience. Accustomed to death-scenes daily, he has seen eight servants of the institution fall in as many weeks, and sometimes threatening symptoms seemed to presage his own speedy dissolution. Scarcely less singular was the religious intolerance which had to be encountered from the only other religious visitor—a Romish priest—who regarded the Protestant with high disfavour. Papist charwomen were even employed to bias the patients against Bible instructions, though in spite of all, even Rome's constituents would say, 'That's a good fellow after all,' and the general results were encouraging. A gentleman-patient was led to take a life-long interest in the City Mission, besides seeking his own eternal welfare, after hearing the gospel in the hospital. 'What you said pricked me so that it has stuck to me ever since,' said another; 'and what with the illness and your visits, it has made another man of me.' A nurse addicted to intemperance, and one who had appropriated the patients' wine, has been known to swallow poison, then to take fever, and on being admitted to the wards, to become benefited for life by the word of the missionary. No object, such as that of merely getting a living, could induce men, not tired of existence, to pass their time in this pestilential air, to go from bed to bed for the purpose of pressing the gospel claims on the attention of numbers who will listen to the message for the last time. Then, occasionally, the disappearance of well-known faces from among the nurses, or the death of physicians, adds additional gloom to the awful shades of the infirmary. 'I marvel at my own existence,' wrote the missionary referred to, after the epidemic of 1866. 'During the cholera months I went every day to the wards, expecting it would be the last of my visitation there. I even delayed the purchase of several articles of clothing which I needed, from the thought that I should never live to wear them. My chief danger I felt to be in the effect produced by witnessing scenes so harrowing to the mind, and the increased sensitiveness to the effects of foul air, which depression occasioned. For days I scarcely tasted any distinction in different articles of food, so vitiated had my palate become.'

Thus it appears that those who visit and sympathise with the poor share their burdens, and share them not in a sentimental sense merely. Hence they are patient endurers of ills and crosses. Their experience during epidemics, or in hospitals set apart for loathsome diseases, may be of an exceptional kind; but how repeatedly are horrors of the worst type encountered in the common street in ordinary course of visitation.

A missionary once entered a dilapidated hovel at the

east-end of the town, and as the windows of the lower part were gone, one would scarcely have expected to find the place inhabited. There were inhabitants above, however, but to gain ingress, you stepped on to a plank laid across a tub, and so clambered up as best you could. On entering the room it was found to be a retreat of virulent typhus fever, several persons representing different stages of the distemper. A coffin by the wall contained one of the family, while another child lay in the throes of death. The father also was prostrated; but the wife, who was recovering, sat by a poor fire attending to four children. Altogether the spectacle was most surprising, filth and destitution adding to its horrible novelty. This man, unlike other subjects of this chapter, traced his calamities to waste and profligacy; so that the case is given here, only as illustrative of the self-denial of those who dare explore such scenes, with the Bible in one hand and their lives in the other! 'I am going to hell, as the wages of my sin,' said the husband, in tones of anguish and repentance, until hope dawned as he listened to the Bible message in the penitential expressions of the Fifty-first Psalm. As the case was one of literal starvation, life necessaries were speedily provided; and the man, on his restoration to health, declared that the missionary had been the means of saving both his body and his soul.

Many allusions of this chapter direct our thoughts to the sanitary condition of the homes of the poor. Much as social reformers have done for London, and while their efforts justly engender gratitude, we hope we see in them promises of better things and a plea for greater effort in the work of amelioration. The sanitary arrangements of good neighbourhoods show the power of science and wealth under a reign of high civilisation; but if only from instinct of self-preservation, the rich should protect the poor, whose districts too often court small-pox, fever, and cholera, whenever an epidemic sweeps through city and village. It is surely a stain on our national honour when people are allowed to herd together in filth and misery, and to pay in proportion higher rents for their houses than the rich occupants of terraces and squares. It is notorious that many landlords grow rich on the exorbitant rents taken from the subjects of wretchedness in the crumbling tenements of over-crowded and pestiferous rookeries. Let us hope that a better day is near, meanwhile doing what we are able to hasten its approach, and always remembering that 'Blessed is he that considereth the poor.'

CONCLUSION.

CONCLUSION.

IN the spring of 1835 there arrived in London a gentleman of middle age, whose immediate object, when explained to many good and far-seeing men, seemed to be unique, if not Utopian. But a great work was about to be inaugurated, and the visitor and his lady—he was accompanied by his wife—set about fulfilling their mission in a business-like manner. The lady retired to her father's house in Kent, while her husband proceeded to furnish a humble dwelling at Hoxton. The gentleman—he was no other than David Nasmith—had already been instrumental in establishing several town missions, and was now desirous of crowning his work by founding a great association for London. Plans of operation for the proposed society were subjected to the inspection of many leading men, and by the majority were pronounced impracticable. Nor need we be surprised at their judgment, when we consider the natural difficulties attending the founding of a great work, and the slight social standing of the seemingly ambitious agent.

A small band of philanthropic friends in Dublin being

the occasion of David Nasmith's visiting London, arranged that he should come by way of experiment for three years. The task allotted was in itself one of great difficulty, and at that conjuncture, the relation of the Established Church to Dissent put new obstacles in the way of separate bodies of Christians working harmoniously. 'I very much fear that in the present circumstances of the Church you will find yourself repelled at every step in *any* plan which contemplates the co-operation of different denominations,' was the language of one of the most eminent of the evangelical clergy. Even Dr. Campbell, who was not of a temperament to be dismayed at trifles, not thinking the Mission possible, declined helping it forward until he utterly failed at dissuasion. Then, as it invariably happens, when a great scheme is afloat, there was the usual distrust and misgiving. The best friends of David Nasmith rather tremulously pointed out the obstacles to success besetting his path. Other societies existed for attaining similar ends to those now aimed at; and unluckily, just at that time, Episcopacy and Dissent would not work together, even for so unsectarian an object as the evangelisation of the perishing thousands of London. Then reasons, too numerous to be mentioned, were given why the contemplated Mission should be dropped, and why it would fail if undertaken; so that had he been a novice instead of a veteran, Nasmith, as he himself confessed, would have hurried away from London, discouraged or in utter despair. The sayings and doings of men among the most excellent of the earth in those days, show, when viewed from our present standpoint, that the best advice of able thinkers may sometimes nip a great work in the bud. Happily it was beyond the power of human objectors to hinder the progress of David Nasmith. 'I carried with me not only the divine warrant, but the divine command,' he says; 'assured that He who had wrought by me in fifty other places would be with me here also. I took courage.'

The broad stream of evangelical truth which now sends its cleansing waters into the forbidding recesses of the great city, first issued from a not very promising spring. This agency, whose sum of work, during thirty-seven years, will bear favourable comparison with the operations of any other philanthropic organisation, and the success of which, in seeking the lost, in reclaiming the despairing, and in blessing outcasts in general, has probably even exceeded that of any modern institution, had the humblest of beginnings. No public excitement marked its birth. No public meeting, with an eminent chairman and popular speakers, announced to England the planting of the LONDON CITY MISSION.

'The kingdom of God,' says the Great Teacher, 'cometh not with observation.' This truth was well illustrated in the rise of this society. The auspicious day was May the 16th, 1835, and the place, a small apartment of a house in the vicinity of the Regent's-canal—Canning-terrace, Hoxton. A company of three, there assembled, founded the Mission, and a fourth would have attended had he been able to find the unfashionably situated house. In this manner was the good work begun; but for a time the entire staff of agents and officers were not too numerous to take tea together in the parlour of the little mansion in Canning-terrace. But so good a work, undertaken in faith, was sure to extend its empire. A step in advance was taken when Sir T. F. Buxton assumed the treasurership, for his name attracted subscriptions. Beginning with ten agents, forty were employed at the end of the first year, and before two years they numbered sixty-three.

David Nasmith was a liberal-minded and large-hearted man. Abhorring party bickerings, his one aim being to promote Christianity, he had no notion of choosing an agent for any other reason than moral fitness. But this procedure did not always give satisfaction. Many persons of station and character objected to the management when the members of the committee were too exclusively of one party. It mattered not to David Nasmith to what party a man belonged, if he were only possessed of piety and proper mental capacity. Imagining the rule too arbitrary which obliged the Board to be composed of Churchmen and Nonconformists in equal number, he resigned his office in 1837.

At the first annual meeting of the society, held in the Music-hall, Store-street, Bedford-square, the chair was occupied by the Hon. and Rev. B. W. Noel, who in the course of an able speech adopted an apologetic strain. Some persons contemned a paid agency, others demanded a purely clerical staff, and it was necessary to set at rest, as far as possible, the objections of either party.

Besides the prejudices and objections of parties and persons, a formidable opposition to the society was raised by the Bishop of London. Adhering strictly to the letter of the Anglican order, his lordship condemned the Mission on many grounds, even while evincing considerable anxiety to relieve the abounding destitution. He disapproved of lay agency, and also of Churchmen harmoniously working with Dissenters. Other reasons given need not be repeated; for being obsolete, they would only expose the scruples of a conscientious High Church Prelate of thirty years ago. But, meanwhile, the infant Mission fared little better at the hands of extreme Nonconformists. Said one to the other, 'It is a churchified society: let it alone.' Here then were the proverbial 'two stools,' between which there was some danger of falling to the ground.

The prejudice of contending parties at length wore itself out, and the Church at large now recognises the evil to be combated as something too momentous to justify bickerings which only hinder progress.

The conquests achieved year by year speak for themselves, and plead for increased aid to the good cause more eloquently than could any words of mine. The facts and startling histories of this volume carry a moral which the right-minded reader will know how to apply. 'Let us not be high-minded, but fear,' are the closing words of a recent Report of the Committee, and with these I bid my reader farewell:—

'The storm has burst over our sister city. And we are yet spared. But dark clouds, by the eye of faith, are to be seen over our heads, hovering around us. The Lord grant that they may be averted from us. Would we escape the tempest's fury? Let us work the works of Christ while the day is yet fair.'

Yet a little while is the bright light with us. May we labour for our blessed Lord while we have the light, lest darkness come upon us. Then shall the work of righteousness have as its result "peace; and the effect of righteousness" shall be to us "quietness and assurance for ever."'

THE END.

UNWIN BROTHERS, THE GRESHAM PRESS, CHILWORTH AND LONDON.

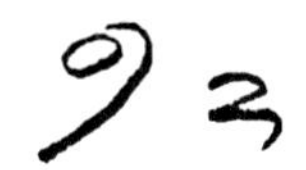

CPSIA information can be obtained at www.ICGtesting.com
Printed in the USA
LVOW12s2122051213

364128LV00012B/115/P

9 781290 356565